The Nature of the Firm

9500440

The Nature
of the Firm
Origins, Evolution, and Development

Edited by

OLIVER E. WILLIAMSON

SIDNEY G. WINTER

New York   Oxford
OXFORD UNIVERSITY PRESS   1993

Oxford University Press

Oxford   New York   Toronto
Delhi   Bombay   Calcutta   Madras   Karachi
Kuala Lumpur   Singapore   Hong Kong   Tokyo
Nairobi   Dar es Salaam   Cape Town
Melbourne   Auckland   Madrid

and associated companies in
Berlin   Ibadan

First issued as an Oxford University Press paperback, 1993

Oxford is a registered trademark of Oxford University Press

Library of Congress Cataloging-in-Publication Data
The Nature of the firm : origins, evolution, and development
edited by Oliver E. Williamson, Sidney G. Winter.
p.   cm.   Includes bibliographical references and index.
ISBN 0-19-508356-3 (pbk.)
1. Industrial organization (Economic theory)
I. Williamson, Oliver E.
II. Winter, Sidney G.
HD2326.N38   1993
338.5 — dc20   92-38007

9 8 7 6 5 4 3 2 1

Printed in the United States of America
on acid-free paper

Preface

Ronald H. Coase's classic article "The Nature of the Firm" was first published in 1937. That article and the proceedings from a 1987 conference that was organized to celebrate the fiftieth anniversary of "The Nature of the Firm" are reprinted here. It was our great privilege and pleasure to organize that conference. A grant from the Alfred P. Sloan Foundation to the Yale School of Organization and Management was used to support the conference, for which grant we express our appreciation.

Professor Coase possesses an unusual mind. In addressing some of the most basic issues of the day, he manages to transform the dialogue permanently. He has done this not once but repeatedly. The formula evidently entails first thinking the unthinkable, then penetrating and examining its essence, and finally explicating the issues in a more fundamental way than was hitherto possible.

To be sure, this can be embarrassing to others. What is one to do with a "gift" that is patently right, eludes analysis, and upsets foundations? One judicious response is to cite certain papers in footnotes without heeding their message in the text. Sooner or later, however—later, as it turned out, in this instance—the strain must be addressed.

Professor Coase has never been deterred by the fact that he was ahead of his time. It has always been better, in his judgment, to expose strains than to bury them. Those of us who work on or are concerned with problems of economic organization—which, directly and indirectly, takes in the entire economics profession—are in his everlasting debt.

The first chapter in this book provides an overview of the volume. That is followed by Coase's 1937 article and the three lectures that he presented at the conference. Six conference papers and two other papers that were inspired by the conference conclude the volume. The *Journal of Law, Economics, and Organization* 4 (Spring 1988) featured all but the introduction and the 1937 article. Permission from Oxford University Press to reprint these materials as well as the 1937 article is gratefully acknowledged.

As the conference and related papers disclose, research on the economics of organization is currently in a state of ferment. Real progress notwithstanding, many issues remain unsettled and some are just beginning to be addressed. Considering the variety of approaches and research talents that are being applied to this area, we look forward with confidence to the next ten and even fifty years. All of the conference participants, as well as the economics profession more generally, count ourselves fortunate that Ronald Coase continues to take an active part in these developments.

Berkeley, California   O. E. W.
July 1990   S. G. W.

Contents

Contributors

Ronald H. Coase
  University of Chicago, Emeritus

Harold Demsetz
  University of California, Los Angeles

Oliver D. Hart
  Massachusetts Institute of Technology

Paul L. Joskow
  Massachusetts Institute of Technology

Benjamin Klein
  University of California, Los Angeles

Scott E. Masten
  University of Michigan

Sherwin Rosen
  University of Chicago

Oliver E. Williamson
  University of California, Berkeley

Sidney G. Winter
  General Accounting Office, U.S. Government

The Nature of the Firm

1

Introduction

OLIVER E. WILLIAMSON

"The Nature of the Firm," the rudiments of which had already taken shape in Ronald Coase's mind and had appeared in his correspondence by 1932, was first published in 1937. That was a seminal event — although it took a very long time for its full importance to register. The fiftieth anniversary of that event was celebrated at a 1987 conference. Coase's 1937 article, the three lectures that he gave at the conference, and the conference papers are brought together here. I briefly examine each of these in that order and offer some observations about work in progress and the research agenda.

1. THE 1937 PAPER

The "main advantage which an economist brings to the other social sciences is simply a way of looking at the world" (Coase, 1978:210). But while a shared world view holds economists together — indeed, may be said to define membership in the club — a few economists venture beyond and reshape the worldview, which temporarily upsets the status quo. Ronald Coase is one of those reshapers; his 1937 article on "The Nature of the Firm" is recognized as a classic because it changed the way people think about economic organization.

Coase describes his purpose in writing the article as that of developing a theory of the firm that is both realistic and tractable. Whereas it is customary in economics to think of "the economic system as being coordinated by the price mechanism" (19), that is only a partial description. The economic system is also made up of subsystems, of which the large corporation is a conspicuous member. What distinguishes the firm, in Coase's view, is that when "a workman moves from department Y to department X, he does not go because of a change in relative prices, but because he is ordered to do so" (19). Evidently there are at least two coordinating mechanisms: within markets the price system signals (decentralized) resource allocation needs and opportunities; but firms employ a different organizing principle — that of hierarchy — whereupon authority is used to effect resource reallocations.

3

What determines which activities a firm chooses to do for itself and which it procures from others?

A simple answer to that question is that the natural boundaries of the firm are defined by technology—economies of scale, technological nonseparabilities, and the like. The firm-as-production function is in this tradition. But Coase would have none of that. He insisted, correctly, that firm and market were *alternative* modes for organizing the very same transactions (19). In mundane terms, the issue is that of make-or-buy. What is it that determines which transactions are executed how?

That posed a deep puzzle for which the firm-as-production function approach had little to contribute. To be sure, firms sometimes internalize transactions because this serves to relieve monopoly strains (an efficient factor proportions argument), to reinforce monopoly advantage (a strategic entry deterrent argument), to evade sales taxes, or to escape interfirm trading quotas. All of these features can be and have been interpreted in applied price theory terms. But applied price theory in combination with technological determinism explain only a minuscule fraction of the total range of activities in which firms engage. What explains the remainder?

Whereas others ignored "the remainder," Coase would not. Instead, he posed both of the key questions that—both then and now—are at the heart of the research agenda on economic organization: "Why is there any [internal] organization?" (19); and "Why is not all production carried on by one big firm?" (23). He furthermore implicated transaction costs in his answers to both questions.

To be sure, the transaction cost particulars that Coase advanced in 1937 have withstood the test of time less well than the general argument that markets and hierarchies differ in transaction cost respects. Thus Coase answered the first question by asserting, "The main reason why it is profitable to establish a firm is that it would seem to be that there is a cost of using the price mechanism. The most obvious cost of 'organizing' production through the price mechanism is that of discovering what the relevant prices are" (21). And Coase cited earlier treatments by Nicholas Kaldor (1934) and E. A. G. Robinson (1934) as authorities for the proposition that firm size is limited because of "diminishing returns to management" (23).

Although the failure of the price mechanism to reflect spillover costs or benefits may occasion merger between otherwise unrelated firms (Davis and Whinston, 1962), that is very different from the argument that the main cost of using markets is that of ascertaining market prices. Interestingly, however, the study of spillover (externalities; market failure) leads into and/or invites attention to information asymmetries, uncertainty, incomplete contracting, bilateral dependencies, the limits of third-party enforcement, and the like—all of which have transaction cost origins and have a great deal of relevance for studying comparative economic organization. Also, explicating vaguely described diminishing returns to management is a transaction cost exercise. A theory of bureaucracy in which the sources and consequences of comparative bureaucratic cost *differences* between firm and market mediation (of the very same transactions) is needed. The upshot is that whereas transaction cost differences are at the very essence of recent efforts to assess the comparative efficacy of alternative governance structures (expressed as a function of the transactions to be organized), the transaction cost particulars to which Coase referred in 1937 have not figured prominently in the exercise.

Be that as it may, Coase nevertheless posed the fundamental inquiries that invite follow-on research. But responses to the twin puzzles posed by Coase were slow to materialize. Frequent references to "The Nature of the Firm" notwithstanding, the theory of the firm was mainly devoid of transaction cost content during the ensuing thirty-five years. That lapse was noted by Coase in his National Bureau address (1972:63) and again in his 1987 lectures.

2. THE 1987 LECTURES

The three lectures that Coase prepared for the 1987 conference dealt with the origin, meaning, and influence of "The Nature of the Firm." Rather than review each of these in the order presented by Coase, I examine the lectures in terms of Coase and his times, the "main case," the core issues, and research needs and opportunities as perceived by Coase.

2.1. Autobiography

Coase's lectures are autobiographical and disclose a great deal about his background and intellectual development. Thus, although everyone knows that the "Nature of the Firm" was published in 1937, Coase discloses he had already been lecturing on the subject and had worked out many of the main ideas in 1932 — at the age of twenty-one! Coase also remarks that his college program in economics was rather unusual. Because he lacked preparation in Latin and had an aversion to mathematics, he took no courses in economics during his first two years at the London School of Economics but studied "courses in French, accounting, business administration, works and factory accounting and cost accounts, the raw materials of industry and trade, problems of modern industry, the financing of industry, industrial law, and industrial psychology" (36) — subjects which today sound like those of an M.B.A. program. It was not until later, especially as a result of courses that he took with Arnold Plant, that Coase got exposed to economics and developed an economic approach to the study of organization.

Also interesting is the anecdote that Coase relates concerning Abba Lerner's visit "to Mexico to see Trotsky to persuade him that all would be well in a communist state if only it reproduced the results of a competitive system and prices were set equal to marginal cost" (39). Such was the state of economic thinking in the 1930s.

Indeed, the prevailing attitude about economic institutions, as revealed by Lionel Robbins's influential views on *The Nature and Significance of Economic Science* (1932), was that economics should concern itself with "high theory" and that institutions were largely irrelevant (54). The firm-as-production function orientation flourished in such an intellectual environment — which helps to explain why Coase's 1937 article was an aberration. By contrast, the new theories of monopolistic/imperfect competition worked out of a production function setup and enjoyed spectacular success—partly because the "new theoretical apparatus had the advantage that one could cover the blackboard with diagrams and fill the hour in one's lectures without the need to find out anything about what happened in the real world" (51).

2.2. The Main Case

Coase was massively influenced by Arnold Plant, who taught him that "producers maximize profits, that producers compete, and therefore that prices tend to equal costs and the composition of output to be that which consumers value most highly. Plant also explained that governments often served special interests, promoted monopoly rather than competition, and commonly imposed regulations which made matters worse" (37). Coase further remarks that "my basic position was (and is) the same as Plant's, that our economic system is in the main competitive. Any explanation therefore for the emergence of the firm had to be one which applied to competitive conditions, although monopoly might be important in particular cases" (54). Coase thus insisted that the theory of economic organization needed to be grounded on an examination of costs (rather than monopoly) and that costs needed to be investigated comparatively (59). Accordingly, comparative economizing on transaction costs was held to be the main case—to which monopoly and other explanations could be added as refinements, qualifications, extensions, and the like, but none of which qualify for main-case standing.

2.3. Core Issues

The question, then, was how to respond to this formulation. Although Coase was sympathetic with Plant's view that competition provides the requisite coordination for the economic system to work itself, he nevertheless regarded this approach as incomplete: it left "obscure the role of business management and of the employer-employee relationship" (38). Coase used his Cassel travelling scholarship for the academic year 1932–1933 to study vertical and lateral integration in the United States. He visited a number of large U.S. manufacturing firms, collecting and interpreting "data" of a more microanalytic and comparative kind than is customary in economics (44).

Although Coase was intrigued with the possibility that the characteristics of the assets played a crucial role in the choice of firm or market and in the design of long-term contracts (43, 45–46, 70–71), he decided against making this a central feature. That was because the hazards of opportunism posed by specialized investments are "usually effectively checked by the need to take account of the effect of the firm's actions on future business" (71). His inquiries disclosed that "there were 'many contractual devices' which would avoid the risk associated with making capital investments to supply one customer, and in fact independent firms commonly made such investments" (46).

Rather than investigate when such reputation effects work well or poorly, which condition is arguably pertinent — even central — to a theory of firm and market organization, Coase assumed that they worked well and held that "the distinguishing mark of the firm is the supersession of the price mechanism" (56). Accordingly, the nature of the employment relation, whereby one contract is substituted for many and employees "agree to obey the directions of an entrepreneur" within limits (56), was made the central focus. Limits to firm size result when "people working in a large firm . . . find the conditions of work less attractive than in a small firm and therefore will require a higher remuneration to compensate them for this" (59). A predictive theory of firm, market, and hybrid organization — *which transactions would be organized by which mode of organization and why* — was plainly not Coase's concern in 1937. Instead, a very general comparison of the benefits and costs of firms (in relation to markets) was what concerned him (66–67).

2.4. The Research Agenda

As Coase looks to the future, however, he regards the main weakness of his 1937 article to be the "use of the employer-employee relationship as the archetype of the firm" (64) and notes that the financing of the firm "by acquiring, leasing, or borrowing [capital was] not examined" (65). More generally, his 1937 article led to an "undue emphasis on the firm as a purchaser of the inputs it uses," as a consequence of which "economists have tended to neglect the main activity of a firm, running a business" (65). The need that he perceives now is to go beyond an explanation of "why there were firms," which is what Coase was preoccupied with in 1937, to investigate "how the functions which are performed by firms are divided up among them" (73). He observes in this connection that the costs incurred by a firm in managing any particular activity are "presumably largely determined by the other activities that the [firm is] undertaking" (67).

The pressing need and research opportunity is to achieve "a theoretical scheme which would link together all these factors into a coherent theoretical system" (67). It is pertinent that "all these interrelationships are affected by the state of the law" (73). A combined law, economics, and organizations approach to the issues is thus contemplated.

3. THE CONFERENCE PAPERS

Six papers were prepared for the conference, and two other papers were inspired by the conference. The first conference paper is by Sherwin Rosen, who examines "Transaction Costs and Internal Labor Markets." Rosen begins with the observation that Coase's reported aversion to mathematics is surprising — considering the mathematical nature of many of his arguments (75). The choice of language, however, is a means to an end. The objective, after all, is to develop important ideas in disciplined ways. Although mathematics is a disciplined language, Coase has an unusually meticulous and subtle mind and has successfully communicated his ideas to a broad audience with the disciplined use of prose.

Rosen recalls the tension between the use of the price system to elicit spontaneous coordination and recourse to hierarchy to effect conscious coordination. Why is it that we have both? Which transactions go where? Rosen responds by tracing the rationale for the firm to conditions of firm-specific human and nonhuman capital (77). He thus invites his readers to consider a hypothetical assembly line in which each worker owns or rents his position on the line. Rosen then queries whether a decentralized price system could implement the efficient program in such an organization. He concludes that such would be very complicated (80) and would impose unrealistic knowledge requirements (81).

Rosen then entertains the possibility that decentralization within firms could be effected through penalty and reward schemes of a self-enforcing kind. If feasible, that would avoid the need for monitoring and is the modern agency theory approach. Upon examination, however, that too leads to complications and makes unreasonable knowledge assumptions (84). This leads Rosen to advance a theory of internal labor markets in which conscious coordination is featured: "Incentives, testing, career assignments, and rewards must be analyzed in the context of a dynamic personnel *system*" (87).

My paper, entitled "The Logic of Economic Organization," deals with efforts to operationalize the Coasian insight that transaction cost differences are mainly responsible for market, hierarchy, and hybrid modes of organization. The key trade-off that characterizes the shift of a transaction from market to hierarchy is that incentive intensity is sacrificed in favor of greater (bilateral) adaptability.

Both parts of that trade-off are discovered only upon an examination of microanalytic process differences that distinguish firms and markets. Thus incentive intensity is degraded within firms because of the "impossibility of selective intervention," and markets are limited in adaptability respects by the Fundamental Transformation—which obtains for those transactions for which a large numbers ex ante bidding competition is transformed into a small numbers exchange relation during contract execution and at contract renewal intervals.

The operationalization of transaction cost economics entails three key moves: the basic unit of analysis needs to be declared, the rudimentary attributes of human nature need to be identified, and the intertemporal process transformations of organization need to be described. My response to the first of these is to adopt John R. Commons's (1934) suggestion to make the transaction the basic unit of analysis, whereupon attention is directed to the dimensionalization of transactions. The twin assumptions of bounded rationality and opportunism are the behavioral attributes on which transaction cost economics relies.

A predictive theory of economic organization will align transactions (which differ in their attributes) with governance structures (which differ in their costs and competencies) in a discriminating (mainly, transaction cost–economizing) way. Applications of the argument (in which the above-described process transformations are featured) to vertical integration and to the discriminating use of debt and equity are sketched.

Paul Joskow's paper deals with "Asset Specificity and the Structure of Vertical Relationships: Empirical Evidence." He begins with reflections on his own intellectual development and recalls grave skepticism that transaction cost arguments would ever be used in disciplined ways (118). Even upon being persuaded that a comparative institutional approach to industrial organization had a good deal to recommend it, especially for purposes of rethinking and reshaping antitrust enforcement, he did not see that the approach had relevance for his own interests in regulation (118–119). That changed, however, when regulation was posed as a contracting problem and transaction cost economics was used to assess the efficacy of franchise bidding for natural monopoly. Thereafter Joskow (in collaboration with Richard Schmalensee) examined vertical integration in the electric power industry in comparative contracting terms (123–124). The regulation-deregulation dialogue has been significantly transformed as a result.

Joskow then surveys recent empirical studies of vertical integration and long-term contracting in which the type and degree of asset specificity is an explanatory variable (126–133). Difficult data collection and measurement problems notwithstanding, empirical research of this kind has steadily progressed. The cumulative evidence supports the proposition that the governance of contractual relations varies systematically with the degree of asset specificity. Thus markets are preponderantly used to mediate nonspecific transactions, hybrid contracting forms appear as asset specificity builds up, and hierarchy (vertical integration) is reserved for transactions where bilateral dependency is especially great.

Oliver Hart's chapter is titled "Incomplete Contracts and the Theory of the Firm." Whereas agency theory is able to relate easily and effectively to the condition of opportunism (in the forms of adverse selection and moral hazard), it has been loath to come to terms with the condition of bounded rationality. The reason for that is simple: all comprehensive contracting theories, of which agency theory is one, concentrate all of the contracting action on the ex ante incentive alignment. The central lesson of bounded rationality for the study of economic organization, however, is that all complex contracts are unavoidably incomplete. Accordingly, express provision for ex post governance is needed if bounded rationality is to be admitted.

That lesson was long resisted, however—not least of all because formal models of incomplete contracting are formidably difficult. Sanford Grossman and Oliver Hart's 1986 paper developed new models of an incomplete contracting kind and broke with the earlier contracting tradition. A central result of that paper and of Hart's conference paper is that ownership matters. As Hart puts it, "Incompleteness of contract opens the door to a theory of ownership" (141)—whereas ownership is irrelevant under a comprehensive contracting setup.

Hart's conference paper builds on earlier work of a transaction cost kind in which asset specificity is featured. The theory focuses attention entirely on the ownership of physical assets and uses the concept of residual rights of control to explain both the costs and the benefits of vertical integration. Three examples are provided, each of which demonstrates that the assignment of ownership has productivity consequences — for a single asset, for two laterally related assets, and for vertical integration. Hart concludes with the observation that the research future for work of this kind is very exciting (154).

Harold Demsetz's chapter provides an overview of the theory of the firm — past, present, and prospective. As he observes, the neoclassical theory of markets regards the firm as a "rhetorical device adopted to facilitate discussion of the price system" (161). Although the need to simplify the theory of the firm for this purpose is very real, the resulting gains come at a huge cost. What was an analytically *convenient* theory of the firm for purposes of studying markets and equilibrium came to be treated as an *adequate* theory of the firm for purposes of understanding economic organization. The advantages of an all-purpose theory of the firm notwithstanding, the latter was a fateful mistake.

That lapse could not forever go unnoticed. Coase's 1937 paper expressly protested that condition, and more recent work has attempted to redress it. In Demsetz's judgment, however, recent work — of team theory (Alchian and Demsetz, 1972), agency theory (Jensen and Meckling, 1976), and transaction cost kinds — has not gone far enough.

One of the problems that Demsetz has with transaction cost economics is terminological: rather than use transaction costs symmetrically to describe cost differences among alternative forms of governance, he urges that the term *transaction cost* should be reserved for markets and *management cost* be used for firms. The absence of a generic cost category complicates comparisons, however, especially when hybrid forms of organization (franchising, joint ventures, etc.) are introduced.

More importantly, Demsetz is not persuaded that asset specificity has the explanatory power that has been ascribed to it. The key question that needs to be but has not been asked is the following: "When is a nexus of contracts *more firm-like*?" (170). He avers that three factors are distinctively associated with firm-like coordination: specialization, continuity of association, and reliance on direction. Interestingly, the first two of these are closely related to the condition of asset specificity. (A rose by another name smells not the same?) The third, moreover, in conjunction with the first two, appears to concede the efficacy of fiat. If so, Demsetz joins Armen Alchian (1984) in revising earlier insistence that fiat is not a distinguishing feature of the firm (Alchian and Demsetz, 1972).

Be that as it may, Demsetz argues that future work on the theory of the firm needs to be more concerned with the economics of acquiring and using knowledge. He observes in this connection that those "who produce on the basis of specialized knowledge . . . [need] not be possessed of it themselves." That is because the activities of others can be "directed by those who possess . . . [greater] knowledge" (172). Accordingly, the role of management needs to be given a much greater prominence in subsequent work on the theory of the firm.

Sidney Winter's chapter is titled "On Coase, Competence, and the Corporation." Like Demsetz, Winter contrasts the orthodox theory of the firm that is featured in microeconomic theory textbooks with the needs of a theory in which the distinctive productive features of the firm are expressly addressed. He then examines four critiques of orthodoxy — methodological individualism, failure to address the core Coasian queries, unrealism, and failure to recognize the firm as a repository of competence — before discussing evolutionary and transaction cost perspectives on the firm.

Whereas transaction cost economics draws its inspiration from Coase's 1937 article, evolutionary economics is inspired by Alchian's classic paper, "Uncertainty, Evolution, and Economic Theory" (1950). Interestingly, both of these papers (hence both of these approaches) work out of a bounded rationality setup. But whereas the paradigm problem for transaction cost economics is the make-or-buy decision, which has the effect of decomposing the enterprise into its constituent parts, evolutionary economics adopts a systems view of the enterprise in which knowledge acquisition and utilization are featured. Since "it is the performance of the system as a whole to which the most important feedback relates, it is quite possible that a very good solution to [a subsystem] . . . problem can carry, at least for a time, the cost burdens of a number of blunders in other areas [of the whole system]" (191).

Suboptimization is a chronic problem in the study of organization and is sometimes an unavoidable concession to the limits of bounded rationality. But suboptimization can sometimes be remedied — by embedding and reassessing local solutions in the context of the larger system of which they are a part. Path dependency considerations also need to be factored in. And Winter, like Demsetz, also emphasizes the importance of knowledge acquisition and its utilization in future work on the theory of the firm.

Scott Masten's paper on "A Legal Basis for the Firm" and Benjamin Klein's paper on "Vertical Integration as Organizational Ownership" complete the volume. Masten takes exception with the widely held view that the firm is merely a "nexus of contracts." He argues that firm and market differ in kind because of legal rule differences that apply to an employment relation as compared with a commercial contract. Thus, whereas commercial law is designed to preserve considerable autonomy between the parties, the law applicable to internal organization is designed to break down autonomy — whence there are "mechanisms or sanctions available in employment transactions that are not similarly available to independent contractors" (Masten, 1988:199). Accordingly, the laws governing the employment contract have "the intent of making the employee, to as great an extent as possible, an extension of the employer" (1988:208). The upshot is that firm and market differ because an employer has legal bases whereby greater obedience, loyalty, respect, and faithfulness can be expected from his employees (200). A firm is more than a neutral nexus of contract as a result.

Contrary to Coase and Demsetz, Benjamin Klein contends that the contracting hazards posed by asset specificity do have a significant influence on economic organization. To be sure, everyone agrees that firms will not breach contracts or otherwise behave opportunistically without making due allowance for reputation effect penalties in markets. To deter opportunism is not, however, to eliminate it. The fact that opportunism is "usually effectively checked" by reputation effect penalties (Coase: 71) is not, therefore, dispositive. The issue is one of the comparative efficacy of alternative forms of organization. Klein reexamines the Fisher Body–General Motors experience with interfirm contracting in the 1920s and concludes that "the long-term, fixed price formula, exclusive dealing contract" that Fisher Body and GM had negotiated was not only defective but created an enormous potential for Fisher to hold up General Motors—which is precisely what Fisher did (216). Market reputation effect penalties notwithstanding, vertical integration of these two stages of production was needed to relieve the strain.

Klein also distinguishes physical from human asset specificity and points out that the latter poses more severe contracting problems. Consonant with Winter's treatment of the firm as a nexus for knowledge acquisition and utilization, Klein urges that the "organization is embedded in the human capital of [its] employees" and that the management team is "greater than the sum of its parts" (220).

4. THE RESEARCH AGENDA

So what do we conclude from this volume in its treatment of past, current, and prospective research on the study of economic organization? One conclusion, on which there is unanimity, is that Ronald Harry Coase is one of the most influential economists of his day. His seminal thinking has pushed economics to reconsider its primitives. The core Coasian messages, which Coase tells with great subtlety, are these: the choice between firm and market organization is neither given, nor largely determined, by technology but mainly reflects efforts to economize on transaction costs; the study of transaction costs is preeminently a comparative institutional undertaking; and this very same comparative contractual approach applies to the study of economic organization quite generally—including hybrid forms of economic organization, externalities, and regulation.[1]

The past fifteen years have witnessed an increase of interest in and research relating to the microeconomics of organization. The once-orthodox view that the firm is a production function and that prices and output are the relevant data remains serviceable but is also limited. The study of economic organization in all of its forms through the lens of transaction cost economizing has made headway. There is growing agreement, moreover, with the need to engage data of a much more microanalytic kind than was hitherto thought to be necessary. Indeed, there is reason to believe that the elusive "science of organization" to which Chester Barnard made reference fifty years ago (1938:290) may take shape during the 1990s. Pertinent in this connection are the following observations and proposals:[2]

A. The Theory of Economic Organization
  1. *Comparative governance.* If the firm is a governance structure, then the boundary of the firm ought to be set with reference to the capacity of the firm (as compared with the market) to provide useful organizational functions. A comparative transaction cost economizing theory of the firm thus

needs to take its place alongside a technological theory of the firm. That has been occurring.

2. *Systems considerations.* Lest the analysis of subsystems fail to make allowance for team considerations, intraorganizational effects, intertemporal effects, or legal and political considerations, the analysis of transaction costs needs to be embedded in a larger context. The ways and reasons why the business enterprise as a whole is larger than and different from the sum of the parts need to be explicated. New analytical tools need to be devised, and the added ramifications need to be worked out. That too has been occurring.

3. *Safeguards.* If the benefits of supplying contractual safeguards against breakdown and premature breach vary systematically with the attributes of transactions, then an economic theory of contract will prescribe significant safeguards for some transactions and fewer safeguards for others. It does, and the data line up.[3]

4. *Generality.* If the above theory of contract has general application, it should apply—with variation—to labor, intermediate product, and capital market transactions alike.

   a. *Labor.* The collective organization of labor (unions) and the governance structures that appear within internal labor markets should vary systematically with the attributes of labor. The preliminary evidence suggests that they do.

   b. *Intermediate product.* Make or buy decisions should vary systematically with the attributes of transactions. There is abundant evidence that they do.[4]

5. *Leakage.* The need to seal off some technologies or protect some investments against loss of appropriability will predictably elicit leakage attenuation of a discriminating kind. It does.[5]

6. *The limits of internal organization.* Lest internal organization be overused with adverse cost-increasing consequences, internal organization needs to be used in a discriminating way. The powers and limits of both markets and hierarchies need to be worked out. The basic trade-offs need to be displayed. The data need to be worked up. Nuances need to be discovered. More generally, market failure and organizational failure need to be put on a parity. Work of this kind is in progress.

7. *Integrity.* The relentless emphasis on efficiency should not obscure the human needs of individuals—especially for personal integrity. The integrity respecting (or demeaning) attributes of markets and hierarchies of different kinds need to be worked out.

B. Applications to Functional Areas

1. *Finance.* Debt and equity can be described as financial instruments. But it is misleading to think of debt and equity only in financial terms if the critical economic differences between these two instruments turn also on their governance structure differences. A combined theory of corporate finance and corporate governance is needed. Alliance capitalism issues are implicated. Work on these matters has been progressing.[6]

2. *Marketing.* A contractual approach to marketing should lead to a discriminating theory of forward integration into distribution, the use of franchising, the use of agents, and so on. Work of this kind and evidence that pertains thereto are coming along.[7]

3. *Comparative systems.* Various approaches to the study of comparative economic systems have been employed with varying degrees of success. An assessment of the incentive and bureaucratic features of capitalism and socialism — the powers, limits, contradictions of each — is sorely needed.

4. *Economic development.* The time has come and the apparatus is at hand to examine economic development in a more institutionally oriented and microanalytic way. Older theories — of neoclassical, rent-seeking, and property rights kinds — simply fail to address, much less come to grips with, many of the pertinent institutional issues.

5. *Business strategy.* Strategic thinking is always appealing. But a lot of strategizing is mistaken and can be costly. A discriminating theory of strategizing — when it pays; when it does not; what are the instruments; how do they work — is needed. A comparative contractual approach supplies some of the needed framework.

6. *Business history.* Business history ought both to inform and be informed by the combined study of economics and organization. Business history is a field which appears to be experiencing a new life.

C. Applications to Contiguous Disciplines

1. *Politics.* Contractual theories of how to organize regulatory agencies and how federalism should be structured would greatly add to our understanding of politics. Work of both kinds is in progress.[8] Also, a combined assessment of political institutions, credible contracting, and economic development is sorely needed. That too has begun to take shape.[9]

2. *International.* Reconceptualizing the modern corporation in governance structure/organizational terms has ramifications for the way in which the multinational corporation is interpreted. The selective use of the multinational corporation to facilitate technology transfer is one example. More generally, the multinational corporation is usefully thought of in transnational terms — which has ramifications for the theory of the nation-state.[10]

3. *Sociology.* The new economics of organization has brought economics and sociology into active contract with one another whereas they used to operate at a distance. A rich dialogue is needed and is in prospect.[11]

4. *The law.* In addition to antitrust and regulation, the new economics of organization has an important bearing on corporate governance and on contract law. Among other things, new interpretations of "excuse doctrine," a satisfactory rationale for which has been elusive, need to be worked out.

D. Public Policy

1. *Antitrust.* Public policy toward business needs to be informed and reformed accordingly. This too has been going on. Antitrust has already been reshaped (especially with respect to vertical integration and vertical contract-

ing practices) and more is in prospect — joint research ventures being an example.[12]

2. *Regulation*. If contracts work well in some circumstances but predictably break down in others, then the merits of deregulation (moving out of regulation into autonomous contracting) ought to be susceptible to analysis. Deregulation — including mistaken deregulation — should be examined along these lines.[13]

3. *Micro/macro*. The microfoundations of macroeconomics also need to be reexamined in a comparative contractual way. That surface has barely been scratched.[14]

NOTES

1. These three points are based on my review of Coase's book, *The Firm, the Market, and the Law* (Williamson, 1989: 223–24).

2. The material here relies on my chapter on "Chester Barnard and the Incipient Science of Organization" (Williamson, 1990).

3. See especially the papers by Joskow (1985; 1987; 1988) and references therein.

4. Much of this is summarized in Williamson (1985, ch. 5).

5. See David Teece (1986) and Jan Heide and George John (1988).

6. See Michael Gerlach (1987), Masahiko Aoki (1988), and Eric Berglof (1989).

7. See Erin Anderson and David Schmittlein (1984) and George John and Burton Weitz (1988).

8. See Terry Moe (1990) and Weingast and Marshall (1988).

9. See Douglass North and Barry Weingast (1989) and Gary Miller (1989).

10. See Robert Keohane (1984) and Beth and Robert Yarborough (1987).

11. See Mark Granovetter (1985) and Williamson (1988).

12. On the latter, see Thomas Jorde and David Teece (1989).

13. See Williamson (1985, ch. 13) and Joskow and Schmalensee (1983).

14. See Arthur Okun (1981), Michael Wachter and Williamson (1978), and Williamson (1986).

REFERENCES

Alchian, Armen. 1950. "Uncertainty, Evolution and Economic Theory," 58 *Journal of Political Economy* 211–21.

———. 1984. "Specificity, Specialization, and Coalitions," 140 *Journal of Economic Theory and Institutions* 34–49.

———, and H. Demsetz. 1972. "Production, Information Costs, and Economic Organization," 62 *American Economic Review* 777–95.

Anderson, Erin, and David Schmittlein. 1984. "Integration of the Sales Force: An Empirical Examination," 15 *The Rand Journal of Economics* 385–95.

Aoki, Masahiko. 1988. "The Nature of the Japanese Firm as a Nexus of Employment and Financial Contracts: An Overview," 3 *Journal of the Japanese and International Economies* 345–66.

Berglof, Eric. 1989. "Capital Structure as a Mechanism of Control: A Comparison of Financial Systems." In Masahiko Aoki, Bo Gustafsson, and Oliver Williamson, eds., *The Firm as a Nexus of Treaties*. London: Sage Publications.

Coase, Ronald H. 1937. "The Nature of the Firm," 4 *Economica N.S.* 386–405 [chapter 2 of this volume].

———. 1972. "Industrial Organization: A Proposal for Research." In V. R. Fuchs, ed., *Policy Issues and Research Opportunities in Industrial Organization*. New York: National Bureau of Economic Research.

———. 1978. "Economics and Contiguous Disciplines," 7 *Journal of Legal Studies* 201–11.

———. 1988. *The Firm, the Market, and the Law*. Chicago: University of Chicago Press.

Commons, John R. 1934. *Institutional Economics*. Madison: University of Wisconsin Press.

Gerlach, Michael. 1987. "Business Alliances and the Strategy of the Japanese Firm," 30 *California Management Review* 126–42.

Granovetter, Mark. 1985. "Economic Action and Social Structure: The Problem of Embeddedness," 91 *American Journal of Sociology* 481–501.

Grossman, Sanford J., and Oliver D. Hart. 1986. "The Costs and Benefits of Ownership: A Theory of Vertical and Lateral Integration," 94 *Journal of Political Economy* 691–719.

Heide, Jan, and George John. 1988. "The Role of Dependence Balancing in Safeguarding Transaction-Specific Assets in Conventional Channels," 52 *Journal of Marketing* 20–35.

Jensen, Michael, and William Meckling. 1976. "Theory of the Firm: Managerial Behavior, Agency Costs, and Capital Structure, 3 *Journal of Financial Economics* 305–60.

John, George, and Barton Weitz. 1988. "Forward Integration into Distribution," 4 *Journal of Law, Economics, and Organization* 337–56.

Jorde, Thomas, and David Teece. 1989. "Innovation, Cooperation, and Antitrust." Unpublished manuscript.

Joskow, Paul L. 1985. "Vertical Integration and Long-term Contracts," 1 *Journal of Law, Economics, and Organization* 33–80.

———. 1987. "Contract Duration and Relationship-Specific Investments," 77 *American Economic Review* 168–85.

———. 1988. "Asset Specificity and the Structure of Vertical Relationships: Empirical Evidence," 4 *Journal of Law, Economics, and Organization* 95–117 [chapter 8 of this volume].

———, and Richard Schmalensee. 1983. *Markets for Power*. Cambridge, Mass.: MIT Press.

Kaldor, Nicholas. 1934. "The Equilibrium of the Firm," 44 *Economic Journal* 70–91.

Keohane, Robert. 1984. *After Hegemony: Cooperation and Discord in the World Political Economy*. Princeton, N.J: Princeton University Press.

Miller, Gary. 1989. "Confiscation, Credible Commitment and Progression Reform in the United States," 145 *Journal of Institutional and Theoretical Economics* 686–92.

Moe, Terry. 1990. "The Politics of Structural Choice: Toward a Theory of Public Bureaucracy." In Oliver Williamson, ed., *Organization Theory*. New York: Oxford University Press.

North, Douglass, and Barry Weingast. 1989. "Constitutions and Commitment: The Evolution of Institutions Governing Public Choice in Seventeenth-Century England," 49 *Journal of Economic History* 803–32.

Okun, A. 1981. *Prices and Quantities: A Macroeconomic Analysis*. Washington, DC: The Brookings Institution.

Robbins, Lionel. 1932. *An Essay on the Nature and Significance of Economic Science.* London: Macmillan.

Robinson, E. A. G. 1934. "The Problem of Management and the Size of Firms," 44 *Economic Journal* 240–54.

Teece, David J. 1986. "Profiting from Technological Innovation," 15 *Research Policy* 285–305.

Wachter, Michael, and O. E. Williamson. 1978. "Obligational Markets and the Mechanics of Inflation," 9 *Bell Journal of Economics* 549–71.

Weingast, Barry, and William Marshall. 1988. "The Industrial Organization of Congress," 96 *Journal of Political Economy* 132–63.

Williamson, Oliver E. 1985. *The Economic Institutions of Capitalism.* New York: Free Press.

_____. 1986. "A Microanalytic Assessment of 'The Share Economy,'" 95 *Yale Law Journal* 627–37.

_____. 1988. "The Economics and Sociology of Organization: Promoting A Dialogue." In George Farkas and Paula England, eds., *Industries, Firms, and Jobs.* New York: Plenum.

_____. 1989. "Review of Ronald Coase's The Firm, the Market, and the Law," 77 *University of California Law Review* 2223–31.

_____. 1990. *Organization Theory: From Chester Barnard to the Present and Beyond.* New York: Oxford University Press.

Yarborough, Beth, and Robert Yarborough. 1987. "Institutions for the Governance of Opportunism in International Trade," 3 *Journal of Law, Economics, and Organization* 129–39.

2

The Nature of the Firm (1937)

R. H. COASE

Economic theory has suffered in the past from a failure to state clearly its assumption. Economists in building up a theory have often omitted to examine the foundations on which it was erected. This examination is, however, essential not only to prevent the misunderstanding and needles controversy which arise from a lack of knowledge of the assumptions on which a theory is based, but also because of the extreme importance for economics of good judgment in choosing between rival sets of assumptions. For instance, it is suggested that the use of the word "firm" in economics may be different from the use of the term by the "plain man."[1] Since there is apparently a trend in economic theory towards starting analysis with the individual firm and not with the industry,[2] it is all the more necessary not only that a clear definition of the word "firm" should be given but that its difference from a firm in the "real world," if it exists, should be made clear. Mrs. Robinson has said that "the two questions to be asked of a set of assumptions in economics are: Are they tractable? and: Do they correspond with the real world?"[3] Though, as Mrs. Robinson points out, "More often one set will be manageable and the other realistic," yet there may well be branches of theory where assumptions may be both manageable and realistic. It is hoped to show in the following paper that a definition of a firm may be obtained which is not only realistic in that it corresponds to what is meant by a firm in the real world, but is tractable by two of the most powerful instruments of economic analysis developed by Marshall, the idea of the margin and that of substitution, together giving the idea of substitution at the margin.[4] Our definition must, of course, "relate to formal relations which are capable of being *conceived* exactly."[5]

I

It is convenient if, in searching for a definition of a firm, we first consider the economic system as it is normally treated by the economist. Let us consider the description of the economic system given by Sir Arthur Salter.[6] "The normal economic system works itself. For its current operation it is under no central control, it needs no central survey. Over the whole range of human activity and human need, supply is adjusted to demand, and production to consumption, by a process that is automatic, elastic and responsive." An economist thinks of the economic system as being co-ordinated by the price mechanism and society becomes not an organization but an organism.[7] The economic system "works itself." This does not mean that there is no planning by individuals. These exercise foresight and choose between alternatives. This is necessarily so if there is to be order in the system. But this theory assumes that the direction of resources is dependent directly on the price mechanism. Indeed, it is often considered to be an objection to economic planning that it merely tries to do what is already done by the price mechanism.[8] Sir Arthur Salter's description, however, gives a very incomplete picture of our economic system. Within a firm, the description does not fit at all. For instance, in economic theory we find that the allocation of factors of production between different uses is determined by the price mechanism. The price of factor A becomes higher in X than in Y. As a result, A moves from Y to X until the difference between the prices in X and Y, except in so far as it compensates for other differential advantages, disappears. Yet in the real world, we find that there are many areas where this does not apply. If a workman moves from department Y to department X, he does not go because of a change in relative prices, but because he is ordered to do so. Those who object to economic planning on the grounds that the problem is solved by price movements can be answered by pointing out that there is planning within our economic system which is quite different from the individual planning mentioned above and which is akin to what is normally called economic planning. The example given above is typical of a large sphere in our modern economic system. Of course, this fact has not been ignored by economists. Marshall introduces organization as a fourth factor of production; J. B. Clark gives the co-ordinating function to the entrepreneur; Professor Knight introduces managers who co-ordinate. As D. H. Robertson points out, we find "islands of conscious power in this ocean of unconscious co-operation like lumps of butter coagulating in a pail of buttermilk."[9] But in view of the fact that it is usually argued that co-ordination will be done by the price mechanism, why is such organization necessary? Why are there these "islands of conscious power"? Outside the firm, price movements direct production, which is co-ordinated through a series of exchange transactions on the market. Within a firm, these markets transactions are eliminated and in place of the complicated market structure with exchange transactions is substituted the entrepreneur-co-ordinator, who directs production.[10] It is clear that these are alternative methods of co-ordinating production. Yet, having regard to the fact that if production is regulated by price movements, production could be carried on without any organization at all, well might we ask, why is there any organization?

Of course, the degree to which the price mechanism is superseded varies greatly. In a department store, the allocation of the different sections to the various locations in the building may be done by the controlling authority or it may be the result of competitive price bidding for space. In the Lancashire cotton industry, a weaver can rent power and shop-room and can obtain looms and yarn on credit.[11]

This co-ordination of the various factors of production is, however, normally car-ried out without the intervention of the price mechanism. As is evident, the amount of "vertical" integration, involving as it does the supersession of the price mecha-nism, varies greatly from industry to industry and from firm to firm.

It can, I think, be assumed that the distinguishing mark of the firm is the supersession of the price mechanism. It is, of course, as Professor Robbins points out, "related to an outside network of relative prices and costs,"[12] but it is impor-tant to discover the exact nature of this relationship. This distinction between the allocation of resources in a firm and the allocation in the economic system has been very vividly described by Mr. Maurice Dobb when discussing Adam Smith's concep-tion of the capitalist: "It began to be seen that there was something more important than the relations inside each factory or unit captained by an undertaker; there were the relations of the undertaker with the rest of the economic world outside his immediate sphere . . . the undertaker busies himself with the division of labour inside each firm and he plans and organises consciously," but "he is related to the much larger economic specialisation, of which he himself is merely one specialised unit. Here, he plays his part as a single cell in a larger organism, mainly uncon-scious of the wider rôle he fills."[13]

In view of the fact that while economists treat the price mechanism as a co-ordinating instrument, they also admit the co-ordinating function of the "entrepre-neur," it is surely important to enquire why co-ordination is the work of the price mechanism in one case and of the entrepreneur in another. The purpose of this paper is to bridge what appears to be a gap in economic theory between the assumption (made for some purposes) that resources are allocated by means of the price mechanism and the assumption (made for other purposes) that this allocation is dependent on the entrepreneur-co-ordinator. We have to explain the basis on which, in practice, this choice between alternatives is effected.[14]

II

Our task is to attempt to discover why a firm emerges at all in a specialized exchange economy. The price mechanism (considered purely from the side of the direction of resources) might be superseded if the relationship which replaced it was desired for its own sake. This would be the case, for example, if some people preferred to work under the direction of some other person. Such individuals would accept less in order to work under someone, and firms would arise naturally from this. But it would appear that this cannot be a very important reason, for it would rather seem that the opposite tendency is operating if one judges from the stress normally laid on the advantage of "being one's own master."[15] Of course, if the desire was not to be controlled but to control, to exercise power over others, then people might be willing to give up something in order to direct others; that is, they would be willing to pay others more than they could get under the price mechanism in order to be able to direct them. But this implies that those who direct pay in order to be able to do this and are not paid to direct, which is clearly not true in the majority of cases.[16] Firms might also exist if purchasers preferred commodities which are produced by firms to those not so produced; but even in spheres where one would expect such preferences (if they exist) to be of negligible importance, firms are to be found in the real world.[17] Therefore there must be other elements involved.

The main reason why it is profitable to establish a firm would seem to be that there is a cost of using the price mechanism. The most obvious cost of "organizing" production through the price mechanism is that of discovering what the relevant prices are.[18] This cost may be reduced but it will not be eliminated by the emergence of specialists who will sell this information. The costs of negotiating and concluding a separate contract for each exchange transaction which takes place on a market must also be taken into account.[19] Again, in certain markets, e.g., produce exchanges, a technique is devised for minimizing these contract costs; but they are not eliminated. It is true that contracts are not eliminated when there is a firm but they are greatly reduced. A factor of production (or the owner thereof) does not have to make a series of contracts with the factors with whom he is co-operating within the firm, as would be necessary, of course, if this co-operation were as a direct result of the working of the price mechanism. For this series of contracts is substituted one. At this stage, it is important to note the character of the contract into which a factor enters that is employed within a firm. The contract is one whereby the factor, for a certain remuneration (which may be fixed or fluctuating), agrees to obey the directions of an entrepreneur *within certain limits*.[20] The essence of the contract is that it should only state the limits to the powers of the entrepreneur. Within these limits, he can therefore direct the other factors of production.

There are, however, other disadvantages — or costs — of using the price mechanism. It may be desired to make a long-term contract for the supply of some article or service. This may be due to the fact that if one contract is made for a longer period, instead of several shorter ones, then certain costs of making each contract will be avoided. Or, owing to the risk attitude of the people concerned, they may prefer to make a long rather than a short-term contract. Now, owing to the difficulty of forecasting, the longer the period of the contract is for the supply of the commodity or service, the less possible, and indeed, the less desirable it is for the person purchasing to specify what the other contracting party is expected to do. It may well be a matter of indifference to the person supplying the service or commodity which of several courses of action is taken, but not to the purchaser of that service or commodity. But the purchaser will not know which of these several courses he will want the supplier to take. Therefore, the service which is being provided is expressed in general terms, the exact details being left until a later date. All that is stated in the contract is the limits to what the persons supplying the commodity or service is expected to do. The details of what the supplier is expected to do is not stated in the contract but is decided later by the purchaser. When the direction of resources (within the limits of the contract) becomes dependent on the buyer in this way, that relationship which I term a "firm" may be obtained.[21] A firm is likely therefore to emerge in those cases where a very short-term contract would be unsatisfactory. It is obviously of more importance in the case of services —

labor—than it is in the case of the buying of commodities. In the case of commodities, the main items can be stated in advance and the details which will be decided later will be of minor significance.

We may sum up this section of the argument by saying that the operation of a market costs something and by forming an organization and allowing some authority (an "entrepreneur") to direct the resources, certain marketing costs are saved. The entrepreneur has to carry out his function at less cost, taking into account the fact that he may get factors of production at a lower price than the market transactions which he supersedes, because it is always possible to revert to the open market if he fails to do this.

The question of uncertainty is one which is often considered to be very relevant to the study of the equilibrium of the firm. It seems improbable that a firm would emerge without the existence of uncertainty. But those, for instance, Professor Knight, who make the *mode of payment* the distinguishing mark of the firm—fixed incomes being guaranteed to some of those engaged in production by a person who takes the residual, and fluctuating, income—would appear to be introducing a point which is irrelevant to the problem we are considering. One entrepreneur may sell his services to another for a certain sum of money, while the payment to his employees may be mainly or wholly a share in profits.[22] The significant question would appear to be why the allocation of resources is not done directly by the price mechanism.

Another factor that should be noted is that exchange transactions on a market and the same transactions organized within a firm are often treated differently by Governments or other bodies with regulatory powers. If we consider the operation of a sales tax, it is clear that it is a tax on market transactions and not on the same transactions organized within the firm. Now since these are alternative methods of "organization"—by the price mechanism or by the entrepreneur—such a regulation would bring into existence firms which otherwise would have no *raison d'être*. It would furnish a reason for the emergence of a firm in a specialized exchange economy. Of course, to the extent that firms already exist, such a measure as a sales tax would merely tend to make them larger than they would otherwise be. Similarly, quota schemes, and methods of price control which imply that there is rationing, and which do not apply to firms producing such products for themselves, by allowing advantages to those who organize within the firm and not through the market, necessarily encourage the growth of firms. But it is difficult to believe that it is measures such as have been mentioned in this paragraph which have brought firms into existence. Such measures would, however, tend to have this result if they did not exist for other reasons.

These, then, are the reasons why organizations such as firms exist in a specialized exchange economy in which it is generally assumed that the distribution of resources is "organized" by the price mechanism. A firm, therefore, consists of the system of relationships which comes into existence when the direction of resources is dependent on an entrepreneur.

The approach which has just been sketched would appear to offer an advantage in that it is possible to give a scientific meaning to what is meant by saying that a firm gets larger or smaller. A firm becomes larger as additional transactions (which could be exchange transactions co-ordinated through the price mechanism) are organized by the entrepreneur and becomes smaller as he abandons the organization of such transactions. The question which arises is whether it is possible to study the forces which determine the size of the firm. Why does the entrepreneur not organize one less transaction or one more? It is interesting to note that Professor Knight considers that:

> the relation between efficiency and size is one of the most serious problems of theory, being, in contrast with the relation for a plant, largely a matter of personality and historical accident rather than of intelligible general principles. But the question is peculiarly vital because the possibility of monopoly gain offers a powerful incentive to *continuous and unlimited* expansion of the firm, which force must be offset by some equally powerful one making for decreased efficiency (in the production of money income) with growth in size, if even boundary competition is to exist.[23]

Professor Knight would appear to consider that it is impossible to treat scientifically the determinants of the size of the firm. On the basis of the concept of the firm developed above, this task will now be attempted.

It was suggested that the introduction of the firm was due primarily to the existence of marketing costs. A pertinent question to ask would appear to be (quite apart from the monopoly considerations raised by Professor Knight), why, if by organizing one can eliminate certain costs and in fact reduce the cost of production, are there any market transactions at all?[24] Why is not all production carried on by one big firm? There would appear to be certain possible explanations.

First, as a firm gets larger, there may be decreasing returns to the entrepreneur function, that is, the costs of organizing additional transactions within the firm may rise.[25] Naturally, a point must be reached where the costs of organizing an extra transaction within the firm are equal to the costs involved in carrying out the transaction in the open market, or, to the costs of organizing by another entrepreneur. Secondly, it may be that as the transactions which are organized increase, the entrepreneur fails to place the factors of production in the uses where their value is greatest, that is, fails to make the best use of the factors of production. Again, a point must be reached where the loss through the waste of resources is equal to the marketing costs of the exchange transaction in the open market or to the loss if the transaction was organized by another entrepreneur. Finally, the supply price of one or more of the factors of production may rise, because the "other advantages" of a small firm are greater than those of a large firm.[26] Of course, the actual point where the expansion of the firm ceases might be determined by a combination of the factors mentioned above. The first two reasons given most probably correspond to the economists' phrase of "diminishing returns to management."[27]

The point has been made in the previous paragraph that a firm will tend to expand until the costs of organizing an extra transaction within the firm become equal to the costs of carrying out the same transaction by means of an exchange on the open market or the costs of organizing in another firm. But if the firm stops its expansion at a point below the costs of marketing in the open market and at a point equal to the costs of organizing in another firm, in most cases (excluding the case of "combination"[28]), this will imply that there is a market transaction between these two procedures, each of whom could organize it at less than the actual marketing costs. How is the paradox to be resolved? If we consider an example the reason for this will become clear. Suppose A is buying a product from B and that both A and B could organize this marketing transaction at less than its present cost. B, we can assume, is not organizing one process or stage of production, but several. If A therefore wishes to avoid a market transaction, he will have to take over all the processes of production controlled by B. Unless A takes over all the processes of production, a market transaction will still remain, although it is a different product that is bought. But we have previously assumed that as each producer expands he becomes less efficient; the additional costs of organizing extra transactions increase. It is probable that A's cost of organizing the transactions previously organized by B will be greater than B's costs of doing the same thing. A therefore will take over the whole of B's organization only if his cost of organizing B's work is not greater than B's cost by an amount equal to the costs of carrying out an exchange transaction on the open market. But once it becomes economical to have a market transaction, it also pays to divide production in such a way that the cost of organizing an extra transaction in each firm is the same.

Up to now it has been assumed that the exchange transactions which take place through the price mechanism are homogeneous. In fact, nothing could be more diverse than the actual transactions which take place in our modern world. This would seem to imply that the costs of carrying out exchange transactions through the price mechanism will vary considerably as will also the costs of organizing these transactions within the firm. It seems therefore possible that quite apart from the question of diminishing returns the costs of organizing certain transactions within the firm may be greater than the costs of carrying out the exchange transactions in the open market. This would necessarily imply that there were exchange transactions carried out through the price mechanism, but would it mean that there would have to be more than one firm? Clearly not, for all those areas in the economic system where the direction of resources was not dependent directly on the price mechanism could be organized within one firm. The factors which were discussed earlier would seem to be the important ones, though it is difficult to say whether "diminishing returns to management" or the rising supply price of factors is likely to be the more important.

Other things being equal, therefore, a firm will tend to be larger:

a. the less the costs of organizing and the slower these costs rise with an increase in the transactions organized.

b. the less likely the entrepreneur is to make mistakes and the smaller the increase in mistakes with an increase in the transactions organized.

c. the greater the lowering (or the less the rise) in the supply price of factors of production to firms of larger size.

Apart from variations in the supply price of factors of production to firms of different sizes, it would appear that the costs of organizing and the losses through mistakes will increase with an increase in the spatial distribution of the transactions organized, in the dissimilarity of the transactions, and in the probability of changes in the relevant prices.[29] As more transactions are organized by an entrepreneur, it would appear that the transactions would tend to be either different in kind or in different places. This furnishes an additional reason why efficiency will tend to decrease as the firm gets larger. Inventions which tend to bring factors of production nearer together, by lessening spatial distribution, tend to increase the size of the firm.[30] Changes like the telephone and the telegraph which tend to reduce the cost of organizing spatially will tend to increase the size of the firm. All changes which improve managerial technique will tend to increase the size of the firm.[31/32]

It should be noted that the definition of a firm which was given above can be used to give more precise meanings to the terms "combination" and "integration."[33] There is a combination when transactions which were previously organized by two or more entrepreneurs become organized by one. This becomes integration when it involves the organization of transactions which were previously carried out between the entrepreneurs on a market. A firm can expand in either or both of these two ways. The whole of the "structure of competitive industry" becomes tractable by the ordinary technique of economic analysis.

III

The problem which has been investigated in the previous section has not been entirely neglected by economists and it is now necessary to consider why the reasons given above for the emergence of a firm in a specialized exchange economy are to be preferred to the other explanations which have been offered.

It is sometimes said that the reason for the existence of a firm is to be found in the division of labor. This is the view of Professor Usher, a view which has been adopted and expanded by Mr. Maurice Dobb. The firm becomes "the result of an increasing complexity of the division of labour. . . . The growth of this economic differentiation creates the need for some integrating force without which differentiation would collapse into chaos; and it is as the integrating force in a differentiated economy that industrial forms are chiefly significant."[34] The answer to this argument is an obvious one. The "integrating force in a differentiated economy" already exists in the form of the price mechanism. It is perhaps the main achievement of economic science that it has shown that there is no reason to suppose that specialization must lead to chaos.[35] The reason given by Mr. Maurice Dobb is therefore inadmissible. What has to be explained is why one integrating force (the entrepreneur) should be substituted for another integrating force (the price mechanism).

The most interesting reasons (and probably the most widely accepted) which have been given to explain this fact are those to be found in Professor Knight's *Risk, Uncertainty and Profit*. His views will be examined in some detail.

Professor Knight starts with a system in which there is no uncertainty:

acting as individuals under absolute freedom but without collusion men are
supposed to have organised economic life with the primary and secondary
division of labour, the use of capital, etc., developed to the point familiar in
present-day America. The principal fact which calls for the exercise of the
imagination is the internal organisation of the productive groups or establish-
ments. With uncertainty entirely absent, every individual being in possession
of perfect knowledge of the situation, there would be no occasion for anything
of the nature of responsible management or control of productive activity.
Even marketing transactions in any realistic sense would not be found. The
flow of raw materials and productive services to the consumer would be entirely automatic.[36]

Professor Knight says that we can imagine this adjustment as being "the result
of a long process of experimentation worked out by trial-and-error methods alone,"
while it is not necessary "to imagine every worker doing exactly the right thing at the
right time in a sort of 'pre-established harmony' with the work of others. There
might be managers, superintendents, etc., for the purpose of co-ordinating the
activities of individuals," though these managers would be performing a purely
routine function, "without responsibility of any sort."[37]
Professor Knight then continues:

With the introduction of uncertainty—the fact of ignorance and the necessity
of acting upon opinion rather than knowledge—into this Eden-like situation,
its character is entirely changed. . . . With uncertainty present doing things,
the actual execution of activity, becomes in a real sense a secondary part of
life; the primary problem or function is deciding what to do and how to do
it.[38]

This fact of uncertainty brings about the two most important characteristics of
social organization.

In the first place, goods are produced for a market, on the basis of entirely
impersonal prediction of wants, not for the satisfaction of the wants of the
producers themselves. The producer takes the responsibility of forecasting
the consumers' wants. In the second place, the work of forecasting and at the
same time a large part of the technological direction and control of production are still further concentrated upon a very narrow class of the producers,
and we meet with a new economic functionary, the entrepreneur. . . . When
uncertainty is present and the task of deciding what to do and how to do it
takes the ascendancy over that of execution the internal organisation of the
productive groups is no longer a matter of indifference or a mechanical detail.
Centralisation of this deciding and controlling function is imperative, a process of "cephalisation" is inevitable.[39]

The most fundamental change is:

the system under which the confident and venturesome assume the risk or insure the doubtful and timid by guaranteeing to the latter a specified income in return for an assignment of the actual results. . . . With human nature as we know it it would be impracticable or very unusual for one man to guarantee to another a definite result of the latter's actions without being given power to direct his work. And on the other hand the second party would not place himself under the direction of the first without such a guarantee. . . . The result of this manifold specialisation of function is the enterprise and wage system of industry. Its existence in the world is the direct result of the fact of uncertainty.[40]

These quotations give the essence of Professor Knight's theory. The fact of uncertainty means that people have to forecast future wants. Therefore, you get a special class springing up who direct the activities of others to whom they give guaranteed wages. It acts because good judgment is generally associated with confidence in one's judgment.[41]

Professor Knight would appear to leave himself open to criticism on several grounds. First of all, as he himself points out, the fact that certain people have better judgment or better knowledge does not mean that they can only get an income from it by themselves actively taking part in production. They can sell advice or knowledge. Every business buys the services of a host of advisers. We can imagine a system where all advice or knowledge was bought as required. Again, it is possible to get a reward from better knowledge or judgment not by actively taking part in production but by making contracts with people who are producing. A merchant buying for future delivery represents an example of this. But this merely illustrates the point that it is quite possible to give a guaranteed reward providing that certain acts are performed without directing the performance of those acts. Professor Knight says that "with human nature as we know it, it would be impracticable or very unusual for one man to guarantee to another a definite result of the latter's actions without being given power to direct his work." This is surely incorrect. A large proportion of jobs are done to contract, that is, the contractor is guaranteed a certain sum providing he performs certain acts. But this does not involve any direction. It does mean, however, that the system of relative prices has been changed and that there will be a new arrangement of the factors of production.[42] The fact that Professor Knight mentions that the "second party would not place himself under the direction of the first without such a guarantee" is irrelevant to the problem we are considering. Finally, it seems important to notice that even in the case of an economic system where there is no uncertainty Professor Knight considers that there would be co-ordinators, though they would perform only a routine function. He immediately adds that they would be "without responsibility of any sort," which raises the question by whom are they paid and why? It seems that nowhere does Professor Knight give a reason why the price mechanism should be superseded.

IV

It would seem important to examine one further point and that is to consider the relevance of this discussion to the general question of the "cost-curve of the firm."

It has sometimes been assumed that a firm is limited in size under perfect competition if its cost curve slopes upward,[43] while under imperfect competition, it is limited in size because it will not pay to produce more than the output at which marginal cost is equal to marginal revenue.[44] But it is clear that a firm may produce more than one product and, therefore, there appears to be no prima facie reason why this upward slope of the cost curve in the case of perfect competition or the fact that marginal cost will not always be below marginal revenue in the case of imperfect competition should limit the size of the firm.[45] Mrs. Robinson[46] makes the simplifying assumption that only one product is being produced. But it is clearly important to investigate how the number of products produced by a firm is determined, while no theory which assumes that only one product is in fact produced can have very great practical significance.

It might be replied that under perfect competition, since everything that is produced can be sold at the prevailing price, then there is no need for any other product to be produced. But this argument ignores the fact that there may be a point where it is less costly to organize the exchange transactions of a new product than to organize further exchange transactions of the old product. This point can be illustrated in the following way. Imagine, following von Thunen, that there is a town, the consuming center, and that industries are located around this central point in rings. These conditions are illustrated in the following diagram in which A, B, and C represent different industries.

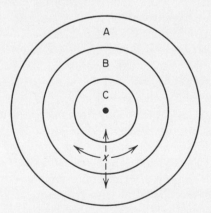

Imagine an entrepreneur who starts controlling exchange transactions from x. Now as he extends his activities in the same product (B), the cost of organizing increases until at some point it becomes equal to that of a dissimilar product which is nearer. As the firm expands, it will therefore from this point include more than one product (A and C). This treatment of the problem is obviously incomplete,[47] but it is necessary to show that merely proving that the cost curve turns upwards does not give a limitation to the size of the firm. So far we have only considered the case of perfect competition; the case of imperfect competition would appear to be obvious.

To determine the size of the firm, we have to consider the marketing costs (that is, the costs of using the price mechanism), and the costs of organizing the different entrepreneurs and then we can determine how many products will be produced by each firm and how much of each it will produce. It would, therefore, appear that Mr. Shove[48] in his article on "Imperfect Competition" was asking questions which Mrs. Robinson's cost curve apparatus cannot answer. The factors mentioned above would seem to be the relevant ones.

V

Only one task now remains; and that is, to see whether the concept of a firm which has been developed fits in with that existing in the real world. We can best approach the question of what constitutes a firm in practice by considering the legal relationship normally called that of "master and servant" or "employer and employee."[49] The essentials of this relationship have been given as follows:

(1) the servant must be under the duty of rendering personal services to the master or to others on behalf of the master, otherwise the contract is a contract for sale of goods or the like.

(2) The master must have the right to control the servant's work, either personally or by another servant or agent. It is this right of control or interference, of being entitled to tell the servant when to work (within the hours of service) and when not to work, and what work to do and how to do it (within the terms of such service) which is the dominant characteristic in this relation and marks off the servant from an independent contractor, or from one employed merely to give to his employer the fruits of his labour. In the latter case, the contractor or performer is not under the employer's control in doing the work or effecting the service; he has to shape and manage his work so as to give the result he has contracted to effect.[50]

We thus see that it is the fact of direction which is the essence of the legal concept of "employer and employee," just as it was in the economic concept which was developed above. It is interesting to note that Professor Batt says further:

That which distinguishes an agent from a servant is not the absence or presence of a fixed wage or the payment only of commission on business done, but rather the freedom with which an agent may carry out his employment.[51]

We can therefore conclude that the definition we have given is one which approximates closely to the firm as it is considered in the real world.

Our definition is, therefore, realistic. Is it manageable? This ought to be clear. When we are considering how large a firm will be the principle of marginalism works smoothly. The question always is, will it pay to bring an extra exchange transaction under the organizing authority? At the margin, the costs of organizing within the firm will be equal either to the costs of organizing in another firm or to the costs involved in leaving the transaction to be "organized" by the price mechanism. Business men will be constantly experimenting, controlling more or less, and in this way, equilibrium will be maintained. This gives the position of equilibrium for static analysis. But it is clear that the dynamic factors are also of considerable importance, and an investigation of the effect changes have on the cost of organizing within the firm and on marketing costs generally will enable one to explain why firms get larger and smaller. We thus have a theory of moving equilibrium. The above analysis would also appear to have clarified the relationship between initiative or enterprise and management. Initiative means forecasting and operates through the price mechanism by the making of new contracts. Management proper merely reacts to price changes, rearranging the factors of production under its control. That the business man normally combines both functions is an obvious result of the marketing costs which were discussed above. Finally, this analysis enables us to state more exactly what is meant by the "marginal product" of the entrepreneur. But an elaboration of this point would take us far from our comparatively simple task of definition and clarification.

NOTES

1. Joan Robinson, *Economics Is a Serious Subject* (1932), 12.

2. See N. Kaldor, "The Equilibrium of the Firm," 44 The Economic Journal (1934) 60–76.

3. Op. cit., 6.

4. J. M. Keynes, *Essays in Biography* (1933), 223–24.

5. L. Robbins, *Nature and Significance of Economic Science* (1935), 63.

6. This description is quoted with approval by D. H. Robertson, *Control of Industry* (1923), 85, and by Professor Arnold Plant, "Trends in Business Administration," 12 *Economica* (1932) 45–62. It appears in *Allied Shipping Control*, pp. 16–17.

7. See F. A. Hayek, "The Trend of Economic Thinking," 13 *Economica* (1933) 121–37.

8. See F. A. Hayek, op. cit.

9. Op. cit., 85.

10. In the rest of this paper I shall use the term entrepreneur to refer to the person or persons who, in a competitive system, take the place of the price mechanism in the direction of resources.

11. *Survey of Textile Industries*, 26.

12. Op. cit., 71.

13. *Capitalist Enterprise and Social Progress* (1925), 20. Cf., also, Henderson, *Supply and Demand* (1932), 3–5.

14. It is easy to see when the State takes over the direction of an industry that, in planning it, it is doing something which was previously done by the price mechanism. What is

usually not realized is that any business man in organizing the relations between his departments is also doing something which could be organized through the price mechanism. There is therefore point in Mr. Durbin's answer to those who emphasize the problems involved in economic planning that the same problems have to be solved by business men in the competitive system. (See "Economic Calculus in a Planned Economy," 46 *The Economic Journal* [1936] 676–90.) The important difference between these two cases is that economic planning is imposed on industry while firms arise voluntarily because they represent a more efficient method of organizing production. In a competitive system, there is an "optimum" amount of planning!

15. Cf. Harry Dawes, "Labour Mobility in the Steel Industry," 44 *The Economic Journal* (1934) 84–94, who instances "the trek to retail shopkeeping and insurance work by the better paid of skilled men due to the desire (often the main aim in life of a worker) to be independent" (86).

16. None the less, this is not altogether fanciful. Some small shopkeepers are said to earn less than their assistants.

17. G. F. Shove, "The Imperfection of the Market: a Further Note," 44 *The Economic Journal* (1933) 113–24, n. 1, points out that such preferences may exist, although the example he gives is almost the reverse of the instance given in the text.

18. According to N. Kaldor, "A Classificatory Note of the Determinanteness of Equilibrium," 1 *The Review of Economic Studies* (1934) 122–36, it is one of the assumptions of static theory that "All the relevant prices are known to all individuals." But this is clearly not true of the real world.

19. This influence was noted by Professor Usher when discussing the development of capitalism. He says: "The successive buying and selling of partly finished products were sheer waste of energy." (*Introduction to the Industrial History of England* (1920), 13.) But he does not develop the idea nor consider why it is that buying and selling operations still exist.

20. It would be possible for no limits to the powers of the entrepreneur to be fixed. This would be voluntary slavery. According to Professor Batt, *The Law of Master and Servant* (1933), 18, such a contract would be void and unenforceable.

21. Of course, it is not possible to draw a hard and fast line which determines whether there is a firm or not. There may be more or less direction. It is similar to the legal question of whether there is the relationship of master and servant or principal and agent. See the discussion of this problem below.

22. The views of Professor Knight are examined below in more detail.

23. *Risk, Uncertainty and Profit*, Preface to the Re-issue, London School of Economics Series of Reprints, No. 16 (1933).

24. There are certain marketing costs which could only be eliminated by the abolition of "consumers' choice" and these are the costs of retailing. It is conceivable that these costs might be so high that people would be willing to accept rations because the extra product obtained was worth the loss of their choice.

25. This argument assumes that exchange transactions on a market can be considered as homogeneous; which is clearly untrue in fact. This complication is taken into account below.

26. For a discussion of the variation of the supply price of factors and production to firms of varying size, see E. A. G. Robinson, *The Structure of Competitive Industry* (1932). It is sometimes said that the supply price of organizing ability increases as the size of the firm increases because men prefer to be the heads of small independent businesses rather than the heads of departments in a large business. See Jones, *The Trust Problem* (1921), 531, and Macgregor, *Industrial Combination* (1935), 63. This is a common argument of those who

advocate Rationalization. It is said that larger units would be more efficient, but owing to the individualistic spirit of the smaller entrepreneurs, they prefer to remain independent, apparently in spite of the higher income which their increased efficiency under Rationalization makes possible.

27. This discussion is, of course, brief and incomplete. For a more thorough discussion of this particular problem, see N. Kaldor, "The Equilibrium of the Firm," 44 *The Economic Journal* (1934) 60–76, and E. A. G. Robinson, "The Problem of Management and the Size of the Firm," 44 *The Economic Journal* (1934) 242–57.

28. A definition of this term is given below.

29. This aspect of the problem is emphasized by N. Kaldor, op. cit. Its importance in this connection had been previously noted by E. A. G. Robinson, *The Structure of Competitive Industry* (1932), 83–106. This assumes that an increase in the probability of price movements increases the costs of organizing within a firm more than it increases the cost of carrying out an exchange transaction on the market — which is probable.

30. This would appear to be the importance of the treatment of the technical unit by E. A. G. Robinson, op. cit., 27–33. The larger the technical unit, the greater the concentration of factors and therefore the firm is likely to be larger.

31. It should be noted that most inventions will change both the costs of organizing and the costs of using the price mechanism. In such cases, whether the invention tends to make firms larger or smaller will depend on the relative effect on these two sets of costs. For instance, if the telephone reduces the costs of using the price mechanism more than it reduces the costs of organizing, then it will have the effect of reducing the size of the firm.

32. An illustration of these dynamic forces is furnished by Maurice Dobb, *Russian Economic Development* (1928), 68. "With the passing of bonded labour the factory, as an establishment where work was organised under the whip of the overseer, lost its raison d'être until this was restored to it with the introduction of power machinery after 1846." It seems important to realize that the passage from the domestic system to the factory system is not a mere historical accident, but is conditioned by economic forces. This is shown by the fact that it is possible to move from the factory system to the domestic system, as in the Russian example, as well as vice versa. It is the essence of serfdom that the price mechanism is not allowed to operate. Therefore, there has to be direction from some organizer. When, however, serfdom passed, the price mechanism was allowed to operate. It was not until machinery drew workers into one locality that it paid to supersede the price mechanism and the firm again emerged.

33. This is often called "vertical integration," combination being termed "lateral integration."

34. Op. cit., 10. Professor Usher's views are to be found in his *Introduction to the Industrial History of England* (1920), 1–18.

35. Cf. J. B. Clark, *Distribution of Wealth* (1899), 19, who speaks of the theory of exchange as being the "theory of the organisation of industrial society."

36. *Risk, Uncertainty and Profit*, 267.

37. Op. cit., 267–68.

38. Op. cit., 268.

39. Op. cit., 268–95.

40. Op. cit., 269–70.

41. Op. cit., 270.

42. This shows that it is possible to have a private enterprise system without the existence of firms. Though, in practice, the two functions of enterprise, which actually influences

the system of relative prices by forecasting wants and acting in accordance with such forecasts, and management, which accepts the system of relative prices as being given, are normally carried out by the same persons, yet it seems important to keep them separate in theory. This point is further discussed below.

43. See Kaldor, op. cit., and Robinson, *The Problem of Management and the Size of the Firm*.

44. Mr. Robinson calls this the Imperfect Competition solution for the survival of the small firm.

45. Mr. Robinson's conclusion, op. cit., 249, n. 1, would appear to be definitely wrong. He is followed by Horace J. White, Jr., "Monopolistic and Perfect Competition," 26 *The American Economic Review* (1936) 645, n. 27. Mr. White states "It is obvious that the size of the firm is limited in conditions of monopolistic competition."

46. *Economics of Imperfect Competition* (1934).

47. As has been shown above, location is only one of the factors influencing the cost of organizing.

48. G. F. Shove, "The Imperfection of the Market," 43 *The Economic Journal* (1933), 115. In connection with an increase in demand in the suburbs and the effect on the price charged by suppliers, Mr. Shove asks " . . . why do not the old firms open branches in the suburbs?" If the argument in the text is correct, this is a question which Mrs. Robinson's apparatus cannot answer.

49. The legal concept of "employer and employee" and the economic concept of a firm are not identical, in that the firm may imply control over another person's property as well as over their labor. But the identity of these two concepts is sufficiently close for an examination of the legal concept to be of value in appraising the worth of the economic concept.

50. Batt, *The Law of Master and Servant*, 6.

51. Op. cit., 7.

3

The Nature of the Firm: Origin

R. H. COASE

"It is difficult for a man to speak long of himself without vanity." So said David Hume at the beginning of his autobiography. If David Hume felt such a warning to be necessary, a man who, according to Adam Smith, approached "as nearly to the idea of a perfectly wise and virtuous man, as perhaps the nature of human frailty will permit," it is hardly to be expected that my lectures will be free from vanity. However, a natural tendency to be overindulgent in dealing with my own work will be somewhat curbed by a real desire on my part to understand why "The Nature of the Firm" has been treated by the economics profession in the way it has. It is an article which is usually referred to with respect, has been reprinted in a number of books of reading, including *Readings in Price Theory*, sponsored by the American Economic Association, but which, until comparatively recently, has been largely without influence. It has had what the French call "un succès d'estime." To understand why this has been the case would be more difficult, if not indeed impossible, if I did not deal honestly with the circumstances surrounding its writing, with the ideas that it was intended to convey and with how they were expressed.

There is no problem in discovering when I formulated the ideas to be found in "The Nature of the Firm." They must have crystallized in my mind sometime in the summer of 1932. In October 1932 (or thereabouts) I was appointed an assistant lecturer at the Dundee School of Economics and Commerce. Duncan Black, the other assistant lecturer, has recalled that I arrived in Dundee with my head full of my ideas on the firm. His recollection is confirmed by a letter I wrote on October 10, 1932, to my friend Ronald Fowler, who was an assistant lecturer at the London School of Economics. It went as follows:

October 10, 1932

Dear Fowler,

Thanks very much for your letter. I am very sorry that I have not written to you before but I am terribly busy preparing lectures at the moment. Think of three courses all starting now! I am snowed under with work.

I am giving a course on organization of the business unit. I have given my first lecture on it. As it was a new approach (I think) to this subject, I was quite pleased with myself. One thing I can say is that I made it all up myself.

I first of all inquired the reason [for] an organization of the business unit which, the business unit, I said existed when anyone produced to sell in a market. This implied exchange and exchange specialization. But this specialization is a specialization of the business unit — it need imply no specialization within the business unit. I then differentiated between the regulation of the efforts of business units and that of individuals within the firm. The effort of business units in a market not organized — supply and demand, etc. I quoted that Salter piece in Plant's article. I pointed out [that] if there were atomistic competition, where every transaction involving the use of another's labour, materials or money was the subject of a market transaction, there would be no need for an organization. In fact, this is not so. Why? I found the reason in the costs of conducting these marketing transactions. Think of the inconvenience (increased cost) if every time someone worked with someone else, there had to be a market transaction. But if the transactions are not to be governed by the price mechanism directly there *has* to be an organization. Since under market conditions, the greatest use is made of the factors of production, [the] object of the organization was to reproduce market conditions, but production would be greater because of lowered costs. I then asked — if by eliminating market transactions, costs were lowered, why were there market transactions at all? That is, why are there separate firms? two reasons —

1. Increasing cost for each additional market transaction until cost of organizing marginal market transaction was equal to marketing cost of that transaction.
2. That as transactions increased, might not carry out its object of reproducing market conditions.

Then said, could not eliminate *ever* cost of selling to final consumer unless eliminated consumer's choice. Talked about organization in Russia, etc., etc. Concluded that object of organization was

(a) to reproduce distribution of factors under atomistic competition within the business unit
(b) to do so at a cost which is less than the marketing transactions it supersedes.

Of course, I was much fuller than the above. But I believe it was quite a good lecture. It certainly succeeded in linking up organization with cost. I intend to work up this argument a bit more. What do you think of the idea?

It is clear that this lecture, given when I was twenty-one, contained the main points which were later to appear in "The Nature of the Firm": the choice of the transaction as the unit of analysis, the concept of transaction costs, the distinction between the allocation of resources within the firm and through the market, the comparison of the costs of organizing a transaction within the firm and by means of a market transaction, and so on. The letter from which this account of the lecture is taken forms part of a correspondence with Ronald Fowler. In reconstructing the evolution of my ideas on the firm, I am relying to a considerable extent on this correspondence. It will be deposited in the Regenstein Library of the University of Chicago along with my other papers, notwithstanding that the boyish enthusiasm and juvenile expressions displayed therein now make me wince.

For some, their academic achievements have the character of inevitability. Had they not been attained by one route, they would have been by another. There was nothing inevitable about my writing "The Nature of the Firm." It came about as the result of a series of accidents. At my school (the Kilburn Grammar School, which would have been called a high school in the United States), after matriculating, which I did at sixteen, the normal age, it was possible to spend two additional years preparing for the external intermediate degree examinations of the University of London (the equivalent of the first year of university work). My inclination was to take a degree in history but having come into the school at twelve rather than at the usual age of eleven, there was no question of my taking Latin at school. This lack of Latin barred me from taking an arts degree (or at any rate the one I wanted to take). I therefore started to work for a science degree, with the intention of specializing in chemistry. However, I soon found that mathematics, a requirement for a science degree, was not to my taste, and I switched to the only alternative open to me at school, working for a commerce degree. This move was undoubtedly made easier by the fact that I was at that time a socialist and the interest in social problems that this implies made the prospect of studying economics (a requirement for a commerce degree) attractive. During the next two years I studied economics, geography, French, English economic history and accounting (this through a correspondence course since accounting was not taught at my school). Although I knew next to nothing about these subjects, I managed to pass the examinations, the standard required obviously being rather low. In 1929, I went, aged eighteen, to the London School of Economics (LSE) to continue work for a commerce degree.

In 1929-1930, I worked for Part 1 of the final examination, taking courses in British foreign trade, the principles of currency, the theory of production, industrial relations, the economic development of the overseas dominions, India and the tropical dependencies, commercial law, statistical method, the organization of transport and psychology. In 1930-1931, I decided to take group D (industry) in Part 2 of the Bachelor of Commerce, a group which was recommended for those wishing to enter the engineering and metal trades, distributing trades (in certain instances), and generally for those engaged in works and factory management. It was a choice of occupation for which I was singularly ill-suited, but what else was there for someone to do who did not know Latin and did not like mathematics? In studying for Part 2 in 1930-1931, I took courses in French, accounting, business administration, works and factory accounting and cost accounts, the raw materials of industry and trade, problems of modern industry, the financing of industry, industrial law, and industrial psychology.

It will have been noticed that during my two years at LSE I studied a great variety of subjects, devoting therefore very little time to each and inevitably doing no systematic reading. I took no course in economics, and although some of the courses had an economics content, most did not. The courses to which I devoted the most time were those on law, particularly industrial law. I was fascinated by the cases and by legal reasoning. As a result of taking the B. Com., I knew a little about economics as well as a little about law, accounting, and statistics, a mixture of subjects which was not without effect on my subsequent work. But it was the teaching of Arnold Plant that had the greatest influence on me at LSE. I was the beneficiary of this by an extraordinary piece of luck. Plant, who had held a professorship in commerce at the University of Cape Town, South Africa, was appointed a professor of commerce (with special reference to business administration) at LSE in 1930. I attended Plant's lectures on business administration, but it was what he said in his seminar that really influenced me. I can still remember the impact of the first meeting of the seminar which Plant held. At a conference in Los Angeles in 1981 I described the dramatic effect this had on me: "We had been having a seminar previously by a man called Sargent. . . . Plant said, 'What have you been discussing?' And I said, 'Oh, we've been discussing policy in the oil industry. We've been contrasting the fine conservation policies which are carried out by the Anglo-Persian oil company with the wasteful policies they pursue in the United States.' And Plant said, 'Well, that is very interesting,' and then he started asking a few questions. After a little bit we discovered that the oil companies weren't maximizing their profits. And then we discovered that the government knew more about the oil industry than the oil companies did. That seemed odd. Even worse, that we knew more than the oil companies did. That was hard to take. Then we learned . . . that . . . a large part of the cost of producing oil is the present discounted value of the future receipts, and so on."[1] This seminar took place some five months before I took Part 2 of the final examination. Until I met Plant my economic views were extremely woolly. From him I learned that producers maximize profits, that producers compete, and therefore that prices tend to equal costs and the composition of output to be that which consumers value most highly. Plant also explained that governments often served special interests, promoted monopoly rather than competition, and commonly imposed regulations which made matters worse. He made me aware of the benefits which flow from an economy directed by the pricing system. Clearly, I did not need Chicago.

If Plant gave me my basic approach, I learned such economics as I knew mainly from discussions with fellow students. Chief among them was Ronald Fowler, who had been away in France on a Cassel travelling scholarship during my first year at LSE but had returned to follow the same courses that I did during my second year. Fowler had a fine analytical mind and I greatly benefited from our discussions. I also benefited from discussion with other students, particularly those specializing in economics, among whom were Vera Smith (later Vera Lutz), Abba Lerner, and Victor Edelberg. Ronald Fowler and I were particularly interested in costs and the construction of cost curves. However, the subject which dominated the discussion of economics at LSE in the last few months before the final examinations was far from my main interest. It was the structure of production—not the organizational structure of production that was going to absorb me but the Austrian capital structure of production, both teachers and students at LSE having been captivated by Hayek's public lectures given at LSE in February 1931, which were later published in *Prices and Production*. My performance in the final examinations was undistinguished but was at least sufficient for me to be awarded a Cassel travelling scholarship for the academic year 1931–1932. As I had spent only two years at LSE and three years' residence was required for a degree I was not awarded the B. Com. until 1932, my year on the Cassel scholarship being counted as a year's residence at LSE.

I proposed to spend this year in the United States and to study what I termed vertical and lateral integration in industry. My choice of subject (and it was my choice) undoubtedly resulted from the fact that Plant had referred to the different ways in which industries were organized. What stimulated my interest was that we seemed to lack any theory which would explain why those industries were organized in the way they were. My year in the United States was essentially devoted to a search for a theory of integration. This is quite explicit in my letters to Fowler. But there was another question which, while not directly concerned with the ways in which different industries were organized, was in my own mind related to it. Plant was critical of the rationalization schemes that were at that time advocated for a number of industries in Britain, and he was particularly hostile to proposals for the coordination of the various means of transport, a subject on which he presented a paper to the Institute of Transport in 1931. Plant argued that competition would provide all the coordination needed. Yet we had in economics a factor of production, management, whose function was to coordinate. Plant in his inaugural lecture at LSE in October 1931 spoke of the consumer as the "ultimate employer" in the economic system and he quoted Arthur Salter: "The normal economic system works itself."[2] (This passage was referred to in my Dundee lecture and later cited in "The Nature of the Firm.") Plant's point of view seemed to me to leave obscure the role of business management and of the employer-employee relationship. I did not dispute what Plant was saying. Indeed, it made a lot of sense. But it seemed somehow incomplete.

What was essentially the same puzzle presented itself to me in another form which can be summed up in one word, Russia. It would be very easy to someone today to have a mistaken idea about the situation as we saw it in 1931. The storming of the Winter Palace in St. Petersburg had taken place in October 1917, some fourteen years previously. After a period of war and civil strife and an initial period of centralized control, Lenin had instituted the New Economic Policy. He died in 1924 and Stalin did not become the undisputed leader of Russia until 1928 when Trotsky was exiled. The first five year plan was not adopted until 1928. So, at the time I was a student at LSE, from 1929 to 1931, it was not easy to form a view of how planning in Russia would actually work. We had heard of the construction of the vast Dnieper Dam on the Volga and I went to see its giant generators being made, at the General Electric works in Schenectady. But detailed knowledge was hard to get. Lenin had said that the economic system in Russia would be run as one big factory. Although it was undoubtedly a good deal easier to find out what was happening in Russia then than now, there was very little experience of economic organization in Russia to go on and economists in the West were engaged in a grand debate on the subject of planning, some maintaining that to run the economy as one big factory was an impossibility. And yet there were factories in England and America. How did one reconcile the impossibility of running Russia as one big factory with the existence of factories in the western world? At the time I considered myself to be a socialist and one of the people I went to see in the United States was Norman Thomas, the socialist candidate for president. One may ask how I reconciled my socialist sympathies with acceptance of Plant's approach. The short answer is that I never felt the need to reconcile them. I would only recall that a fellow student, Abba Lerner, who, in the preface to his *Economics of Control*, acknowledges Plant's influence in the development of his views, went to Mexico to see Trotsky to persuade him that all would be well in a communist state if only it reproduced the results of a competitive system and prices were set equal to marginal cost. In my case my socialist views fell away fairly rapidly without any obvious stage of rejection.

During my time in the United States I attended very few classes and although I visited a number of universities, most of my time was spent in visiting businesses and industrial plants. Before I went to America, Ernest Bevin, the secretary of the biggest trade union in Britain, the Transport and General Workers Union, had approached Bruce Gardner of the Bank of England on my behalf. Gardner gave me letters of introduction to various businessmen in the United States, and as a result I had little difficulty in meeting them. I still remember one most instructive day I spent in the office of a purchasing agent, I think at Union Carbide, listening to his telephone conversations, a visit which gave me a lively sense of the possibilities of substitution. While in the United States I read the reports of the Federal Trade Commission and books describing the organization of different industries, such as Copeland's study of the cotton textile industry. I also read trade periodicals and used more unusual sources (for an economist), such as the yellow pages of the telephone directory, where I was fascinated to find so many specialist firms operating within what we thought of as a single industry as well as such interesting combinations of activities as those represented by coal and ice companies. What I was in fact doing in America was looking for clues which would enable me to solve the puzzles that I took there with me. The extraordinary thing is that I think I succeeded.

In recounting how this came about I am fortunate in being able to use my correspondence with Fowler. Not all the letters in the correspondence have been preserved, but enough have survived to indicate what I was thinking about as I investigated the problem of integration. The correspondence is not, of course, wholly concerned with this subject. Fowler told me about Viner's article in the *Zeitschrift für Nationalökonomie* for September 1931, an article that, after I had read it, I described as a "magnificent achievement." He told me of Yntema's article in the *Journal of Political Economy* for 1928, which Hicks had been discussing at LSE and which disputed Viner's conclusion that dumping would not affect the price in the home market. As a letter to Fowler shows, I completely failed to understand Yntema's argument. I was also baffled by Fowler's reference to a "marginal receipts curve." In addition, Fowler discussed his own work on the economics of depreciation that was later to result in his *Depreciation of Capital*. This led to a discussion of more general questions, such as the utility of a concept of "profit" or a "dynamic surplus." Nonetheless, the main question considered in my own letters was the development of a theory of integration. It is somewhat embarrassing to me to quote from these letters in which my innermost thoughts are expressed with great frankness and without of course any expectation that they would ever be published. As I quote from these letters I can only hope that readers will treat the aspirations of this young man as sympathetically as I do.

I must first mention some thoughts in my letters which, while they did not lead directly to the breakthrough that enabled me to solve my puzzles, yet played their part in the evolution of my ideas and certainly came into their own once that breakthrough had been made. In a letter dated February 28, 1932, I said: "I am developing a theory that economic integration is the result of the limitations of small-scale production—in essence it is the joining up of small-scale producers in different industries in order to get the advantages of large-scale production. Therefore I would regard the linking up of units already producing on a large scale as most probably unsound." Within less than a month, however, I was expressing uneasiness about the concept of integration and its analysis. On March 24, 1932, I said that I had been thinking of integration as "the bringing together under one control of different functions." However, it wasn't clear to me how this fitted in with our view of the role of specialization. In any case I thought the way to proceed was to examine the effect on costs of bringing various combinations of functions under one control, and I illustrated my position with diagrams somewhat in the manner of Stigler in his 1951 article, "The Division of Labor Is Limited by the Extent of the Market," although of course without any of his sophistication. This led me to argue that the distinction between vertical and horizontal integration was without value. "What is important is that different functions are in fact brought together under one control, what stage they are in being of little account."

Fowler, in replying to this letter, gave a particularly clear account of the relation, as he saw it, between integration and specialization. He said: "The whole problem of integration seems to be this. All economies, lowering of costs by more efficient methods are as a rule due to greater specialization. Horizontal expansion depends for its greater productivity on the greater productivity of specialization and in fact you can say that specialization and horizontal expansion are two aspects of the same phenomenon. The difficult question is why do we get economies from vertical integration since it is quite clearly a reversal of the process of specialization. Of course the easy cases such as vertical integration in iron and steel between smelting and rolling are due to special technical considerations which cannot be generalized into any concept such as specialization. Lavington, I believe it was, wrote an article denying any general tendency towards vertical integration (I mean apart from attempts to obtain monopoly). If one is of the opinion that there is a *general* tendency to vertical integration, one has got to admit that there is a general tendency to eliminate the middleman, in other words that *in competition* two middlemen are more efficient than 3 middlemen. It really amounts to denying the greater economy of specialization."

To this I replied as follows: "I am not so sure how far all economies are as a rule due to greater specialization. . . . I started with this attitude but found it was not very helpful since it is not clear really whether modern business is more or less specialized than it used to be. It is more probably true that manual operations are more specialized but what about management? . . . This question is rather—what is the economic degree of integration? And this you can only analyze . . . by saying in what ways can the joining together of two tasks hitherto separate affect the shape of the resultant cost curves. I think that this form of analysis will get you some-where. The other concepts are too hazy to be of more than general use."

Fowler then commented: "I think it would be worthwhile going into the rea-sons for decreasing returns to managerial ability under conditions of equilibrium. Do decreasing returns arise from increasing complexity (the reverse of specializa-tion) as you suggest or from some other cause? If, for example, you are a firm specializing in the production of a particular commodity you go on expanding to a point where decreasing returns from managerial ability arise. Is it possible that these decreasing returns are due to the fact that the firm now has become not more specialized but less? For a likely cause of decreasing returns lies in the wider range of markets which are now supplied by the firm. A wide range of markets means less specialization, greater complexity. Where different markets require different treat-ment because of different conditions, there must be a tendency inducing specializa-tion for each market among producers." I responded to this point with enthusiasm: "I think your remark about decreasing returns to managerial ability arising not because the firm is more specialized but because it is less hits the nail on the head. There may be technical advantages in increasing complexity but it is decreasing returns to managerial ability which seems to set the limit." I go on to give an example: "When I was looking into the rubber tire industry, I considered the posi-tion of chemicals for the industry. Now, when you read American trade journals, it was obvious that these chemicals were marketed by the firms themselves. You could gather this from the advertisements. But if you looked at English trade publica-tions, the advertisement for the particular chemical appeared under the heading— X and Co.—Agents for XYZ Chemicals. That is to say, the selling in a foreign market was left to people who specialized in that market. The chemicals considered were, of course, American chemicals."

Fowler also said that my approach "to the question—what is the economic degree of integration?—by means of finding out in what ways the joining together of two tasks hitherto separate can affect the shape of the resultant cost curve is a very good one. I hope however that you will be able to generalize the results in some form or other." To this I did not reply and for what I believe was a good reason—the approach, so promising, was going nowhere. What the correspondence with Fowler had done was to indicate some of the problems. Why was it that what seemed to be a movement away from specialization was more efficient? Why should we make a distinction between vertical and horizontal integration? And why was it that costs could be lowered by grouping together certain activities under one control? I was very conscious that I had not got a handle on these problems. In my letter of March 24, 1932, after characterizing my own approach via the effect on costs of putting different functions under one control as "very weak," I go on to lament the lack of help I received from economists either in discussion or through a study of their writings. "The ignorance of the academic world on this subject is amazing. I think it is true to say that I have yet to discuss this question with any professor who has clearer ideas on it than I have." I add in the margin, "I am very hazy." I continue: "This becomes obvious when we go on to discuss the major part of the problem — the classification of the reasons for the change in the shape of the cost curve. Some of the reasons they give are absolutely untenable. If you want to know the type of thing just read the literature of the subject — it is absolute bilge." What I undoubtedly meant by characterizing the literature as "bilge" was that it made assumptions which contravened some of Plant's basic positions. I have forgotten the specifics, but examples would be arguments which assumed implicitly that producers were not maximizing profits or that producers in one industry knew more about the problems of some other industry than the producers in that industry. I continued after the reference to "bilge": "The above may seem very boastful to you but it does not come from a particularly joyful heart. My criticism of the literature has been destructive, not constructive. But I still have hope of constructing a theory of integration (if it exists!)."

The route which was ultimately to take me to a theory of integration is a curious one, and the more so because it came about in part as a result of examining the role in promoting vertical integration of what is now called asset-specificity. Let me start by quoting once again from my letter of March 24, 1932, which was written in Cleveland, where I was visiting the Union Carbide and Carbon Company: "Before leaving New York, I went and saw Wassily Leontief, the mathematical economist whom I think I have mentioned to you before [this earlier letter has not been preserved]. He used an argument for integration that I had already rejected as not at all satisfactory. He said, suppose a company has a steady demand of a certain amount and fluctuating demand above this. Then it might pay the company to produce the steady demand and buy the fluctuating demand outside. My arguments against this were as follows — Following on Plant's usual mode of attack, if it would pay to produce this amount, why does not the raw material producer set up a plant or whatever the equipment is, and produce this regular amount?" I then noted that it might be cheaper to operate two plants, each with a moderately fluctuating output, rather than one with a constant and the other with a greatly fluctuating output but went on to introduce a qualification which I said "might be of some importance." This qualification was that Plant's argument that I had deployed "assumed that the cost to the original producer and the original consumer who later produces, is the same." However, "if, for instance, one sets up a plant to cope with the steady demand of one consumer, there is obviously the risk that the consumer will cease to demand your product." I then noted that "it is obvious that many of the risks are borne ultimately by whoever produces the product, but that the risks inherent in this condition of bilateral monopoly may make the capital costs so high that it is cheaper for the original consuming firm to produce itself even though the actual operating efficiency is less. I have in mind certain actual examples of this same thing that I have come across." A remark follows that indicates the direction in which my mind was moving and that would start up a line of inquiry which would ultimately lead to the thesis of "The Nature of the Firm": "The above has suggested to me that I should investigate long-term contracting between firms. This may in many instances be considered as an alternative to actual operating integration, and [it] seems well worth the trouble of trying to get any information." I added that, although obtaining information is difficult, "occasionally I am well rewarded as when the other day in the case of a power plant which had integrated with some coal-mines, I was shown actual cost curves that they had constructed." Although I don't say this in my letter to Fowler, the power company concerned was the Duquesne Power and Light Company of Pittsburgh, and some years later I adapted their figures for use in an article on the rationale of cost accounting.

Fowler did not understand my argument about the "risks inherent in this condition of bilateral monopoly" making the capital costs greater for the producing firm. I replied: "I don't think the term bilateral monopoly is a good one and it may have confused you. The case I am considering is this. Suppose the production of a particular product requires a large capital equipment which is, however, specialized insofar that it can only be used for the particular product concerned or can only be readapted at great cost. Then the firm producing such a product for one consumer finds itself faced with one great risk—that the consumer may transfer his demand elsewhere or that he may exercise his monopoly power to force down the price—the machinery has no supply price. Now this risk must mean that the rate of interest paid on this capital is that much higher. Now, if the consuming firm decides to make this product this risk is absent and it may well be that this difference in capital costs may well offset the relative inefficiency in actual operating. An example of this reason for integration is to be found in the Ford Motor Company. I am well aware of the many other factors that have to be considered and this is rather a specialized case (at one time for certain products Ford was such a large consumer that he might be considered the only consumer)."

This was written in Detroit but at a time when I had not as yet visited the Ford Motor Company. No doubt what I said about Ford was based on what I had read or heard. I was later to visit the Ford Motor Company, but before I did so I visited General Motors, where no doubt I discussed their relations with suppliers, and I certainly saw a Fisher Body plant, Fisher Body having been acquired by General Motors about six years before. I wish I could now repeat what I was told by General Motors officials about their reasons for acquiring Fisher Body, but nothing appears in the correspondence except that I had visited General Motors. My recollection is that I was told that the main reason for the acquisition was to make sure that the body plants were located near General Motors assembly plants. That I say nothing about my visit to Fisher Body is not surprising since the vast majority of my visits to businesses and industrial plants are not mentioned and my letters deal mainly with economic analysis.

My Detroit letter, in a passage written later than the one I have just quoted, does however contain a detailed account of my visit to the Ford Motor Company but this was only because I wanted to tell Fowler how it was possible to make such a visit and obtain the information which I was seeking without having a letter of introduction. This is what I said: "I went over to the Ford Motor Company today. You may be interested in the tactics I adopted to get the information I wanted. You must first understand that I had no letter of introduction to the Ford Company and since the type of information I want can only be obtained by seeing more or less responsible officials I was in a little doubt as to how to approach the company. A certain Mr. Lansburgh of Detroit whose book on Factory Management you may or may not have read advised me to go about the job in the following way. When I arrived at the Administration Building of the Ford Company, I went in and asked if I could see Mr. Edsel Ford. Edsel is Henry Ford's son and he is now President of the Ford Motor Company and is worth in his own right about 500,000,000 dollars. I was told that he was out of town—I did not expect that he would be in town, of course. So I asked if I could see his secretary. I then filled out a form in which I said I was from England—I had come all the way to see Edsel sort of thing. A few minutes later a man arrived to see me and I then explained exactly who I was. You see, once you are in a firm, that is, have seen someone of importance, you are quite all right. I then had a short talk to this man about integration. By the way, I am quite a lawyer in my craftiness in putting questions. I can get admissions regarding costs out of them without them realizing that they have done so. Of course, I am aided in this by the fact that I do not want statistics. All I want are statements that are suggestive from the point of view of fitting into a theory of integration. After this I had lunch in the Ford cafeteria and was afterwards provided with a special man to show me anything I wanted to see in the plant. After going round the plant, I said I wanted to see someone in the purchasing department. So I was handed over to a gentleman who is, I imagine, the head of the purchasing department. I then discussed the problems connected with contracting for supplies, purchasing schedules and the like for about an hour and a half. Why I am mentioning this is not because of my treatment there being exceptional—I can always get almost whatever I want—but because I got all this without any introduction at all. . . . I really did get some most interesting points with regard to the relations of the Ford Company with its suppliers. Tomorrow, I am going to get the other side of the picture—I am going to visit one of Ford's suppliers. Of course, the Ford Company did not know this."

My next letter came from Chicago. While there I visited the steel works at Gary as well as Sears Roebuck, Montgomery Ward, and the stockyards in Chicago itself. I also went to Milwaukee where I visited Allis Chalmers and, what made a great impression on me, the A. O. Smith plant. But I did not omit to visit the University of Chicago. I attended a few classes of Frank Knight, who was talking about planning. I quote in my letter what I describe as a characteristic statement, "Property, competition and freedom are names for the same thing," a remark which did not do much to aid me in the search for a theory of integration. The only person with whom I discussed this was Jacob Viner. Viner had the reputation of being sharp with students but he was very kind to me. However, I'm not sure what I gained from him. I report in the letter to Fowler from Chicago that Viner said in discussing integration that it was not right to assume that producers were rational. In response I argued that one could normally assume rationality on the part of producers since if *one* producer were rational, his competitors would have to be (presumably because a rational producer would be more profitable and would displace his irrational and less profitable competitors). Of course I did not mean that firms would not sometimes follow mistaken policies. I report to Fowler a study I made of the purchases of rubber plantations by a rubber company, in which they purchased plantations when the price of rubber was high and disposed of them when the price was low. What I meant in not accepting Viner's point was that practices persistently followed in an industry would be those that were profitable. I also recall (which is not mentioned in the correspondence) that Viner suggested that there might be cases, such as the construction of a bridge, in which, say, a choice between two locations was a matter of indifference to almost everyone except one producer whose profits would be much affected by the location selected. This producer would have an incentive to build the bridge in the location most profitable to him. Viner, as I remember it, did not explain why the producer had to become the operator of the bridge rather than make a financial arrangement with the person or organization proposing to build it. It may well be that reflecting on this example had an important influence on the development of my views — but of this I cannot be sure.

As Fowler was still disputing my argument that integration might reduce risk, I set out in a letter from Chicago on May 7, 1932, a careful restatement of my position, with the accompanying remark that Viner thought it was sound. "Assume a producer of some finished product finds he needs a special part. Then, he has two alternatives. One, to produce it himself and two, to let a supplier produce it. Now, this specialized part requires a large capital equipment which is highly specialized, e.g., a special die [misspelt "dye" in my letter]. Now to an outside supplier, there is the risk that the consumer, that is, the producer of the finished product, may change his demand to another producer. If the consumer transfers his demand elsewhere, then the outside producer will find that he has a large amount of capital invested on which he is unable to get a return. Because of this risk, he will expect a higher return on his capital. But there will not be this risk in the case where the consumer, that is, the producer of the finished product, makes the part himself. Insofar as this one risk is removed, then to this extent, a saving is made." However, in this same letter are some remarks which very much reduce the practical importance of this argument: "As a matter of fact, my queries about the form of contracts for products requiring large capital equipment has shown me that contractual arrangements can be made to avoid this risk. Thus, the consuming firm may buy the particular equipment itself, even though it is in another company's plant. There are a number of other contractual devices which tend to get over this difficulty." To prevent Fowler from concluding that my argument about risk had no practical significance, I instance the case in which the "most economic production would occupy the whole of one plant" and I ask, "Is the consuming firm to buy the whole plant?" I also point out that if only one customer is supplied, there will be much capital investment which is of an intangible character. "When one is engaged in supplying only one producer the whole of the energies of the firm are turned in one direction — think of the goodwill invested in your market — I am thinking of goodwill as being created by capital investment." In such a case, "the only solution seems to be for the producing company to be bought by the consuming company." I add: "There is no doubt of the fact that suppliers will refuse to take too great a proportion of their business from one consumer even though there would be an actual saving in operating expenses if they did so. The risks could be too great! I have come across many instances of this."

There is only one more letter from America after the one I have just quoted (or at any rate only one that has been preserved), and this does not add much to what has gone before. The next letter in the correspondence is the one from Dundee from which I quoted at the beginning of this lecture. Lest I give a false impression of the extent of this correspondence, I should explain that there are only seven letters totaling sixty-four pages sent from America. The first letter, in which I talked of the risks of bilateral monopoly and the need to investigate long-term contracting between firms, was written on February 28, 1932, and the last letter from which I quoted, in which I spoke of the existence of contractual arrangements which avoided this risk, was dated May 7, 1932, so the period involved in the correspondence from which I have quoted was just over two months long.

The position at the beginning of the summer of 1932 was that I had developed this theory about the risk inherent in a situation in which a firm, in order to supply a particular customer, had to make a large capital investment. Viner thought the argument was sound but, what is more to the point, I thought it was sound. Furthermore, my inquiries had uncovered evidence to support it. I had come across "many instances" of suppliers refusing to take too great a proportion of their business from one customer. However, my inquiries had uncovered something else. They had shown that there were "many contractual devices" which would avoid the risk associated with making capital investments to supply one customer, and in fact independent firms commonly made such investments. The A. O. Smith plant furnished an example of this. On the other hand it seemed likely that this situation did sometimes lead to integration, and the acquisition of Fisher Body by General Motors might well have been an example of this.

The puzzle needing to be solved was clear. What was it that determined whether this problem would be handled by contractual arrangements between independent firms or by integration, the alternative which was already in my mind by the end of February 1932? There was also the problem posed by the usual economic analysis in which it is assumed that, in Salter's phrase, "the normal economic system works itself," and which apparently left no room for firms. I cannot say exactly how I came to hit upon the solution; getting an idea is the kind of process in which you don't know what you're doing until you've done it. The solution was to realize that there were costs of making transactions in a market economy and that it was necessary to incorporate them into the analysis. This was not done in economics at that time — nor, I may add, is it in most present-day economic theory. However, once taken into account, everything falls into place. The quest on which I had sailed across the Atlantic had been successful. I had reached China. Whether a transaction would be organized within the firm (in the terminology of the letters, whether there would be integration) or whether it would be carried out on the market by independent contractors depended on a comparison of the costs of carrying out these market transactions with the costs of carrying out these transactions within an organization, the firm. As I said in my letter of October 10, 1932, my approach "succeeded in linking up organization with cost."

NOTES

1. Edmund W. Kitch, ed., "The Fire of Truth: A Remembrance of Law and Economics at Chicago, 1932–1970," 26 *Journal of Law and Economics* (1983) 214.

2. Arnold Plant, "Trends in Business Administration," 12 *Economics* (1932) 387.

4

The Nature of the Firm: Meaning

R. H. COASE

The solution to the puzzles that I took with me to America was, as it turned out, very simple. All that was needed was to recognize that there were costs of carrying out market transactions and to incorporate them into the analysis, something which economists had failed to do. A firm had therefore a role to play in the economic system if it were possible for transactions to be organized within the firm at less cost than would be incurred if the same transactions were carried out through the market. The limit to the size of the firm would be set when the scope of its operations had expanded to the point at which the costs of organizing additional transactions within the firm exceeded the costs of carrying out the same trans-actions through the market or in another firm. This statement has been called a "tautology." It is the criticism people make of a proposition which is clearly right.

It was of course obvious to me that the exposition in my lecture of 1932 needed elaboration, and in a letter to Fowler written shortly after I had given it, I indicated that this was what I wanted to do. I completed a draft of "The Nature of the Firm" by early summer in 1934, while I was still at Dundee. Unfortunately I do not possess a copy of this draft. However, very few changes were in fact made before the article was published in *Economica* in 1937. I know I added a footnote reference to an article in the *American Economic Review* by Horace White, who argued that monopolistic competition would set a limit to the size of the firm. I also added a footnote reference to an article by a colleague at LSE, Evan Durbin. No doubt I made some other changes, but they were almost certainly quite minor in character. The article published in 1937 was essentially the same as the draft of 1934.

In transforming my Dundee lecture into an article I elaborated the argument and embellished it with additional illustrations but made no change in the basic approach. However, I wrote a section dealing with alternative explanations for the existence of the firm, those that had been advanced by Dobb and by Knight. It is almost certain that I had not read Dobb's book on *Russian Economic Develop-ment*, from which I quote, before I gave my Dundee lecture. And it is quite certain that I also had not read Knight's *Risk, Uncertainty and Profit* before then. A letter to Fowler, written in May 1933, indicates that I had just read Knight (along with Wicksteed, Babbage, and some Marshall). When I put forward my explanation in 1932 for the existence of the firm, I had not examined these alternative explanations, but after doing so, it is clear that I did not feel it necessary to change my mind. It can, I think, be said with some confidence that Knight played no part in the development of my ideas on the firm, a point I emphasize because some have thought the contrary. What set me going was the approach I learned from Plant, and this no doubt came via Plant from his teacher, Edwin Cannan. It might of course be argued that Knight's ideas were so much in the air at LSE that I would be exposed to them without reading him. And this is true. Everyone at LSE referred to *Risk, Uncertainty and Profit* whether they had read it or not. But what mattered to Robbins (and he was the main expositor of Knight's views at LSE) was the distinction between risk and uncertainty and the analytical scheme and arguments of Part 2 of Knight's book. I doubt very much whether the economists at LSE ever discussed Knight's views on those aspects of economic organization that interested me. Of course, afterwards I read Knight's work with care, and I have little doubt that in my later writings I have been greatly influenced by him, although in what ways it is not easy to say. But in 1932, when I formulated the ideas in "The Nature of the Firm," my analytical system, such as it was, came from Plant.

It may be asked why so much time elapsed between the formulation of these ideas in 1932 and their publication in 1937. The reasons are various. First of all, I have always been reluctant to rush into print. This is no doubt in part due to laziness and the fact that I find writing so difficult but it also comes about because I do not like to publish until I feel that I have things right. Fowler, in a letter written in March 1932, had expressed the hope that I would write a paper or a series of papers on the subject of integration. I replied: "You say that I will want to put all my ideas on integration on paper as soon as possible. Don't you believe it. I want as long as possible. Honestly, Fowler, you never know what is going to turn up which will make you alter what you have written. For instance, this Viner article that you mention and which I will certainly read may make me change much of what I have already decided. I am not going to be in too great a hurry to put myself on paper." I may illustrate my reluctance to rush into print with a tale which has nothing to do with the firm. Late in 1932 I discovered an error in Robertson's *Banking Policy and the Price Level*. My colleagues at Dundee were at first unwilling to believe that there could be any question on which I could be right and Robertson wrong. But in the end they were convinced and I was urged to write a note on the subject and send it to the *Economic Journal*. This I did not want to do. Instead I wrote to Robertson explaining why I thought what he had said was wrong. A month later Robertson replied, saying that I was right. The war intervened but in 1949 a revised edition of *Banking Policy and the Price Level* was published with a new introduction by Robertson. I eagerly secured a copy to find out what Robertson said about the error. To be referred to in Robertson's *Banking Policy and the Price Level*, that was immortality. I discovered that he acknowledged the "glaring error" and set out my argument in summary form. However in his introductory statement Robertson said that the error "was pointed out to me long ago by a correspondent whose name I have ungratefully forgotten. . . . "[1] Immortality was lost. It seems that there is something to be said for rushing into print.

My slowness in writing up my ideas on the firm was, however, in large part due to other factors. As I said in a letter to Fowler from which I quoted in my first lecture, I was giving three courses simultaneously at Dundee. In those days textbooks were not normally used, not at any rate in England, and we were expected to prepare our lectures based on our reading in the subject. Ignorant as I was of the subjects on which I was lecturing, preparation of my lectures took up a lot of my time, although not, I fear, as much as it ought to have done. Then in 1934 I was appointed an assistant lecturer at the University of Liverpool where I lectured on banking and finance, subjects about which I knew nothing. Mercifully, for me and for the students, in 1935 I was appointed an assistant lecturer in economics at the London School of Economics where I became responsible for the course on the economics of public utilities, a course which had previously been given by Batson, who had left for South Africa. I soon found that very little was known about public utilities in Britain and to discover what the facts were, I began those historical studies which resulted in publications on broadcasting and the post office. I also studied the history of water, gas and electricity supply in Britain, but so far I have not embodied this work in any substantial publications. I also worked in the Department of Business Administration at LSE, of which Plant had become the head, and prepared cases in the manner of the Harvard Business School. I remember preparing one on the manufacture and distribution of gramophone records. I also took part in the formation of the Accounting Research Association (for which the moving spirit was Ronald Edwards) and developed an approach to cost accounting which resulted in a series of articles in *The Accountant*, articles which have since been reprinted and much referred to.

It will have been noticed that I did not seem to have been very particular about the subjects on which I taught and worked. And this is correct. Emerging on the labor market in 1932, the problem was not to find a suitable job but to find a job. LSE was swarming with unemployed graduates. To be particular at that time was not to get a job or secure promotion. The result for me was a constant learning about new subjects. Not that this depressed me. I still found time to undertake a number of research projects. At that time I was very interested in making quantitative investigations, influenced, I believe, by the work of Schultz at the University of Chicago. One project, carried out with Fowler, aimed at discovering what producers' expectations of price actually were, in particular, did they think current prices would continue to apply into the future, as was assumed in many theoretical constructions used by economists? We decided to study the pig-cycle in Britain, in which this assumption was believed to hold. We concluded that pig farmers did not think that current prices would continue, as had been asserted, and we published an article giving our findings in 1935.[2] This article, among other things, advanced, according to Pashigian, "if in a faint outline, the essence of the rational expectations hypothesis which was to blossom thirty-five years later."[3] I cannot forbear to mention some important, but neglected, work by Fowler on the substitution of materials in production. In November 1937 (the same month as saw the publication of "The Nature of the Firm") he published an article in the *Quarterly Journal of Economics* on "The Substitution of Scrap for Pig-iron in the Manufacture of Steel." Had this kind of work been taken up and continued, it might have breathed life into input-output analysis and would certainly have greatly improved our analysis of the working of a competitive system. But this was not to be.

I must not omit to mention another development which came to occupy our time and our attention. In 1933 were published Mrs. Robinson's *Economics of Imperfect Competition* and Chamberlin's *Theory of Monopolistic Competition*. These two books were a great success in England. Mrs. Robinson's book in particular gave us a new set of tools with which to analyze the working of a pricing system. I published in 1935 an article written early in 1934 in which I used Mrs. Robinson's new approach to analyze the duopoly problem as discussed by Chamberlin. This new theoretical apparatus had the advantage that one could cover the blackboard with diagrams and fill the hour in one's lectures without the need to find out anything about what happened in the real world. There can be no question that these two books were a major interest of economists in England in the early 1930s, before Keynes came along to occupy the scene, and I was swept along with the others. I was appointed an assistant lecturer at LSE in 1935, the same year that Hicks left for Cambridge. Hicks had lectured on monopoly, and I was given his course along with my course on public utilities and my work in the Department of Business Administration. Out of my lectures in Hicks's old course came an article on monopoly price published in 1937[4] and an article entitled "Monopoly Pricing with Interrelated Costs and Demands" which, owing to the war, did not appear until 1946.[5] All in all, given the demands on my time, it is not difficult, I think, to understand why my ideas on the nature of the firm, conceived in 1932, were not published until 1937 and why, when they were published, they were very little revised.

On the day that the issue of *Economica* was published in which "The Nature of the Firm" appeared, on the way to lunch I was congratulated by Sargent and Plant, the professors of commerce. Neither ever referred to the article again or discussed it with me, although I worked closely with Plant and he thought of me as a member of his "team." Robbins, the head of my department, never mentioned the article to me and neither did Hayek, although my relations with both of them were quite cordial. The article was not an instant success. This did not discourage me, and Duncan Black has recalled in correspondence with Elzinga my saying of this article in the early 1940s, "I don't believe I will ever do anything so important as that in my life again."

There were some citations to the article in the 1940s and more in the 1950s after the article had been chosen by Stigler to be reprinted in the American Economic Association's *Readings in Price Theory*. The article continued to be cited in footnotes in the 1960s, although without any noticeable effect on what was written in the text, so that my paper at the National Bureau's Fiftieth Anniversary Colloquium on Industrial Organization, I felt justified in referring to my article as "much cited and little used." In the 1970s, however, the article was not only cited but also discussed, and this has continued into the 1980s. There has without question been more discussion of my article in the past ten years than in the preceding forty. However, given that none of the economists discussing my article could have known the circumstances of its writing or my concerns at the time and that many will not be aware of the state of economics in the early 1930s in England, it is hardly surprising that there should have been some misconceptions about what I had in mind when I wrote "The Nature of the Firm."

What strikes me in rereading this article is its extreme simplicity. There is no subtle or complicated argument to tax the brain and no concepts difficult to under-stand. My article starts by making a methodological point: it is desirable that the assumptions we make in economics should be realistic. Most readers will pass over these opening sentences (Putterman omits them when reprinting my article), and others will excuse what they read as a youthful mistake, believing, as so many modern economists do, that we should choose our theories on the basis of the accuracy of their predictions, the realism of their assumptions being utterly irrele-vant. I did not believe this in the 1930s and, as it happens, I still do not. In my Warren Nutter lecture, delivered in 1981, I argue that economists do not, could not, and, if they could, should not choose their theories on the basis of the accuracy of their predictions. In "The Nature of the Firm," I refer to a long-forgotten pamphlet by Mrs. Robinson, *Economics Is a Serious Subject*, which came out in 1932. She argued, and it is difficult to disagree with her, that if we are to have any economic theory at all, its assumptions must be manageable. But then Mrs. Robinson ap-pears to argue that if the only assumptions we can handle are unrealistic, we have no choice but to use them. In effect what this comes down to is that when econo-mists find that they are unable to analyze what is happening in the real world, they invent an imaginary world which they are capable of handling. It was not a proce-dure that I wanted to follow in the 1930s. It explains why I tried to find the reason for the existence of the firm in factories and offices rather than in the writings of economists, which I irreverently labeled as "bilge." In interpreting the argument of my article it is necessary to keep in mind that my aim was to discover a "realistic assumption." I therefore ignored Mrs. Robinson's main argument and eagerly fas-tened onto one of her phrases, claiming that my concept of the firm was both "realistic and manageable."

In saying that my concept of the firm was manageable, what I had in mind was that, looking at the firm in this way, we could analyze its activities using standard economic theory. This is what I meant when I said in the letter to Fowler in which I described my Dundee lecture that I had succeeded in linking up organization with cost. I ended the introductory section of "The Nature of the Firm" with a quotation from Robbins's *Nature and Significance of Economic Science*, which I had not read when I formulated my ideas on the firm but which I must have read shortly thereafter, since it appeared in 1932. The quotation was to the effect that the concepts we use in economics must be defined in such a way that they "relate to formal relations which are capable of being conceived exactly." At the time I consid-ered that this was what I was doing and that my analysis was consistent with Robbins's point of view. I must have thought that he would be sympathetic to my argument in "The Nature of the Firm." I can now see that I was wrong to expect him to respond in this way. Consider what he says in *Nature and Significance*. After having said that the older economists divided our subject into the Theory of Production and the Theory of Distribution, Robbins commented: "We have all felt, with Professor Schumpeter, a sense almost of shame at the incredible banalities of much of the so-called theory of production – the tedious discussions of the various forms of peasant proprietorship, factory organization, industrial psychology, technical education, etc., which are apt to occur in even the best treatises on general theory arranged on this plan. One has only to compare the masterly sweep of Book V of Marshall's *Principles*, which deals with problems which are strictly economic in our sense, with the spineless platitudes about manures and the 'fine natures among domestic servants' of much of Book IV to realise the insidious effect of a procedure which opens the door to the intrusions of amateur technology into discussion which should be purely economic. But there is a more fundamental objection to this procedure; it necessarily precludes precision." Robbins later proposes to tell us of the advantages of "the modern treatment of organisation of production." But first he gives us the disadvantages of the old. "The old treatment of this subject was hopelessly unsatisfactory: A few trite generalisations about the advantages of the division of labour copied from Adam Smith, and illustrated perhaps by a few examples from Babbage; then extensive discussions on industrial 'forms' and the 'entrepreneur' with a series of thoroughly unscientific and question-begging remarks on national characteristics – the whole wound up, perhaps, with a chapter on localisation. There is no need to dwell on the insufferable dreariness and mediocrity of all this. But it is perhaps just as well to state definitely its glaring positive deficiencies. It suggests that from the point of view of the economist 'organisation' is a matter of internal industrial (or agricultural) arrangement – if not internal to the firm, at any rate internal to 'the' industry. At the same time it tends to leave out completely the governing factor of all productive organisation – the relationship of prices and cost. . . . In the modern treatment, discussion of 'production' is an integral part of the Theory of Equilibrium. It is shown how factors of production are distributed between the production of different goods by the mechanism of prices and costs, how given certain fundamental data, interest rates and price margins determine the distribution of factors between production for the present and production for the future. The doctrine of division of labour, heretofore so disagreeably technological, becomes an integral feature of a theory of moving equilibrium through time. Even the question of 'internal' organisation and administration now becomes related to an outside network of relative prices and costs."[6]

In the second edition of *Nature and Significance*, Robbins says that he has "endeavoured to eliminate certain manifestations of high spirits no longer in harmony with present moods."[7] It was no doubt a change in mood which led Robbins to omit the patronizing remarks about Book IV of Marshall's *Principles*. But the remainder of his comments on the theory of production of the older economists was not changed. Of course, Robbins's strictures, that their discussion was "amateur technology," lacked precision, and did not explain the choice of industrial arrangements in terms of prices and costs, was not without justification. But, as it happens, what I had tried to do in "The Nature of the Firm" was to link up organization with cost and to do so in a very precise way. However, I do not think that Robbins's description of the treatment of the theory of production by John Stuart Mill and Alfred Marshall (the economists he obviously had in mind) as "banal," "tedious," "unscientific," "dreary," and "mediocre" was due solely to its supposed lack of economic content. Robbins was devoted to high theory, and I believe he felt some distaste, at any rate in the 1930s, for discussions of such mundane subjects as peasant proprietorships and industrial "forms." It was not therefore to be expected that an article entitled "The Nature of the Firm" would attract his attention.

Such an attitude of disdain is not found today among economists, although the practice of some would be consistent with it. However, in the past few years a growing number of economists have begun to take an interest in the institutional structure of production, and this has led them to refer to "The Nature of the Firm" not only in footnotes but also in the text. Given that they could not have known what led me to write the article and that I have not discussed its argument in the past fifty years, it is hardly surprising that there have been some misunderstandings about my views.

I want to start with an aspect of my article on which there has been little or no comment but on which the practice of modern economists is often markedly different from mine in "The Nature of the Firm." This concerns the treatment of monopoly as a rationale for the existence of the firm or, perhaps more usually, for vertical integration. I make no reference to monopoly in that article, although I note that certain kinds of sales tax, quota schemes, and price controls might bring firms into existence or make them larger than they would otherwise be. I could easily have included monopoly in this list since the argument for vertical integration would be essentially the same as for the cases mentioned. That I did not do so was undoubtedly the result of Plant's teaching. Plant thought that monopoly tended to be transitory and generally unimportant except when promoted and supported by the state. Of course, in practice we did not keep our minds as clean as this would suggest. The literature on industrial organization was largely American and laid emphasis on the effects of monopoly, and it must have had an influence on our thinking. I remember that in Plant's classes, when discussing the Pittsburgh-plus system of pricing, the main book we used was Fetter's *Masquerade of Monopoly*, published in 1931. And I have no doubt that while in America I took seriously what was said in the reports of the Federal Trade Commission. But my basic position was (and is) the same as Plant's, that our economic system is in the main competitive. Any explanation therefore for the emergence of the firm had to be one which applied in competitive conditions, although monopoly might be important in particular cases. In the early 1930s I was looking for an explanation for the existence of the firm which did not depend on monopoly. I found it, of course, in transaction costs.

Klein, Crawford, and Alchian in an article published in 1978 say this: "Once we attempt to add empirical detail to Coase's fundamental insight that a systematic study of transaction costs is necessary to explain particular forms of economic organization, we find that his primary distinction between transactions within a firm and transactions made in the marketplace may often be too simplistic. Many long-term contractual relationships (such as franchising) blur the line between the market and the firm."[8] Klein and his colleagues imply that in distinguishing between transactions carried out within the firm and in the market, I believed that all that existed were these polar and clear-cut cases. This is incorrect. Indeed, I was quite explicit about it. In "The Nature of the Firm" I state that "it is not possible to draw a hard and fast line which determines whether there is a firm or not. There may be more or less direction."[9] Similarly, I also say in the first section of the article that "the degree to which the price mechanism," in current terminology, the market, "is superseded varies greatly. In a department store, the allocation of the different sections to the various locations in the building may be done by the controlling authority or it may be the result of competitive price bidding for space. In the Lancashire cotton industry, a weaver can rent power and shop-room and can obtain looms and yarn on credit."[10] Of course, as I indicated, this was not the normal way of running a cotton mill. It is true that I do not mention franchising, but this did not become a common method of distribution until the 1950s and, although it existed, was certainly unknown to me in 1932. Over the years I have come across numerous examples of markets found within firms, but one which particularly amused me was the discovery of a kind of market operating in the heart of a nationalized industry in England, the electricity supply industry. I quote from a lecture given by an official of the Central Electricity Generating Board in July 1961: "The outputs of the generating stations in England and Wales are co-ordinated [note the word] by a National Control Centre in London, through seven Regional Control Centres. . . . In arranging each day's load, the National Control Room becomes in effect an auction room, with the National Control Engineer asking the Regional Centres to quote the price at which they could supply a certain number of kilowatts at specified periods during the following day. . . . Wherever possible he accepts the lowest bid, and the Regions plan the operations of their generating stations on the programmes for the interchange of energy which are prepared by the National Control Engineer."[11]

An analogous situation may, of course, be found within a privately owned firm in which separate departments of divisions may supply one another as a result either of instructions from a higher authority or of what are essentially market transactions between them. When there are extensive market transactions, the question has been raised as to whether we are dealing with a single firm or a group of associated firms. No doubt for some purposes it is better to think of a single firm and for others of a group of firms. But if we do think in terms of a single firm, it is clearly one in which some transactions are coordinated by the price mechanism, to use the terminology of my article, and not as a result of administrative decisions. So, although my aim in "The Nature of the Firm" was to explain why firms emerge within markets, we must also admit that there may be markets within firms. Since the power to direct factors of production by the authorities in the firm, as I explained, will be "within the limits of the contract," this means that what is outside the limits of such a contract will inevitably be governed by market transactions. In consequence it is not surprising that the relationship between those in charge of the firm and the owners of the resources it uses often involves a mixture of direction and market transactions. Franchising may provide an example of this. The existence of such mixed relationships does not mean, for me, that we should abandon the view that "the distinguishing mark of the firm is the supersession of the price mechanism," as I put it in "The Nature of the Firm," or that the distinction between the allocation of resources through the market or within the firm is without value, even though it is not possible to draw a hard and fast line which determines whether the relationship between the user and the owners of the factors of production should be considered a firm. In much the same way, the distinction between male and female is serviceable for many purposes notwithstanding the existence of inter-mediate or aberrant categories which, in Klein's phrase, "blur the line."

A number of economists have said in recent years that the problem of the firm is essentially a choice of contractual arrangements. I have never thought otherwise. As I said in "The Nature of the Firm," contracts are not eliminated when there is a firm but they are greatly reduced." This is accomplished by the use of a special kind of contract. "A factor of production (or the owner thereof) does not have to make a series of contracts with the factors with whom he is cooperating within the firm, as would be necessary, of course, if this co-operation were as a direct result of the working of the price mechanism. For this series of contracts is substituted one. . . . It is important to note the character of the contract into which a factor enters that is employed within a firm. . . . The factor, for a certain remuneration (which may be fixed or fluctuating), agrees to obey the directions of an entrepreneur *within certain limits*. . . . Within these limits, he can therefore direct the other factors of production."[12] I also say in the last section of "The Nature of the Firm" that the relationships which constitute the firm, as I conceived it, correspond closely to the legal concept of the relationship of employer and employee, and I quote from a book by Batt on *The Law of Master and Servant* which I had studied in one of my law courses at LSE: "It is this right of control or interference, of being entitled to tell the servant when to work (within the hours of service) and when not to work, and what work to do and how to do it (within the terms of such service) which is the dominant characteristic in this relation and marks off the servant from an independent contractor."[13]

There is other evidence that I thought about the firm in terms of a choice of contractual arrangements. It was my practice as a young man when trying to develop ideas on a subject to sit at the typewriter and type out thoughts about it as they occurred to me. My intention would be to sift these thoughts and combine them later in order to compose a lecture or an article. Some notes that I made in this way have been preserved and will be deposited in Regenstein Library. They have a heading, "A Theory of Contract." Unfortunately, unlike letters, these notes are not dated. But it seems probable, judging from the wording and my own (faint) recollection, that they were written in 1934 after the draft of "The Nature of the Firm" had been completed, although it could be that they were written before then. Certainly the demands on my time in Liverpool and the London School of Economics made it unlikely that I would have paid much attention to contracts after I left Dundee. What we have are some very preliminary notes for use in an article that was never written.

It would be wrong to regard such rough notes, composed without much reflection and never revised, as representing a settled view or one to which much attention should be given. Nonetheless, they indicate the character of my thoughts on contracts and the firm at about the time "The Nature of the Firm" was written. The notes start with the proposition that a contract restricts a person's actions and go on to assert that certainty is acquired at the expense of freedom of action. The latter point now seems dubious to me, because what is secured by giving up freedom of action, though preferred, may be very uncertain. The notes continue by saying that the scope of a contract may be increased by including more operations but that this comes mainly from an increase in the period of time for which the contract runs. The time period may be lengthened to reduce costs by eliminating the need for several shorter contracts or to accommodate the risk preferences of the various parties. There follows a point also found in my article, that the longer the period of the contract, the less possible it becomes to state exactly what the party supplying the service should do, and therefore a contract is entered into that states what the supplier will do in general terms, leaving the details subject to the directions of the user (or employer). I ended this section by saying that the employer-employee contract approaches the firm relationship but that when "several such contracts are made with people and for things which cooperate with one another, you get the full firm relationship."

Up to this point these notes do little more than confirm what a careful reading of my article would have revealed about my views. The next section, entitled "Long Term Contracts and Vertical Integration," does, however, break some new ground. Starting with the view that both integration and long-term contracts are ways of binding people and therefore of reducing risk (the risk that they may act in a way disadvantageous to you), I asked why a certain solution is adopted in some cases but not in others, particularly since at first sight it would appear that all the advantages of integration can be obtained by means of a long-term contract. I then mentioned what I considered to be one disadvantage of long-term contracting, that the other party may die or cease to be effective, whereas integration means that the contractual relationship is guaranteed for the life of entity concerned.

Next came what I now find to be the most interesting part of these notes, a discussion of the risk of being defrauded. "Integration is sometimes said to arise from desire to 'ensure the quality of the product.' Insofar as poor quality is the result of mistakes, there can be no reason for integration, unless it can be shown that an integrated firm is more efficient. The question arises as to whether it would be possible to reduce fraud by integration." My approach to this question was hard-boiled. I set out the factors which determined how much fraud there will be and then considered how these factors would be affected by integration. Fraud, I said, increases the profits of the defrauding firm but reduces custom, that is, reduces its future business. Loss of custom depends on being able to identify the defrauding supplier and on whether, when he is identified, he was still engaged in the same occupation. In a highly mobile society, it is obvious that there is likely to be less honesty. Once when looking through Alfred Marshall's papers I came across a phrase of his that expresses this thought very neatly: "Money is more portable than a good reputation." I summed up the position as I saw it in the following words: "Whether custom will be lost . . . will depend on the class of article being produced and how it is marketed and the speed of economic development in the community considered—this in relation to the time it takes to discover that there is fraud. The fact that this is important may mean the emergence of someone whose job it is to discover who are reliable. Thus, a consuming firm may not know who the producing firms are—but a wholesaler may specialize on discovering who are reliable and who are good customers and thus by using him, a consuming firm may eliminate the effects of fraud. But it is a cost and may be eliminated . . . by integration."

Regarding the factors which determine the amount of fraud, I argued that those in charge of an integrated firm would lack any incentive to commit a fraudulent act in order to increase profits, the underlying thought obviously being that the increased profits that would accrue at one stage (due, for example, to the substitution of a cheaper but inferior material) would be more than offset by the decreased profits of a later stage. However I argued that loss of custom does not exert the same influence in a vertically integrated firm. Such a firm is less easily induced to turn to a competitive supplier of a raw material or component. The result is that competitive pressures work less strongly within the firm, and this leads to increased fraud, "in the sense that employees will not produce what they are expected to produce unless means [are] taken to prevent [them]." Because of this, I concluded that inspection costs may be much the same for an integrated firm as they would be for a firm buying from an independent producer. Grossman and Hart in an article in the *Journal of Political Economy* of August 1986 refer to "Coase's view that integration transforms a hostile supplier into a docile employee,"[14] but this was not my view fifty years ago, as is evident from the passage I have just quoted, nor is it my view today. Suppliers are not hostile and employees are not docile. Both respond in the same way when faced with the same conditions. Integration creates a different institutional setting, and our problem is to discover what effect this has on economic behavior. What I like about these notes is that I used this approach. Whether my tentative conclusion was correct is another matter. I argued that suppliers usually could be identified and that change was not normally so fast as to prevent loss of custom from acting as a significant deterrent to fraud. I concluded that avoidance of fraud was not an important factor in promoting integration.

Some have thought that in "The Nature of the Firm" I had assumed that firms were individual proprietorships and therefore that the analysis could not be applied without modification to corporate or more complex organizations. This impression, which is incorrect, probably resulted from my use of the term *entrepreneur-co-ordinator* to describe those who direct resources in the firm. In a footnote I explained that I used the term *entrepreneur* "to refer to the person or persons who, in a competitive system, take the place of the price mechanism in the direction of resources."[15] What I meant by the entrepreneur is the hierarchy in a business which directs resources and includes not only management but also foremen and many workmen. It is not a particularly good term, but this was the normal usage in England at that time as is apparent from the most important books on price theory published there in the 1930s, Mrs. Robinson's *Economics of Imperfect Competition* and Hicks's *Value and Capital*. In both these books, the word *entrepreneur* is used with this meaning, and the direction of resources is spoken of as if it were carried out by an individual. Mrs. Robinson is quite explicit on this point: "In the following pages the entrepreneur is personified and referred to as an individual. But in a joint stock company no single individual is responsible for the final control of the firm."[16]

A final point refers to the meaning of a "rising supply price" of factors of production, which I said might bring about an increase in the cost of organizing transactions as a firm became larger and thus limit its size. This "rising supply price" has nothing to do with the rising supply price of factors to an industry as normally thought of in economic theory, but relates to the fact that people working in a large firm may find the conditions of work less attractive than in a small firm and therefore will require a higher remuneration to compensate them for this. This does not mean that others, perhaps the majority, may not find working in a large firm more attractive, in which case the supply price would fall. But this would not operate to limit the size of the firm. Similar effects may be found for factors other than labor, for example, in the supply of capital.

I have mentioned some of the misconceptions about the character of my argument in "The Nature of the Firm," some of them, I believe, of quite minor importance. There is, however, one misunderstanding that, I fear, is both widespread and serious, one that relates to the very heart of my thesis. This concerns the source of the gains which accrue through the existence of the firm. My view is, of course, that they come from a reduction in transaction costs. But the main transaction costs that are saved are those which would otherwise have been incurred in market transactions between the factors now cooperating within the firm. It is the *comparison* of these costs with those that would have to be incurred to operate a firm which determines whether it would be profitable to establish a firm.

NOTES

1. The passage to which I objected is to be found in D. H. Robertson, *Banking Policy and the Price Level* (1932), 35–36. In the fourth printing (revised) of 1949, on p. vii of the preface, will be found the passage I quote. Robertson's summary statement of my argument is to be found on pp. xiii and xiv. Robertson's postcard acknowledging receipt of my letter and letter agreeing with my argument will be deposited in Regenstein Library, the University of Chicago, along with any other papers. An abridged version of my letter to Robertson is set out in a letter to Fowler dated December 7, 1932.

2. "Bacon Production and the Pig-Cycle in Great Britain," 2 *Economica* (n.s.) (1935).

3. B. Peter Pashigian, in the article, "The Cobweb Theorem" in the *New Palgrave Dictionary* (1987).

4. "Some Notes on Monopoly Price," 5 *Review of Economic Studies* (1937).

5. "Monopoly Pricing with Interrelated Costs and Demands," 13 *Economica* (n.s.) (1946).

6. Lionel Robbins, *The Nature and Significance of Economic Science* (1932), 65, 69–71.

7. Lionel Robbins, *The Nature and Significance of Economic Science* (1935), preface, xiii.

8. Benjamin Klein, Robert G. Crawford, and Armen A. Alchian, "Vertical Integration, Appropriable Rents, and the Competitive Contracting Process," 21 *Journal of Law and Economics* (1978) 326.

9. "The Nature of the Firm," 4 *Economica* (n.s.) (1937), n. 1.

10. Ibid., 388, n. 9.

11. A. R. Cooper, "The Operation of the British Grid System," Central Electricity Generating Board, pp. 11–12. A copy of this lecture, delivered in July 1961, will be deposited with my other papers in Regenstein Library, the University of Chicago.

12. "The Nature of the Firm," 391 [this volume: 21].

13. Ibid., 404 [this volume: 29].

14. Sanford J. Grossman and Oliver D. Hart, "The Costs and Benefits of Ownership: A Theory of Vertical and Lateral Integration," 94 *Journal of Political Economy* (1986) 693, n. 1.

15. "The Nature of the Firm," 388, n. 2.

16. Joan Robinson, *The Economics of Imperfect Competition* (1933), 25.

5

The Nature of the Firm: Influence

R. H. COASE

Because "The Nature of the Firm" had little or no influence for thirty or forty years after it was published, an assessment of its influence of necessity focuses on the recent past. But I will be interpreting what has been happening in the light of the thoughts and events of fifty years ago.

The initial reception of my article by my elders and betters at the London School of Economics (LSE) was a complete lack of interest. Nor was the response of the rest of the economics profession very different. Stigler reprinted the article in 1952 in *Readings in Price Theory*, which he edited (along with Boulding) for the American Economic Association. This increased the number of footnote references but did not bring about any real interest in the questions raised in that article. The only serious discussion of the firm along somewhat similar lines of which I am aware to appear before the 1970s was the article by Malmgren, "Information, Expectations and the Theory of the Firm," published in the *Quarterly Journal of Economics* in August 1961. The result was that when I was asked to present a paper in November 1970 as part of the fiftieth anniversary celebrations of the National Bureau of Economic Research, at a Roundtable on Policy Issues and Research Opportunities in Industrial Organization, I felt justified in referring to "The Nature of the Firm" as "much cited and little used." I pointed to what I considered to be the parlous state of the study of industrial organization at that time. What was dealt with by economists under that heading had nothing to do with how industry was organized. It had become "a study of the pricing and output policies of firms, especially in oligopolistic situations."[1]

The position is different today, although I do not consider it satisfactory. The majority of economists writing on industrial organization still treat the subject as being mainly concerned with the determination of prices and output, but starting in the 1970s and 1980s, a growing number of economists have grappled with the problems of explaining the organization of industry, and this has been accompanied by more references to "The Nature of the Firm." Cheung has pointed out that the number of citations has increased steadily in the period since 1966 and it is undoubtedly more cited today than at any other time in the fifty years since it was published.[2] The increased interest in the economics of the organization of industry is made manifest by the publication in 1986 of *Organizational Economics*, edited by Barney and Ouchi, and of *The Economic Nature of the Firm*, edited by Putterman, both of which reprint "The Nature of the Firm." Further evidence of the heightened interest in the organization of industry is afforded by Williamson's *Economic Institutions of Capitalism*, published in 1985, and his *Economic Organization*, published in 1986.

Why has there been this renewed interest in the 1970s and 1980s in questions which I raised some fifty years ago? Barzel and Kochin have argued in an unpublished paper that the interest now being shown in "The Nature of the Firm" reflects the influence of my article "The Problem of Social Cost," published in the October 1960 issue of the *Journal of Law and Economics*, and that the recent literature on the organization of industry which is seemingly derived from "The Nature of the Firm" is in fact much more an outgrowth of the argument in "The Problem of Social Cost." Klein indeed has said that "The Problem of Social Cost" was essentially a restatement of the earlier article. The thesis of both articles, according to Klein, was that there was "a missing element in our models" and that the missing element was the concept of transaction costs.[3] But in fact I had no such general aim in mind in these articles. Transaction costs were used in the one case to show that if they are not included in the analysis, the firm has no purpose, while in the other I showed, as I thought, that if transaction costs were not introduced into the analysis, for the range of problems considered, the law had no purpose. While the structure of the argument was similar in both cases, the problems that the concept of transaction costs was used to solve were quite different. In retrospect I think it may well be that the most important contribution of "The Nature of the Firm" to economics will be considered to have been the explicit introduction of the concept of transaction costs into economic analysis but it was not my aim to change the character of economic theory. Indeed, given that the ideas in that article were developed by a young man who knew virtually no economics it is inconceivable that he could have had any such aim in mind. In "The Nature of the Firm" I introduced transaction costs to explain the emergence of the firm, and that was all. Similarly, in "The Problem of Social Cost" I used the concept of transaction costs to demonstrate the way in which the legal system could affect the working of the economic system, and I did not press beyond this. However, unlike "The Nature of the Firm," "The Problem of Social Cost" was an immediate success. It was soon cited and extensively discussed, and this continues to be the case. I do not wish to discuss why these two articles, using so similar an approach, should have been received so differently, but I agree with Barzel and Kochin that the popularity of "The Problem of Social Cost" must have played a very important part in rekindling interest in "The Nature of the Firm."

I cannot say at what point it became apparent to me that the whole of economic theory would be transformed by incorporating transaction costs into the analysis—probably this was a gradual process. At any rate it seems fairly clear from Cheung's recollections of conversations he had with me in the late 1960s that by

then this was my view. How far other economists now share my view of the significance of transaction costs for economic theory I do not know. But there is no
question that, starting in the 1970s, numbers of economists began to explain the
adoption of various business practices (including the emergence of the firm) as a
response to the existence of transaction costs.

Although the attention given to my argument in "The Nature of the Firm" in
the 1970s and 1980s derived in part from the interest in my views generated by the
"Social Cost" article and the greater appreciation of the importance of transaction
costs which it brought about, the writings of Williamson must have had the same
effect. His book, *Corporate Control and Business Behavior*, published in 1970 and
especially his *Market and Hierarchies*, published in 1975, must have made many
economists aware that there was an approach to industrial organization different
from that commonly espoused. The alternative approach that Williamson presented depended on the distinction between markets and hierarchy, incorporated transaction costs into the analysis, and examined in much greater detail than is usual
with economists the problems of the internal organization of the firm. His approach is broadly consistent with "The Nature of the Firm," to which he refers, and
must have led some economists to examine, or re-examine, that article. Williamson
agrees with what he terms my "grim assessment" of the position in 1970. However,
he ascribes the non-use of my thesis, so often acclaimed as a "fundamental insight,"
to the fact that it has not been made "operational." As he said in 1975: "Transaction
costs are appropriately made the centerpiece of the analysis but these are not
operationalized in a fashion which permits one to assess the efficacy of completing
transactions as between firms and markets in a systematic way."[4] Williamson has
reaffirmed this view in 1985 and 1986. I think it is largely correct. Standard economic theory deals by and large with a world of zero transaction costs. Incorporating these costs explicitly into the analysis would have the most profound effects.
Wallis and North have estimated that transaction costs are about 50 percent of the
gross national product. Given that they are so large, their influence on the working
of the economic system is bound to be pervasive. The range of goods and services
supplied, the pricing practices, the contractual arrangements, the forms of economic organization, all will be affected, and affected significantly. Furthermore, these
features of the economic system will be interrelated. The range of goods and
services supplied will depend on the pricing practices, the contractual arrangements, and the forms of economic organization and the pricing practices will
depend on the range of goods and services supplied, the contractual arrangements,
the forms of economic organization, and so on. The incorporation of transaction
costs into economic analysis is therefore a formidable task and it is hardly surprising that, in the early 1930s, knowing hardly any economics, I did not attempt it.

The problem faced in incorporating transaction costs into the analysis can be
illustrated by considering a remark of Duncan Black contained in the preface to his
book, *The Theory of Committees and Elections*. He says: "At a very early stage I
was helpful to find the general lines of development by discussion with my colleague Professor Ronald H. Coase on his view of the nature of the firm."[5] Black
and I were the two assistant lecturers at the Dundee School of Economics in the

years 1932–1934. I discussed my views with him at length, and I know he was impressed by what I said about the firm. Yet his remark puzzled me since the factors I emphasized in analyzing the activities of the firm did not seem to be reflected in *The Theory of Committees and Elections*. Black's explanation in correspondence was as follows: "Partly the absence of visible relation was due to the fact that although in arriving at the theory of the committee I had employed the concept of transaction costs (for example to get a theory of political parties) when it came to publication I chose to reject all material which could not be put in mathematical form." That Black was unable to put transaction costs (or their relationship to the main features of the political system) into mathematical form was not due to an inability on his part to handle the mathematics. Black had taken a degree in physics and mathematics before switching to economics. The problem was to state in a precise way the part which transaction costs play in the working of the political system. As with political science, so it is with economics.

But leaving aside the inherent difficulties of the subject, it now seems to me that there was a weakness in my exposition in "The Nature of the Firm" that hampered further development. I was aware of this weakness at the time the article was published, but it was not until I came to prepare this lecture that I realized how serious this may have been for the development of the subject. It is important to understand that this is the first time that I have done any real thinking on the problems of the firm for over fifty years. I am an economic Rip Van Winkle. It is not therefore to be expected that I will be presenting a definitive statement of my position. Still less can I make an appraisal of the recent contributions to the literature, some of which I have only begun to study and others of which I have not had an opportunity as yet to read. All I can do now is indicate my general position. But my remarks will not lack conviction. I should say straight away that while I think my exposition in "The Nature of the Firm" had weaknesses, commentators that I have read do not seem to have detected them, and a good deal of what is now said on the subject seems to me to be wide of the mark.

I consider that one of the main weaknesses of my article stems from the use of the employer-employee relationship as the archetype of the firm. It gives an incomplete picture of the nature of the firm. But more important, I believe it misdirects our attention. The incompleteness that comes from using the analogy of the employer-employee relationship is something of which I was very much aware in the 1930s. In the last section of my article, in which I attempt to show the realism of my concept of the firm, I compare it to the legal relationship of employer and employee. However I add in a footnote that the legal concept and the economic concept are not identical "in that the firm may imply control over another person's property as well as over their labour."[6] And in my notes written around 1934, I said that the employer-employee contract approaches the firm relationship but that the full firm relationship will not come about unless "several such contracts are made with people and for things which cooperate with one another." Nonetheless, in the text of my article in at least one place I seem to have forgotten this necessary qualification and I write as if all that were involved is the relation of employer to employee. I say this: "It is important to note the character of the contract into which a factor enters that is employed within a firm. The contract is one whereby the factor, for a certain remuneration (which may be fixed or fluctuating), agrees to obey the directions of an entrepreneur *within certain limits*. The essence of the contract is that it should only state the limits to the powers of the entrepreneur. Within these limits, he can therefore direct the other factors of production."[7] The footnote reference which I insert at this point states that without limits we would have "voluntary slavery," and this makes it abundantly clear that in this particular passage the factor of production that I had in mind was labor and the contracts of which I was speaking were those between employers and employees. As a result of the emphasis on the employer-employee relationship, the contracts that enable the organizers of the firm to direct the use of capital (equipment or money) by acquiring, leasing, or borrowing it were not examined, perhaps because, fifty years ago, I did not know enough to be able to handle these problems.

This incompleteness is a blemish but of itself does not do serious harm to my general theoretical scheme. Indeed, for my purpose in "The Nature of the Firm," which was to explain why there are firms, my exposition was quite adequate. But if one is concerned with the further development of the analysis of the firm's activities, the way in which I presented my ideas has, I believe, led to or encouraged an undue emphasis on the role of the firm as a purchaser of the services of factors of production and on the choice of the contractual arrangements which it makes with them. As a consequence of this concentration on the firm as a purchaser of the inputs it uses, economists have tended to neglect the main activity of a firm, running a business. And this has tended to submerge what to me is the key idea in "The Nature of the Firm": the comparison of the costs of coordinating the activities of factors of production within the firm with the costs of bringing about the same result by market transactions or by means of operations undertaken within some other firm.

Let us start by assuming that we have an economic system without firms, difficult though it may be to conceive of such a thing. All transactions are carried out as a result of contracts between factors, with the services to be provided to each other specified in the contract and without any direction involved. Contracts would also be entered into between factors and consumers for the sale of the product. How matters would work out in detail is not easy to describe or even to imagine. One of the factors could be responsible for the sale of the product to consumers, or it could be that one would be responsible for the sale of some component, made by some factors, to other factors, with the sale of the product to the consumers being undertaken by still another, or alternatively, the consumer could contract with all the factors which provide the services to make the product. There are a vast number of possible contractual arrangements but, absent firms, none would involve the direction of factors of production. In such a system, the allocation of resources would respond directly to the structure of prices, but a great part of the available resources would be absorbed in making the arrangements for the contracts needed to bring about these transactions and in providing the information on the basis of which decisions would be made.

The position is completely changed if this theoretical scheme is modified to allow firms to be formed. The organizers of a firm will be able to make contracts with factors of production under which they become subject to their direction if they can pay these factors sufficiently more than they would receive in the previously existing system, and they will be able to sell the resultant product if they can do so at a price lower than that at which it was sold under the previous system. In effect this means that it will be profitable to organize a firm when its costs of operating (including its costs of contracting with the factors of production or other firms and its cost of selling the product) are less than the transaction costs that would be incurred in a complete market system, since this difference is the source from which the higher returns to factors and the lower prices for products will come. In "The Nature of the Firm" I explained why it seemed reasonable to me that this difference would often be sufficiently large to bring about this result: "A factor of production (or the owner thereof) does not have to make a series of contracts with the factors with whom he is co-operating within the firm, as would be necessary, of course, if this co-operation were as a direct result of the working of the price mechanism. For this series of contracts is substituted one."[8] I described the situation differently and perhaps better in "The Problem of Social Cost": "Within the firm individual bargains between the various co-operating factors of production are eliminated and for a market transaction is substituted an administrative decision. The rearrangement of production then takes place without the need for bargains between the owners of the factors of production. . . . In effect, . . . the firm would acquire the legal rights of all the parties and the rearrangement of activities would not follow on a rearrangement of rights by contract, but as a result of an administrative decision as to how the rights should be used."[9] The emergence of the firm leads to very much less complicated contractual arrangements, the character of which is indicated by the phrase "for this series of contracts is substituted one." It is also true, which I certainly had not realized at the time I wrote "The Nature of the Firm," that the emergence of firms has as a consequence, the substitution of interfirm for factor-factor transactions and of firm-consumer for factor-consumer transactions. This must also have the effect of simplifying the contracting process.

Of course, the operating costs of a firm not only have to be lower than the transaction costs that would otherwise be incurred in an economic system in which there were no firms but also lower than the costs that other firms would incur to carry out the same operations. If they were not, other firms would be organized, the amount paid for factors of production would be bid up, and the price at which the product was sold would be reduced until the margin between costs and receipts had narrowed so much that the first firm could not operate profitably. The same argument applies to all groupings of activities that firms might undertake. This results in the institutional structure of production being that which minimizes total costs for the output produced.

What emerges from this interfirm competition for the task of coordinating the activities of factors of production is a situation in which what would have been transactions between factors of production are, for the most part, eliminated and are locked inside the firm, although there may be some markets within firms. It also results in a situation in which, apart from the purchase of the services of factors

of production and retail trade, most market transactions will be interfirm transactions. The alternative to an interfirm market transaction is to bring it within the
purview of a firm, either of one of the firms involved in the transaction or of some
other. It is therefore easy to see why vertical integration has come to be regarded as
one of the major problems of industrial organization. It seems to me, however, that
we will make more solid progress if we investigate the problem of vertical integration within the context of a more comprehensive theoretical structure.

In "The Nature of the Firm" there is no such comprehensive theory. My purpose in that article was simply to explain why there were firms and for this it was
enough to show that there were costs that could be avoided by their formation, now
commonly called transaction costs. Of course, organizing a firm would be profitable only if the costs avoided were greater than the costs that would be incurred by
the firm in coordinating the activities of the factors of production. I did not
attempt to uncover the factors that would determine when this would be so. I was
content to give plausible reasons why it was reasonable to assume that it would
often be the case that the costs of a market transaction between the factors of
production would exceed the costs that would be incurred by a firm in coordinating
the activities of the factors of production to bring about the same result. But this
does not tell us what the institutional structure of production will be. That depends
on which firms can carry out this particular activity at the lowest cost and this is
presumably largely determined by the other activities that the firms are undertaking. I complained in my National Bureau talk in 1970 that we knew very little about
the effect of the activities in which a firm is already engaged on its costs of
undertaking additional activities. My impression is that we still have a long way to
go. What is wanted is a theoretical scheme which would link together all these
factors into a coherent theoretical system. I am not going to present such a theoretical scheme here, but to help in this work I would like to clarify the role of the long-
term contract.

After setting out in "The Nature of the Firm" what I considered to be the basic
reason for the existence of firms (the avoidance of the costs of contracting between
factors of production), I append an argument about long-term contracts not in
their role as an alternative to coordination within a firm but as something which
could bring the firm into existence. Few seem to have noticed its anomalous character, and it seems clear that I was not aware of it at the time I wrote "The Nature of
the Firm." The argument fits awkwardly into the rest of my theoretical scheme. I
argue that a long-term contract may be chosen to avoid the additional costs that
would result from a series of short-term contracts or because it may suit the risk
preferences of the parties involved. I then say that the longer the period covered by
the contract, the less desirable it becomes to specify exactly what the party supplying the service is expected to do. Today we would be inclined to express the thought
in transaction cost terms and would explain that the longer the period covered by
the contract, the more costly it would become to specify in the contract all the
contingencies that might arise and what the supplier of the services would be
expected to do in these various circumstances. I then said that it may be a matter of
indifference to the supplier which of several actions are taken but not to the pur-

chaser. As a consequence, what is to be provided is stated in general terms with the details to be decided later. So far what I said still seems to me to be correct. But I conclude: "When the direction of resources (within the limits of the contract) becomes dependent on the buyer in this way, that relationship that I term a 'firm' may be obtained." I would prefer now to say, as I did in my notes made in the middle 1930s, that such a relationship approaches the firm relationship, that relationship coming about only when the organizer has contracts with several factors whose activities he coordinates. Of course, the same reasons which lead the organizer to make such a contract with one factor would be likely to bring about similar contracts with others, and in consequence a firm would seem to arise quite naturally out of such a situation. The rationale for the existence of a firm in such circumstances would be, as before, to bring about a reduction in transaction costs, but the costs that would be lowered would not be those occasioned by transactions between the factors of production but by transactions between the organizers of the firm and the factors of production it uses. I state in "The Nature of the Firm" that this argument "is obviously of more importance in the cases of services — labour — than it is in the case of the buying of commodities."[10] However, to assume that problems associated with the making of long-term contracts would result in the formation of a firm which would not otherwise exist depends on the cost of contracting between the factors of production engaged in this activity being sufficiently low that a firm would not be formed in any case. Such an assumption does not seem to me to be one which can be safely made. The reasons why the costs would be high for the organizer of the firm contracting with factors of production would also apply to factors of production contracting with each other. So it seems to me unlikely that the desirability of making a long-term contract would normally result in the formation of a firm which would not otherwise exist. I add in "The Nature of the Firm" that this argument applies less to commodities since, unlike labor, "the main items can be stated in advance and the details which will be decided later will be of minor importance." This now seems to me doubtfully true. The times of delivery, the quantities to be dispatched, and the places to which they are to be delivered are not, for purchases of most commodities, matters of "minor importance." Notwithstanding that this is so, I have come to believe that the problems posed by long-term contracts for commodities, to which I allude in "The Nature of the Firm," do not in practice usually seem to result in vertical integration being the more efficient solution. I say this because in 1945 I had occasion to examine a number of long-term contracts and I found that they commonly did not specify such items as times of delivery, quantities (except in total), or the places to which the commodity would be delivered. These were matters to be determined later. And yet there was no question that I was dealing with transactions between independent firms. I did not have an opportunity to discover how these questions were settled in practice, but I came away with the clear impression that firms were able to resolve the problems inherent in long-term contracting, problems which seem to economists so intractable, without having to resort to vertical integration. The long-term contract as a factor promoting the formation of a firm now seems to me relatively unimportant, but the long-term contract and vertical integration as alternative solutions to the interfirm contracting problem still seems to me an important question.

Today many of the economists who write about the problems of the firm seem to believe that vertical integration comes about mainly when there is asset-specificity, because of the incentive for opportunistic behavior to which this gives rise. The situation most commonly envisaged is one in which a firm, in order to supply another firm, has to make investments which have little value to it except in its role as supplier to that purchaser, examples being expenditures on designs, special equipment, or learning about the customer's problems. In such a case it is argued that, once these investments have been made, the purchaser has an incentive to drive down the price to a level which yields no return on such investments since what they produce is of no value other than to serve this particular customer. Realizing that this may happen, the supplier would be loathe to make these investments and this leaves the purchaser in a situation in which he may be unable to obtain the services that these investments would provide except by making them himself. Sometimes that opportunistic behavior is assumed to be carried out not by the purchaser but by the supplier. Once the purchaser has agreed to take his requirements of a commodity or service from a particular supplier and has made his plans accordingly, it becomes costly for the producer to shift to another firm. The supplier is then in a position to raise the price charged above what the producer would have been willing to pay when negotiations were initiated. At times it appears as if the price were being raised and lowered simultaneously, but to prevent confusion and simplify exposition I shall confine myself for the time being to examining the incentive for the purchaser to act opportunistically (the case most commonly cited).

The risk that such action will be taken is real. But the task that faces economists is to discover when it is best handled by long-term contracts and when by vertical integration. The leading modern article dealing with this subject appears to be Klein, Crawford, and Alchian's "Vertical Integration, Appropriable Rents, and the Competitive Contracting Process," published in 1978 and reprinted in the recent books of readings edited by Barney and Ouchi and by Putterman. In their introductory remarks Klein and his coauthors say: "The particular circumstance we emphasize as likely to produce a serious threat of this type of reneging on contracts is the presence of appropriable quasi rents. After a specific investment is made and such quasi rents are created, the possibility of opportunistic behavior is very real. Following Coase's framework, this problem can be solved in two possible ways: vertical integration or contracts." They then continue: "The crucial assumption underlying the analysis of this paper is that, as assets become more specific and more appropriable quasi rents are created (and therefore the possible gains from opportunistic behavior increases), the costs of contracting will generally increase more than the costs of vertical integration. Hence, *ceteris paribus*, we are more likely to observe vertical integration."[11] As Mrs. Robinson has said on a similar occasion, we are not surprised to see the man produce the rabbit out of the hat if we've just watched him put it in. What readers were no doubt hoping to discover about the relation of the costs of contracting and of vertical integration appears as an assumption. Even so, the conclusion they draw from this assumption, if not in error, is, I believe, misleading. What decides whether vertical integration or a long-term contract represents the more efficient solution depends on the absolute relation of the costs of these alternative arrangements. Even though the costs of contracting increase more than the costs of vertical integration as assets become more specific and quasi rents increase, vertical integration will not displace the long-term contract unless the costs of contracting become greater than the costs of vertical integration — and this might never happen for any value of quasi rents actually found. In any case, I am very doubtful whether there is such a systematic relationship as that described.

I emphasize this point because, early in 1932, as I explained in my first lecture, I put forward essentially the same argument as that found in the article by Klein et al. and it was in part as a result of thinking about it, and rejecting it as a general explanation for vertical integration, that I arrived at the thesis of "The Nature of the Firm." In that article there is no trace of the argument about asset-specificity. I will explain why. The tale is particularly interesting since it was thinking about one of the examples which Klein and his colleagues use to illustrate their thesis which settled the matter for me and led me to reject their argument some forty-six years before they expounded it. In a letter to Fowler dated March 24, 1932, I said: "Suppose the production of a particular product requires a large capital equipment which is, however, specialized insofar that it can only be readapted at great cost. Then the firm producing such a product for one consumer finds itself faced with one risk — that the consumer may transfer his demand elsewhere or that he may exercise his monopoly power to force down the price — the machinery has no supply price. Now this risk must mean that the rate of interest paid on this capital is that much higher. . . . If the consuming firm decided to make this product this risk is absent and it may well be that the difference in capital costs may well offset the relative inefficiency in actual operating." I confirmed that the risk was real by discussions with businessmen: suppliers were often unwilling to sell too great a proportion of their output to one customer. However, I soon gathered other information which led me to doubt not the reality of this risk, but its importance. There were many contractual arrangements which avoided the risk. I found that the problem worried me more than the businessmen who had to deal with it. And when I came to write the draft of "The Nature of the Firm" in 1934, another strand of thought must have added to my scepticism. In my second lecture I quoted from some notes probably written about 1934 in which I discussed whether fraud would promote integration. Opportunistic behavior is not necessarily fraud, although it may be, but in estimating the likelihood of opportunistic behavior the same approach can be used. A defrauding firm may make immediate gains but if it can be identified, future business is lost and this, I claimed, would normally make fraud unprofitable. A similar argument suggests that opportunistic behavior of the type we are discussing would also normally be unprofitable and this argument has added force since a firm acting in this way will certainly be identified. That the implementation of long-term contracts is commonly accompanied by informal arrangements not governed by contract (at least that is what my 1945 investigation seemed to show) and that this approach seems to work suggests to me that the propensity for opportunistic behavior is usually effectively checked by the need to take account of the effect of the firm's actions on future business. But, of course, there are also contractual arrangements which reduce the profitability of opportunistic behavior and therefore make it even more unlikely. I instanced in a letter to Fowler in 1932 the arrangement in which the consuming firm paid for specialized equipment, for example, dies. And there were apparently other contractual provisions which had a similar effect, although I did not describe them. All this must have made me sceptical about the asset-specificity argument. But my mind was made up, curiously enough, as a result of considering one of the examples used by Klein, Crawford, and Alchian to illustrate their thesis: the acquisition by General Motors in 1926 of the 40 percent of the shares of Fisher Body that they did not already own (they had owned 60 percent of the shares since 1919). This share purchase is ascribed by Klein and his colleagues to the difficulties that had been encountered in drawing up contracts for the supply of bodies, which on the one hand removed General Motors' incentive for opportunistic behavior without on the other hand creating opportunities "for Fisher Body to take advantage of General Motors." At any rate, General Motors was unhappy with the arrangement. "In addition," as Klein and his co-authors explain, "Fisher refused to locate their body plants adjacent to General Motors assembly plants, a move General Motors claimed was necessary for production efficiency (but which required a large very specific and hence possibly appropriable investment on the part of Fisher)."[12]

I visited General Motors in 1932, about six years after they had obtained complete control of Fisher Body, and I recall being told that the reason they had taken this action was to make sure that the body plants were located near the assembly plants. A few weeks later I visited the A. O. Smith plant in Milwaukee. A. O. Smith was the largest manufacturer of automobile frames in the world, producing about 50 percent of the output in the United States. Their main customer was General Motors. The A. O. Smith plant was the most highly automated plant that I had seen. Steel strip was received and made into automobile frames by a completely automated process. The American businessmen to whom I had introductions considered that it was a plant that a budding English works manager should not fail to visit. It was certainly very impressive. Fortunately for me, 1932 saw the height of the Depression, there were no jobs in industry, and I went to Dundee and became an economist. But the memory of the A. O. Smith plant remained with me. What I had seen was the manufacture of a heavy and important part of an automobile, which was made with expensive and highly specific equipment and was shipped hundreds of miles to General Motors' assembly plants in Michigan — but the manufacturer, A. O. Smith, apparently had harmonious relations with General Motors. This visit, as you can imagine, made me sceptical about what general lesson could be drawn from the Fisher Body case. Subsequent events have not made me change my mind. In 1979, A. O. Smith was still said to be the largest manufacturer or automobile frames in the world and General Motors was a major customer. In 1983, according to A. O. Smith's annual report, of the ten best selling cars in the United States, four were built using frames manufactured by

A. O. Smith, two of which were General Motors cars for which A. O. Smith was the sole supplier of full length separate frames. It is difficult to believe that this business relationship could have continued for over fifty years if either General Motors or A. O. Smith had acted opportunistically.

Details of the contractual arrangements between A. O. Smith and General Motors were set out in a document submitted to the Securities and Exchange Commission in 1970. A. O. Smith is once again described as the largest independent manufacturer of automobile and truck frames in the world, and substantially all its passengers car frames, but not its truck frames, were sold to various divisions of General Motors. We are told that A. O. Smith was not given an order for a definite number of frames but releases of a specific quantity were made throughout the year, an arrangement somewhat similar to those in the long-term contracts I examined in 1945. Prices were determined by annual negotiations but were subject to renegotiation if there were modifications in design or changes in costs. A. O. Smith worked closely with General Motors in designing and testing the frames. Major model changes involve substantial expenditures by A. O. Smith for new tooling, the arrangement of production lines and learning time for production employees. Tooling for frames was either manufactured by A. O. Smith or purchased by them and was then sold to and owned by their customers. Nonetheless, as there were many aspects of their relationship not covered by the tooling arrangement, General Motors was clearly in a position to act opportunistically if it wished to do so. It would appear either that General Motors did not do so or that A. O. Smith was a slow learner.

Support for the view that A. O. Smith does provide a general lesson is to be found in Stigler's remarks on economic organization in England in the nineteenth century contained in his article, "The Division of Labor Is Limited by the Extent of the Market": "Those too numerous people who believe that transactions between firms are expensive but those within firms are free will do well to study the [economic] organization of England during this period of eminence. In Birmingham, the center for the metal trades, specialism was carried out to an almost unbelievable extent." After saying this, Stigler quotes G. C. Allen's account of the organization of the small arms industry in 1860.[13] This is instructive because operators in the metal trades have of necessity to make those highly specific investments which give an incentive for opportunistic behavior, but of course those who succumb would find that they received little repeat business.

Vertical integration is an important subject but as I said earlier I think we will be able to understand it better if we treat it within the context of a more comprehensive theory. All I can do now is to indicate briefly what I think the general character of such a comprehensive theory would be. If we start by imagining a world in which there are only factors of production, firms would emerge naturally to overcome the obstacles to their cooperation represented by extremely high transaction costs. But as these firms come into existence and expand, transaction costs would tend to fall because interfirm transactions would take the place of factor-factor transactions and this would brake their expansion. In addition, bureaucratic rigidities, what in my youth were referred to as diminishing returns to management, would also raise a firm's cost of coordinating the activities of factors as it expanded. This would also tend to limit what it does. But there is more to the process than this. In "The Nature of the Firm" I said that a firm would tend to extend the range of its control as long as its costs were less than the costs of achieving the same result by market transactions or by means of operations within some other firm. But in that article I emphasized the comparison of the costs of transacting with the cost of organizing and did not investigate the factors that would make the costs of organizing lower for some firms than for others. This was quite satisfactory if the main purpose was, as mine was, to explain why there are firms. But if one is to explain the institutional structure of production in the system as a whole it is necessary to uncover the reasons why the cost of organizing particular activities differs among firms.

Like galaxies forming out of primordial matter, we can imagine the institutional structure of production coming into being under the influence of the forces determining the interrelationships between the costs of transacting and the costs of organizing. These interrelationships are extremely complex, involving, as I said earlier, pricing practices, contractual arrangements, and organizational forms. And, as I came to realize when I wrote "The Problem of Social Cost," all these interrelationships are affected by the state of the law, which also needs to be taken into account in the analysis. But it is a theoretical scheme that incorporates these interrelationships that I believe will make my approach in "The Nature of the Firm" operational. It will not have escaped the notice of some readers that this analytical scheme can be put into mathematical form. This should give us hope but only if this analytical power is used to enlighten us about the real rather than an imaginary world. All this will require a great deal of empirical work but this is how I conceive that the basic ideas in "The Nature of the Firm" can be made a living part of economic analysis.

It has been said that young men have visions and old men have dreams. My dream is to construct a theory which will enable us to analyze the determinants of the institutional structure of production. In "The Nature of the Firm" the job was only half done — it explained why there were firms but not how the functions which are performed by firms are divided up among them. My dream is to help complete what I started some fifty-five years ago and to take part in the development of such a comprehensive theory. And so, once my present commitments are out of the way, I propose to put aside the research projects on which I am now engaged and to join those economists who are working in this field. I intend to set sail once again to find the route to China, and if this time all I do is to discover America, I won't be disappointed.

NOTES

1. "Industrial Organization: A Proposal for Research," in Victor R. Fuchs, ed., *Policy Issues and Research Opportunities in Industrial Organization* (National Bureau of Economic Research, 1972), 62.

2. Steven N. S. Cheung, "The Contractual Nature of the Firm," 26 *Journal of Law and Economics* (1983) 1, n. 2.

3. Edmund W. Kitch, ed., "The Fire of Truth: A Remembrance of Law and Economics at Chicago, 1932–1970," 26 *Journal of Law and Economics* (1983) 202.

4. Oliver E. Williamson, *Markets and Hierarchies: Analysis and Antitrust Implications* (1975), 3.

5. Duncan Black, *The Theory of Committees and Elections* (1958), preface, xi.

6. "The Nature of the Firm," n. 3.

7. Ibid., 391 [this volume: 21].

8. Ibid.

9. "The Problem of Social Cost," 3 *Journal of Law and Economics* (1960) 16.

10. "The Nature of the Firm," 392 [this volume: 21–22].

11. Benjamin Klein, Robert G. Crawford, and Armen A. Alchian, "Vertical Integration, Appropriable Rents, and the Competitive Contracting Process," 21 *Journal of Law and Economics* (1978) 298.

12. Ibid., 308–10.

13. George J. Stigler, "The Division of Labor Is Limited by the Extent of the Market," 59 *Journal of Political Economy* (1951) 192–93.

6

Transactions Costs
and Internal Labor Markets

SHERWIN ROSEN

1. INTRODUCTION

Coase's first lecture reveals a surprising aversion toward mathematics. Curious, coming from one of the few economists who has a *theorem* named after him. In fact an easy case can be made that Ronald Coase is responsible for two theorems, a lemma, and, according to some, an identity. *The* Coase theorem is at this point well beyond further discussion. The second theorem is the remarkable one on the time-consistent, subgame perfect equilibrium for a durable goods monopolist — the poor soul who is forced to either destroy some property or else act as a perfect competitor because it is impossible to commit now to actions that are not credible in the future except when monopoly power remains unexploited (Coase, 1972). The lemma is not as well known, but should be. It is stated in some remarkable work with Fowler in 1935, the first known attempt to fit an intertemporal arbitage condition, an Euler equation, to real data. Coase and Fowler were dubious about the rationality of cobweb theory as an explanation for the pig cycle. Raising pigs happens to be a very specialized business. Breeders sell young pigs to feeders, who in turn sell them in the slaughter market after they have grown to the proper size. Coase and Fowler reasoned that easy money could be made in the first-stage transactions unless the average market prices paid for young pigs reflected expectations about the price of pork some nine months later, the period in the 1930s (now it is six months) over which animals were held prior to slaughter, and they verified the hypothesis empirically in British data. The work is instantly recognized today as a version of the rational expectations hypothesis and acknowledged as such by Muth in his important paper on the subject.

Though many economists would sell their souls for a theorem, if not an inequality, attached to their name, I suspect that Coase would rather be identified with a *law*. This is not the place to speculate on why laws in economics are so few, but they seem conspicuous by their scarcity. The law of demand is now a theorem about the Slutsky matrix, and most of the laws that are associated with specific names have not fared well. Stigler's law was replaced, for a time, by Laffer's curve, the growth of Los Angeles annihilated Zipf's law, and the takeover and Japanese competition have not been kind to Gibrat's law. Walras and Engel have done better, but then only one of them concerns an empirical phenomenon. I hope Coase claims his law from his renewed interest in the subject at hand.

Many studies have calculated a four-year average half-life of citations of articles in economics. Citations to "The Nature of the Firm" show not only remarkable longevity but also an exceedingly rare decreasing hazard of mortality with age. No doubt this is due to the fundamental questions posed by the work and to the various meanings that can be attached to it. In reading it again I was struck by parallels with the literature of that time on the role of the price system in "spontaneously coordinating" economic activities, to use Hayek's felicitous expression, as compared to the heavy and inefficient hand of coordination through central planning. Coase takes the invisible hand as his point of departure and inquires into the limits of market transactions as a coordinating mechanism. If markets are ideal coordinators, why should we ever observe any nonspontaneous, nonmarket coordination, as we appear ot do within firms?

Coase argues that firms exist because some transactions internal to firms are less costly than similar transactions carried out in markets. The limits of the firm depend on cost comparisons at these margins.

Ultimately, these limits are determined by *market competition* among firms, including the market for corporate control. "Central planning" within firms is disciplined by competition among them, so long as resources are free to move to their highest valued uses. As Alchian argued, firms making superior decisions gain control of more resources at the expense of the less efficient. It is the central role of competition and concern with more aggregate questions of supply and demand that probably accounts for why much of economic theory dispenses with the notion of the firm altogether; for example, general equilibrium theory uses only a very abstract notion of technology.

In what follows, I apply the theme of "The Nature of the Firm" to labor markets. Relation-specific exchange embodies the empirical content of transactions cost in modern industrial organization. Firm-specific human capital is a closely related concept. Section 2 reviews recent research showing that the costs of matching workers to firms and of assembling a team of workers are major components of these investments. Section 3 analyzes the nature of a decentralized market mechanism under these circumstances and shows that efficient allocations require a larger number of transaction-specific prices. The costs and complexity of calculation and implementation make market decentralization impractical. The theme of complexity and a plethora of prices is pursued in section 4, in the context of principal and agent theory. The emphasis here is on incentive rather than selection and allocation problems. Nonetheless, the main results so far share the same conceptual difficulty of excessive complexity and implementation costs. A broader approach which combines incentive, selection, and allocation problems is stated in section 5, within the context of the firm's personnel management policy of its internal labor market. Here changing selection and assignments of workers to positions over the work-life cycle interacts with performance incentives and worker capabilities. Conclusions appear in section 6.

2. TRANSACTIONS COSTS AND SPECIFIC CAPITAL

Coase did not define the empirical content of transactions costs in "The Nature of the Firm" nor tell us how to recognize them when we see them. Much progress has been made since then, especially by Becker and by Williamson (1975), in identifying transactions costs with firm-specific human and nonhuman capital. Shared investment costs requires sharing later returns and can lead to ex post contract enforcement problems due to inefficient, opportunistic behavior. Several empirical observations in the labor market are consistent with the idea of specific human capital, especially the long-term attachments between workers and firms. The longest job of a typical white male worker persists for twenty-five years (Hall). Top-level executives in major U.S. corporations are mostly "home grown," having spent thirty years or more with their firms in lesser positions before breaking into the top echelons (Murphy). It is also otherwise difficult to understand the patterns of layoffs and employment variability among workers. Workers who have higher wages and greater job and firm-specific skills are less likely to be laid off.

So far, however, the magnitude of firm-specific human capital has eluded precise econometric measurement. The latest investigations of this problem by Altonji and Shakotko; Abraham and Farber; Marshall and Zarkin; and Topel suggest that most of the observed effects of firm-specific experience on earnings are due to selection. Highly paid employees have greater tenure with their firms but were also highly paid when first hired. These workers remain with their firms longer and exhibit greater firm-specific experience because their earnings were larger there to begin with. They were better matched to their jobs in the first instance. Workers who were not matched so well earned less and left their firm in search of greener pastures, thus exhibiting less firm-specific experience. When these selection effects are controlled statistically, it is found that the "true" firm-specific experience effect on earnings is about the same as the general labor market experience effect, that is, the same as the general tendency for earnings to rise with age. Now match-specific effects certainly are a type of firm-specific capital, but of a slightly different nature than in the literature that derives inspiration from "The Nature of the Firm."

The measurement of physical capital asset specificity is perhaps easier, especially as it pertains to vertical integration. Joskow's recent study of the contractual relationships between electric utilities and coal suppliers is a good case in point. Nonetheless, there are ambiguities in defining the limits of the firm when asset specificities and transport cost-based rents are regulated by long-term contracts. Are these to be classified as market transactions, transactions internal to the extended family of the firm, or what? Klein, Crawford, and Alchian analyze many examples where asset specificities are internalized by ownership. My favorite was the Hawaiian resort that purchased the adjacent golf course to avoid ex post bargaining costs and opportunism. However, that kind of reasoning won't go very far in accounting for why Yale University is vertically integrated with a splendid golf course (perhaps it is meant as an extra barrier to making tenure among golfers).

As pointed out by Shavell, asset ownership dominates rental when the user's actions can substantially affect its resale or transfer value. Ownership internalizes conflicts of interest over maintenance and reckless use of equipment, which surely is the most important reason why most capital goods are owned outright by the firms that employ them. Some of the remaining cases of capital leasing can be understood on tax grounds (Scholes and Wolfson), but several defy analysis. Rentals of capital services are common in commercial real estate transactions, and greater tax advantages to wealthy individuals compared to businesses probably account for some of this, at least historically. Yet no such consideration applies to the separate ownership of sites and structures. Consider that the World Trade Center sits on rented land. Since those buildings are securely anchored to the bedrock below that part of Manhattan, it is difficult to conceive of more asset specificity than this. There is even more asset specificity in this than in Coase's observations on the contractual relations between General Motors and A. O. Smith in his third lecture. True, the lease on the land is very long-term, running to ninety-nine years. Still, the potential difficulties of renegotiation several years before the lease expires are well illustrated by what has happened in Hong Kong in recent times. These are more than rent-splitting and pure distribution problems, because the building owner can take actions, such as neglect of maintenance, that directly affects the value of the site. Common ownership of both site and structure would eliminate this problem. Why isn't it always observed?

3. LIMITS OF LABOR MARKET DECENTRALIZATION

Contractual difficulties arising from shared ownership of assets is an important case of a more general problem of devising decentralized pricing mechanisms under joint production. If there were no scale economics, transport costs, or economies of joint production, it is difficult to imagine why complete decentralization of labor markets would fail to achieve efficient allocations. Most workers would be, in some sense, self-employed. Coase provides a good example by reference to Stigler's discussion of British gun manufacture in the eighteenth century. Specialization and division of labor in allied trades was virtually complete when guns were manufactured on a small scale in a skilled craft system. Craftsmen were specialized by function: barrels, trigger mechanisms, stocks, sights, and so on. Others specialized in assembly, purchasing inputs from these specialists, producing the finished product, and distributing it to customers. Most of these specialized transactions were carried out by market contracts, all within shouting distance of each other in a small area of Birmingham. Alfred Marshall analyzed this kind of system in his theory of external economies and locational concentration of specialized industries. Whitney's attempt to manufacture standardized guns on a large scale was unsuccessful, but his effort to achieve standardization and interchangeable parts altered gun manufacture forever. Gun-making was thereafter vertically integrated and many of the transactions that had previously been organized through the marketplace were coordinated by more authoritarian methods within firms.

Imagine how markets would have to be organized under these circumstances. A worker would own (or rent) a place in the assembly line, having purchased the rights from its previous owner. Its economic value would reside in the residual rights of contract, the profit gotten from purchasing intermediate products from adjacent upstream sellers and reselling the value-added units to adjacent downstream buyers. A decentralized contracting system confined to single quarters would be very difficult to manage because of the team aspects of the situation and the complicated interconnections of property rights they imply. Downstream workers, obliged to buy from an adjacent seller due to proximity and smaller transport costs, become very interested in the identity of that seller, because the volume and quality of work at each point affects the value of property rights of all others to whom it connects.

An exceedingly complicated contractual system, usually requiring side-payments among participants in the organization, is necessary to achieve efficiency in these circumstances. The number of prices necessary to manage it can be very large indeed. However, a simpler mechanism may be available; one person retains all residual rights, assembles the appropriate team of workers on a contractual basis, assigns them to their most productive positions in the firm, and monitors their work. The terms of these contracts must specify standards for the quality and quantity of work, as well as employment conditions regarding working hours and regularity of employment, these nonprice dimensions of contracts being necessary to internalize technological dependencies among workers. Financial terms of contracts are constrained by competition for workers in the labor market. Concentrating control in this way and establishing a wage system may be a less complicated way of achieving efficiency than designing and monitoring an elaborate accounting system and calculating the individualized prices required by a decentralized internal transfer-pricing mechanism.

To illustrate the nature of the calculations needed, consider an organization where joint production entails complementarities of time spent with coworkers. Let x_i represent the output of worker i and let t_{ij} denote the time that i spends with j (the time that i spends alone is t_{ii}). There are n workers and the output of worker i is

$$x_i = F^i(t_{i1}, t_{i2}, \ldots, t_{in}) \text{ for } i = 1, 2, \ldots, n. \tag{1}$$

The problem is to find an allocation of time $\{t_{ij}\}$ that maximizes total output in the organization, the sum of the x_i's, subject to two kinds of constraints. First, the time allocation of each worker must exhaust total time worked. Ignoring choice of total hours worked and normalizing it to 1.0 for each worker, there are n constraints of the form

$$1 = t_{i1} + t_{i2} + \ldots + t_{in}, \text{ for } i = 1, 2, \ldots, n. \tag{2}$$

In addition, the time that worker i desires to spend with worker j must equal the time that worker j desires to spend with worker i: there are $(n^2 - n)/2$ constraints of the form

$$t_{ij} = t_{ji}, \text{ for } i \neq j. \tag{3}$$

First-order conditions for the efficient time allocation take the following form. For t_{ii} we require

$$F^i_i(t_{i1}, t_{i2}, \ldots, t_{in}) \le \lambda_i, \text{ for } i = 1, 2, \ldots, n \tag{4}$$

where λ_i is the multiplier on constraint (2) for worker i. The equality is binding when $t_{ii} > 0$, so λ_i has the interpretation of the shadow price of i's time. For t_{ij} and t_{ji} we need

$$F^i_j(t_{i1}, t_{i2}, \ldots, t_{in}) \le \lambda_i + \beta_{ij} \text{ for } j = 1, 2, \ldots, n$$
$$F^j_i(t_{j1}, t_{j2}, \ldots, t_{jn}) \le \lambda_j + \beta_{ji} \text{ for } i = 1, 2, \ldots, n \tag{5}$$

with strict equality whenever $t_{ij} > 0$. Here β_{ij} is the multiplier associated with constraint (3) and $\beta_{ij} = -\beta_{ji}$. Since λ_i is the marginal product of own time, (4) and (5) together imply that if it is efficient for i and j to work together ($t_{ij} = t_{ji} < 0$) then

$$\partial F^i / \partial t_{ij} + \partial F^j / \partial t_{ji} = \lambda_i + \lambda_j = \partial F^i / \partial t_{ij} + \partial F^j / \partial t_{jj}. \tag{6}$$

Equation (6) resembles the condition for efficient joint production of a "public good." The right-hand side is the marginal cost of joint production for the pair of workers, the output foregone if both had spent their time alone rather than together. The left-hand side is the marginal value of joint production, the sum of the incremental products of working together.

Conditions (4)–(6) have an important implication, that the decentralized price system that implements the efficient program is very complicated. The fact that (5) and (6) refer to *pairs* of workers means that the marginal product of a given worker's time is *not equated* across all workers to whom he is assigned. The time-price worker i spends with another worker k is $\lambda_i + \beta_{ik}$ and $\beta_{ij} \ne \beta_{ik}$ unless workers j and k are in some sense identical to each other. Hence a pricing system would have to use *different prices* for time charged in each possible pairing. This point is related to the problem of establishing prices in network systems such as landing rights at airports and other assignment problems (Koopmans and Beckmann).

Let w_{ij} be the unit price that worker i charges worker j per unit time, with $w_{ij} = -w_{ji}$, so w_{ji} is the unit price j must pay to i if w_{ij} is positive (or the price that j charges i per unit time if w_{ji} is negative). Taking output as numeraire, the decentralized solution is achieved by letting each worker act as a residual income recipient, selling own output to the owner of the firm at price 1.0 and charging each coworker w_{ij} per unit of time spent with each. Worker i chooses $\{t_{ij}\}$ to maximize

$$F^i(t_{1i}, t_{2i}, \ldots, t_{ni}) + \sum_{i \ne j} w_{ij} t_{ij} \tag{7}$$

subject to (2). The first order condition is

$$-\partial F^i / \partial t_{ii} + \partial F^i / \partial t_{ij} + w_{ij} \le 0, \text{ for } i \ne j. \tag{8}$$

This results in the efficient solution so long as $\beta_{ij} = w_{ij}$, that is, so long as the proper price of time (possibly so large that i and j do not work together) is found for each pair. Since there are $(n^2 - n)/2$ independent shadow values of time, the number of prices necessary to achieve efficiency increases with the square of the number of workers. It would increase even more if triples and higher orders of joint production were considered. Moreover, to calculate and implement this solution requires full knowledge of the underlying technology and productivity of team members in the first place.

If that knowledge is possessed by a specialist, an authoritarian system whereby the specialist-manager allocates workers to each other and monitors their activities may be less expensive to implement than an internal price system. Errors in prices can be more costly than errors in quantities (Weitzman). For example, complementarities may be so large that the optimal t_{ij}'s are easy to calculate, whereas small errors in setting the prices w_{ij}'s could lead to serious misallocations of time among individual workers. Furthermore, agreeing on a price can be time-consuming and divert time and energy away from production even when it is clear that trade should take place. For if exact valuations are private information, then traders have incentives to argue over the distribution of gains from trade. Of course elements of these very same problems arise in interfirm as well as intrafirm transactions. Nevertheless, direct team interactions are far less important in interfirm transactions and they are more easily regulated by contractual arrangements, the monitoring of output quality, and by market competition among alternative sources of supply. The close-quarter interactions of workers and the transport cost savings they imply limit the degree of substitution and competition from outside alternatives. External labor market competition disciplines a firm's internal labor market with respect to overall wages and working conditions but leaves some slack at the micro-transactions level of precise worker interactions.

Such a system is observed in our own backyard, in the organization of the education industry. In modern educational systems, the price mechanism is used largely to allocate students and teachers among schools, and even then it is incompletely used for this purpose: nonprice considerations play an important role in these allocations. It is used hardly at all to allocate students to courses and to teachers *within* schools. Gaining admission and paying tuition entitles a student to fish among a broad range of courses. Committees and other collective bodies determine requirements, course sequencing, class size, and other matters of internal allocations. Transfer prices are seldom used.

It was not always so. The original universities were collections of individual teacher-enterpreneurs, and fees were determined by bargaining and haggling with individual students (Rashdall). As universities emerged out of these crude beginnings, two-part pricing schemes were adopted. Students paid lump-sum tuition charges to enter and a marginal payment to specific teachers in courses of their choice. This is the system that Adam Smith advocated, on incentive and agency grounds. But as far as one can tell, all teachers in the same university charged the same unit prices, whereas efficient allocations of students to teachers almost certainly require different prices for different teachers, as well as price differentials among students within each course. Two-part pricing was entirely abandoned in the twentieth century and replaced with one-part salary and tuition pricing, probably because the bundling and information aspects of modern formal education made it cost effective to ration by queues, prerequisites, and requirements rather than by individually tailored prices (see Rosen [1987] for further elaboration).

4. DECENTRALIZATION AND AGENCY

If the number of prices necessary to decentralize a complex interactive organization increases multiplicatively with size, then the amount and cost of monitoring required to achieve efficiency also must grow with size. Information becomes garbled as it passes through longer chains, and information channels become congested as chains-of-command lengthen (Williamson, 1967). It is the balancing of joint-production and scale economies against increasing costs of control associated with nonmarket transactions costs that determines organization size in traditional theory.

The avoidance of monitoring cost preoccupies the modern literature on agency theory. The main question posed is: Can penalty and reward systems be found that result in self-enforcing contracts? If so, then internal decentralization may be efficient and the size of firms could be very large indeed. A fundamental result proves that multipart pricing is necessary to induce an agent to behave in the interests of the principal. This is the bonding scheme analyzed by Becker and Stigler. The idea is straightforward and rests on the proposition that an agent behaves honestly if confronted by a scheme that makes such behavior consistent with self-interest. Evidently the scheme must either reward good behavior or punish bad behavior (malfeasance).

Considerations of labor market equilibrium dictate the penalty mode rather than the reward mode. For if the agent is given extra monetary rewards for good behavior, the expected utility from holding the job exceeds that available from alternatives and the supply of job applicants exceeds the number of available positions. On the other hand, if a worker posts bond money "up front" and the bond can be seized by the firm if malfeasance occurs, honest behavior is elicited by paying a market wage premium equivalent to interest on the bond, with the bond itself returned at the end of the contract This bond-interest-principle scheme equalizes workers' expected returns among jobs and achieves job-market clearing. An important modification of the argument allows workers to post bond by investing in the firm—by working at a wage less than marginal product in the early years of a career and receiving the return at older ages in the form of wage payments in excess of productivity (Lazear, 1979). Another modification with risk aversion (Mirrlees) also favors the penalty mode because potential monetary losses reduce utility by more than equal monetary gains increase utility.

Potential penalties must increase with the agent's perceived returns to malfeasance to elicit honest behavior in bonding schemes. The temptation toward malfeasance is decreasing in the extent of monitoring and detection activity by the firm as well as in the size of the bond to be lost if malfeasance is detected. It follows that monitoring and the size of the bond are inversely related in bonding schemes. But since monitoring uses real resources (monitors must be hired and taken out of some other productive use of labor), whereas bonds do not, monitoring resources can be driven to zero as the bond increases without limit. The scheme is completely self-enforcing in the limit. For example, penalizing double-parking offenses by execution would reduce the incidence of double-parking to minuscule proportions and very little police time would have to be spent in ticketing offenders. Even apart from the time-inconsistent (incredible) nature of this extreme example, these limiting results are mainly of academic interest. For as the bond grows in size the principal is more likely to find malfeasant behavior when it is not there. This type-II error is itself a manifestation of malfeasance of another kind, for large bonds increase the propensity for the firm to find the employee "guilty" and seize the bond. Hence it is not feasible to eliminate monitoring, and the optimum scheme must involve both penalties and monitoring.

Possibilities for malfeasance by multiple agents in joint production require mutual monitoring and "double" bonding by all participants. This problem has not been completely analyzed, though some interesting work has appeared on the role of reputations in serving as bonds; and agency considerations have been introduced into the analysis of trade unionism, where the union serves as a worker's agent in dealing with the firm. An earlier approach derives from Alfred Marshall's critique of sharecropping, where rewards are stipulated as shares of gross revenue rather than of net profit. Incentives by sharecroppers and landlords are misaligned because both receive only a fraction of their social marginal product in deciding how much labor and effort to supply to the venture. Marginal private return falls short of marginal social return and effort is too small (Johnson; Cheung).

In a multiple sharing arrangement, the socially efficient production outcome occurs only if the marginal share is unity for each party: each receives full marginal product in equilibrium (Groves). Various mechanisms have been studied to implement the efficient solution, including "budget breaking" (Holmstrom, 1982), double-bonds (Kennan), and trigger-strategies in repeated games (Radner), though little empirical research has studied the frequency with which any of them are observed in practice. Since simple sharecropping systems have been historically important in the organization of agriculture and similar institutions are commonly observed in contingent fees for lawyers, the division of reward among doctors (Gaynor and Pauly) and lawyers (Gilson and Mnookin) in group practice, both royalty arrangements, rewards to actors, musicians, and so forth, the survivor principle suggests that the efficiency losses from these schemes must have been kept at tolerable proportions. The simplest hypothesis is that joint monitoring and the adverse effects of shirking on reputations and future business dealings play important roles in resolving these conflicts of interest.

Another approach to the principal-agent problem generalizes decentralized output-reward systems to include considerations of risk sharing (Holmstrom, 1979). The problem is set up to investigate the consequences of hidden actions of the agent. The principal cannot observe the agent's action but can observe the output that is the result of these actions. There cannot be a one-to-one correspondence between output and action or else the principal could infer actions perfectly and the problem is trivial. So output is a mixture of random effects and unobserved actions. If output is large, the principal cannot tell if the agent worked very hard or was very lucky. Similarly, a small output could have been due to bad luck rather than shirking. The worker is risk averse and prefers certain income to risky income, but observability constraints make it impossible to separate insurance from incentives. Paying a strict linear piece rate gives the agent proper incentives to expend effort because the agent realizes the full social product of effort, but at the cost of exposure to excessive risk. Paying a guaranteed wage provides full insurance but does not provide any incentive to work.

The solution is a compromise between these two opposing forces. The earliest treatments (Stiglitz) analyzed two-part tariff solutions, where the principal guarantees the agent a minimum compensation for insurance reasons and a percentage of revenues to provide incentives to work hard. The proportion of pay in each part depends in an obvious way on the extent of risk, the elasticity of output with respect to effort, and the degree of risk aversion. However, when the problem is generalized to allow the form of the payment schedule to be endogenously determined, the solution is extremely complicated: payment need not even be everywhere increasing in output (Grossman and Hart).

The complicated payment schedules predicted by theory are an embarrassment of riches and another manifestation of "too many prices": the schemes we observe, such as salesperson's commissions and contingency fees in legal practice, have very few parameters. These problems would imply complete decentralization and simple linear transfer prices were it not for the presence of risk aversion, so there is a sense in which risk aversion and insurance elements lead the theory astray. One can be properly skeptical that risk aversion and the precise form of preferences are such an important part of the problem. After all, a great virtue of a price system is that it works when utility and production functions are completely private information. Could it be that such simple schemes are observed because they are robust to varieties of preferences? Holmstrom and Milgrom (1987) have recently introduced intertemporal arbitrage considerations to enforce linearity onto the optimal scheme. This is an interesting idea, but the results still depend on special assumptions about risk aversion. None of this theory extends in any obvious way to problems involving joint production among several agents. Furthermore, the analysis assumes that principals possess complete information about preferences of others and is hardly decentralized in that sense.

5. INTERNAL LABOR MARKETS

I have followed Coase (1937) and Alchian and Demsetz in arguing that the expense of implementing quasi-market decentralization within firms forces analysis on the role of performance monitoring in understanding organizational structure. The interactions of personnel within organizations are too complicated to be completely decentralized through a price mechanism. Indeed, if this were not the case then Coase's argument implies that the firm should not exist. This theme is consistent with Williamson's (1975, 1985) criticism of the textbook association of firms as production functions and his idea of a governance structure. The firm's observed production and cost functions are the outcomes of the interaction between production technology, personnel policy, management, and institutional rules and design.

Considerations of the long-term goals and survival of the organization lend additional credence to this view. Since there is substantial earnings growth over the life-cycle and since most job turnover occurs early in the working life-cycle, a large fraction of a person's life-cycle earnings is generated over the course of a career with one firm. Organizational complexity arises from the intertemporal aspects of personnel management systems. Organization dynamics cannot be separated from internal job mobility among overlapping generations of workers and management. All organizations require specialization and division of labor among their members, but job assignments systematically change over a person's tenure with the firm. Institutional memory, specific knowledge, skills, and responsibilities are constantly being transferred from old to young.

The flow and direction of personnel through positions in the firm can be thought of as an "internal labor market." A very good example is provided by the officer corps in the military, where all participants begin at the lowest rank and either move up to higher positions of authority and command or leave for alternative employments outside the military. Most organizations are more complicated than this because lateral entry and exit occur at many points, not simply at one point. Still, most follow a hierarchical design in which ultimate control is concentrated at the top and diffused through the ranks by horizontal and vertical linkages to middle- and lower-level management and to production. In large organizations, it is especially important to assign the most capable and energetic people to top-level positions because top-level decisions percolate through the organization and have much larger effects on organizational productivity than lower-level decisions do.

Top-level decisions have multiplicative effects on productivity in management technologies where authority is limited by a span of control and where monitoring resources are partially economized through lengthy chains-of-command. These multiplicative effects imply that more capable top-level decisionmaking can have enormous effects on the organization and imply that the socially efficient assignment of personnel to positions is hierarchical in ability. The most capable people should control the most resources and direct the largest organizations. Less capable and less energetic people should be assigned to lower-level positions in large firms or higher-level positions in smaller firms. The interaction of talent and scale can support extremely large salaries for top-level managers of large firms on marginal productivity grounds alone (Rosen, 1982), consistent with empirical findings that top executive compensation is systematically increasing with firm size (Murphy; Kostiuk) as well as with profitability.

Monitoring, testing, and performance evaluation take on special significance under these circumstances. Resources must be continually devoted to designing career tracks and to grading, sorting, and assigning workers to their proper positions in the organization. Employees are not passive bystanders in this process because their incomes and status depend on how they are graded. The economics of this combined design and incentive process has begun to be analyzed in the literature on tournaments (Lazear and Rosen), in which the firm optimizes its testing, selection procedures, and wage structure against the competitive efforts of workers to affect their scores, elevate their classifications, and achieve higher-ranking positions. The ordinal quality of this kind of competition follows from the inherent ordering properties of tests and peer comparison when direct output measures are difficult to devise. Ordered or relative performance evaluation also has certain optimality properties in the presence of risk aversion: it eliminates extraneous variance due to measurement error that is common to all participants (Holmstrom, 1982; Green and Stokey; Nalebuff and Stiglitz).

Sequential statistical decisions that rank and order contestants are inherent in the intergenerational dynamics of organizations and lead to a theory of promotions through the ranks as an important motivator of the organization's members. Performance incentives are provided by the wage differentials between hierarchical ranks. Top-ranking prizes (wages) take on special significance in this kind of competition, for they must rise more than in proportion with rank to maintain performance incentives among those competing for the highest-level positions (Rosen, 1986). At early stages of a career a person's performance incentives are propelled by a kind of "option" value, the possibility of achieving not only the next highest position, but all possible positions higher than that. As a successful contestant progresses through the hierarchy and climbs higher in rank and authority, there are fewer places left to attain. The option value falls with rank because there is less distance to travel. Increasing the difference in wages among the topmost-ranking positions maintains incentives by substituting for the option value that propelled performance incentives at lower ranks. In this sense wage structures among top executive positions reflect both the productivity of top-level managers and the productivity induced by the attempts of lower-ranking employees to climb higher.

A problem inherent in performance evaluation and ability testing has received increasing attention in the literature. Since grading, evaluation, and promotion decisions are made by higher-level committees and supervisors, contestants have incentives to increase their scores by exerting unproductive "influence" on the examiners (Milgrom). For example, in relative performance evaluations, there may be gains from unproductive activities that degrade the ranking of competitors and make a contestant look better than others (Lazear, 1986). These adverse "gaming" incentives by contestants apply to any evaluation system (Baker; Breton and Wintrobe) and help to explain some of the bureaucratic procedures adopted by organizations to control them. These bureaucratic costs are properly considered as transactions costs of nonmarket allocations within firms and may ultimately help define the limits of the firm.

6. CONCLUSION

I have argued that the competitive price mechanism necessary to decentralize a complex interacting organization with indivisibilities and joint production is very complicated. So much information and preknowledge is required that more authoritarian "planning" mechanisms are likely to economize on transactions costs within firms. With respect to labor resources, these allocation and contracting problems certainly involve firm-specific human capital. However, much of this appears to arise in the context of assembling a coherent work force and productive team within the firm, collecting and processing information on team members' talents and assigning them to their proper niche in the organization, and transferring productive knowledge between older and younger members of the organization.

Incentives, testing, career assignments, and rewards must be analyzed in the context of a dynamic personnel *system*. Incentives and reward structures cannot be disassociated from testing, personnel assignment, and labor turnover questions in such a system. In combining all of these functions, personnel policies are likely to be inefficient at some margins separately, though they may achieve reasonably good compromises among all goals considered together. Looking at these systems or internal-labor-market aspects of personnel management helps to explain some of the bureaucratic tendencies in organizations as controls on members' attempts to unproductively manipulate the system to personal advantage. Obviously much work remains to be done in this area, but if successful it will improve our understanding of the limits of firms and the limits of markets.

NOTE

I am indebted to Bengt Holmstrom, Edward Lazear, Oliver Williamson, and the referee for comments and criticism of an initial draft and to the National Science Foundation for research support.

REFERENCES

Abraham, Katharine G., and Henry S. Farber. 1987. "Match Quality, Seniority and Earnings," 77 *American Economic Review* 278–97.

Alchian, Armen A. 1950. "Uncertainty, Evolution and Economic Theory," 58 *Journal of Political Economy* 211–21.

———, and Harold Demsetz. 1972. "Production, Information Costs, and Economic Organization," 62 *American Economic Review* 777–95.

Altonji, Joe, and Robert Shakotko. 1984. "Do Wages Rise with Job Seniority?" Unpublished paper, Columbia University.

Baker, George P. 1987. "Monitoring Costs and Compensation Structure." Unpublished paper, Harvard Business School.

Becker, Gary S. 1964. *The Theory of Human Capital: A Theoretical and Empirical Analysis.* New York: Columbia University Press.

_____, and George J. Stigler. 1974. "Law Enforcement, Malfeasance, and Compensation of Enforcers," 3 *Journal of Legal Studies* 1–18.

Breton, Albert, and Ronald Wintrobe. 1986. "The Bureaucracy of Murder Revisited," 94 *Journal of Political Economy* 905–26.

Cheung, Steven N. 1969. *The Theory of Share Tenancy*. Chicago: University of Chicago Press.

Coase, Ronald. 1937. "The Nature of the Firm," 4 *Economica* n.s. 386–405 [chapter 2 of this volume].

_____. 1972. "Durability and Monopoly," 15 *Journal of Law and Economics* 143–49.

_____, and R. H. Fowler. 1935. "Bacon Production and the Pig Cycle in Great Britain," 2 *Economica* 142–67.

Gaynor, Martin, and Mark Pauly. 1987. "Alternative Compensation Arrangements and Productivity Efficiency in Partnerships: Evidence from Medical Group Practice." National Bureau of Economic Research.

Gilson, Ronald J., and Robert H. Mnookin. 1985. "Sharing among the Human Capitalists: An Economic Inquiry into the Corporate Law Firm and How Partners Split Profits," 37 *Stanford Law Review* 313–97.

Green, Jerry, and Nancy Stokey. 1983. "A Comparison of Tournaments and Contracts," 91 *Journal of Political Economy* 349–65.

Grossman, Sanford J., and Oliver Hart. 1983. "An Analysis of the Principal-Agent Problem," 51 *Econometrica* 7–45.

Groves, Theodore. 1973. "Incentives in Teams," 41 *Econometrica* 617–32.

Hall, Robert E. 1982. "The Importance of Lifetime Jobs in the U.S. Economy," 72 *American Economic Review* 716–27.

Holmstrom, Bengt. 1979. "Moral Hazard and Observability," 10 *Bell Journal of Economics* 74–91.

_____. 1982. "Moral Hazard in Teams," 13 *Bell Journal of Economics* 324–40.

_____, and Paul Milgrom. 1987. "Aggregation and Linearity in the Provision of Intertemporal Incentives," 55 *Econometrica* 303–29.

Johnson, D. Gale. 1950. "Resource Allocation under Share Contract," 68 *Journal of Political Economy* 111–23.

Joskow, Paul L. 1987. "Contract Duration and Relation-Specific Investments: Empirical Evidence from Coal Markets," 77 *American Economic Review* 168–85.

Kennan, John. 1979. "Bonding and Enforcement of Labor Contracts," *Economics Letters* 61–66.

Klein, Benjamin, Robert G. Crawford, and Armen A. Alchian. 1981. "Vertical Integration, Appropriate Rents and the Competitive Contracting Process," 89 *Journal of Political Economy* 615–41.

Koopmans, Tjalling, and Martin Beckmann. 1957. "Assignment Problems and the Location of Economic Activities," 25 *Econometrica* 53–76.

Kostiuk, Peter. 1985. "Firm Organization and Compensation of Corporate Executives," Ph.D. dissertation, University of Chicago, 1985.

Lazear, Edward P. 1986. "Pay Equality and Industrial Politics." Unpublished paper, Hoover Institution.

_____. 1979. "Why Is There Mandatory Retirement?" 87 *Journal of Political Economy* 1261–84.

_____, and Sherwin Rosen. 1981. "Rank Order Tournaments as Optimum Labor Contracts," 89 *Journal of Political Economy* 841–64.

Marshall, Alfred. 1930. *Principles of Economics*, 8th ed. London: Macmillan.

Marshall, Robert C., and Gary A. Zarkin. 1985. "The Effects of Job Tenure on Wage Offers." Unpublished paper, Duke University.

Milgrom, Paul. 1987. "Employment Contracts, Influence Activities and Efficient Organization Design." Unpublished paper, University of California, Berkeley.

Mirrlees, James A. 1976. "The Optimum Structure of Incentives and Authority within an Organization," 7 *Bell Journal of Economics* 105–31.

Murphy, Kevin J. 1984. "Ability, Performance and Compensation: A Theoretical and Empirical Investigation of Managerial Compensation." Ph.D. dissertation, University of Chicago.

Nalebuff, Barry J., and Joseph E. Stiglitz. 1983. "Prizes and Incentives: Toward a General Theory of Compensation and Competition," 14 *Bell Journal of Economics* 21–43.

O'Keeffe, Mary, W. Kip Viscusi, and Richard J. Zeckhauser. 1984. "Economic Contests: Comparative Reward Schemes," 2 *Journal of Labor Economics* 27–56.

Radner, Roy. 1981. "Monitoring Cooperative Agreements in a Repeated Principal-Agent Relationship," 49 *Econometrica* 1127–48.

Rashdall, Hastings. 1895. *The Universities in Europe in the Middle Ages*. Oxford: Oxford University Press.

Rosen, Sherwin. 1982. "Authority, Control and the Distribution of Earnings," 13 *Bell Journal of Economics* 311–23.

_____. 1986. "Prizes and Incentives in Elimination Tournaments," 76 *American Economic Review* 701–15.

_____. 1987. "Some Economics of Teaching," 5 *Journal of Labor Economics* 561–75.

Scholes, Myron S., and Mark A. Wolfson. 1986. "Taxes and Organization Theory." Unpublished paper, Stanford University.

Shavell, Steven. 1979. "Risk Sharing and Incentives in the Principal and Agent Relationship," 10 *Bell Journal of Economics* 55–73.

Stigler, George J. 1951. "The Division of Labor Is Limited by the Extent of the Market," 59 *Journal of Political Economy* 185–93.

Stiglitz, Joseph E. 1975. "Incentives, Risk and Information: Notes toward a Theory of Hierarchy," 6 *Bell Journal of Economics* 552–79.

Topel, Robert. 1987. "Job Mobility and Earnings Growth: A Reinterpretation of Human Capital Earnings Functions." In R. E. Ehrenberg, ed., *Research in Labor Economics*. Greenwich, Conn.: JAI Press.

Weitzman, Martin. 1974. "Prices versus Quantities," 41 *Review of Economic Studies* 477–91.

Williamson, Oliver. 1967. "Hierarchical Control and Optimum Firm Size," 75 *Journal of Political Economy* 123–39.

_____. 1975. *Markets and Hierarchies: Analysis and Antitrust Implications*. New York: Free Press.

_____. 1985. *The Economic Institutions of Capitalism*. New York: Free Press.

7

The Logic of Economic Organization

OLIVER E. WILLIAMSON

The transaction cost logic of economic organization had its origins in a tautology, which Ronald Coase wryly defines as "a proposition that is clearly right" (1988:19; this volume: 48). The basic insight, first advanced by Coase in his classic 1937 article (1952:341) and restated for this conference, is this: "A firm . . . [has] a role to play in the economic system if . . . transactions [can] be organized within the firm at less cost than if the same transactions were carried out through the market. The limit to the size of the firm . . . [is reached] when the costs of organizing additional transactions within the firm [exceed] the costs of carrying out the same transactions through the market" (1988). Albeit "clearly right," the argument is also subject to the objection that "almost anything can be rationalized by invoking suitably specified transaction costs" (Fisher: 322, n. 5).

That the state of transaction cost economics in 1972 was approximately where Coase had left it in 1937[1] is largely attributable to the failure, for thirty-five years, to operationalize this important concept. That this flat trajectory has been supplanted by exponential growth during the past fifteen years is because recent students of transaction cost economics have insisted that this approach meet the test of refutable implications. Interestingly, these operationalization efforts have spawned a growing empirical literature. As discussed elsewhere (Williamson, 1985), and as Paul Joskow's conference paper (chapter 8) discloses, this empirical literature is broadly corroborative.

Thus although the Coasian insight referred to above was a crucial first step in an effort to devise a comparative logic of economic organization in which transaction cost economizing was made the core feature, follow-up apparatus was thereafter needed. As described below, this entailed (1) identifying the microanalytic factors that are responsible for transaction cost differences among transactions, (2) aligning transactions with governance structures in a discriminating way, and (3) discovering and respecting the crucial intertemporal process features that predictably attend economic organization.

The microanalytic approach to the study of economic organization on which transaction cost economics is based is set out in section 1. The strategy of deriving

90

refutable implications by effecting a "discriminating match" is described in section 2, both in general and with reference to the efficient use of debt and equity. The importance of process analysis is argued and illustrated in section 3. Concluding remarks follow.

1. MICROANALYTICS

Transaction cost economics adopts a comparative contractual approach to the study of economic organization in which the transaction is made the basic unit of analysis and the details of governance structures and human actors are brought under review. This focus on microanalytics plainly comes at a cost, the justifications for which are sometimes questioned. Thus David Kreps and Michael Spence observe that "if one wishes to model the behavior of organizations such as firms, then study of the firm as an organization ought to be high on one's agenda. This study is not, strictly speaking, necessary: one can hope to divine the correct 'reduced form' for the behavior of the organization without considering the microforces within the organization" (374–75).

The Kreps-Spence approach thus relegates the study of microanalytics to others or, alternatively, turns on the hope that economists will be lucky. The main risks with the first of these are that those to whom the study of the details are relegated will either take the wrong observations or will report the right observations in ways that mask their economic significance.[2] Since hoping to get lucky is even more problematic, the need for economists to take the study of organization seriously is herein suggested.

Herbert Simon's contrast between the physical sciences and economics in microanalytic respects is instructive. As he observes (1984:40):

> In the physical sciences, when errors of measurement and other noise are found to be of the same order of magnitude as the phenomena under study, the response is not to try to squeeze more information out of the data by statistical means; it is instead to find techniques for observing the phenomena at a higher level of resolution. The corresponding strategy for economics is obvious: to secure new kinds of data at the micro level.

Transaction costs economics subscribes to Simon's prescription in both conceptual and empirical respects. To be sure, this focus on microanalytics places a great burden on empirical researchers — in that the relevant data rarely appear in standard statistical sources on library shelves and data tapes. The tradeoff of breadth for depth has nevertheless been resolved in favor of greater detail — for which those who have done the underlying data development deserve great credit.

Kenneth Arrow's contrast between the older institutional economics and the New Institutional Economics is pertinent. He inquires, "Why did the older institutional school fail so miserably, though it contained such able analysts as Thorstein Veblen, J. R. Commons, and W. C. Mitchell?" He ventures two answers, one of which is that the issues are intrinsically difficult. More important, the older institutional school lacked a research strategy. By contrast, "the New Institutional Economics movement . . . [does] not consist primarily of giving new answers to the traditional questions of economics—resource allocation and degree of utilization. Rather it consists of answering new questions, why economic institutions have emerged the way they did and not otherwise; it merges into economic history, but brings sharper nanoeconomic . . . ('nano' is an extreme version of 'micro') reasoning to bear than has been customary" (1987:734).

Transaction cost economics maintains that the microanalytics matter in three basic respects: (1) behavioral assumptions, (2) dimensionalizing transactions, and (3) process features. Consider these seriatim.

1.1. Behavioral Assumptions

As discussed at length elsewhere, transaction cost economics employs two critical behavioral assumptions. The first is a cognitive assumption: human agents are assumed to be "*intendedly* rational, but only *limitedly* so" (Simon, 1961:xxiv), which condition is commonly referred to as bounded rationality. This assumption relegates all forms of comprehensive contracting (with and without private information) to the infeasible set. The argument that all viable forms of complex contracting are unavoidably incomplete has massive research ramifications that are only now beginning to be explored (Hart and Holmstrom, 1987).

Much of the confusion that is associated with bounded rationality is due to the mistaken belief that irrationality or satisficing are thereby implied. Inasmuch, however, as boundedly rational agents are attempting effectively to cope, irrationality (except, perhaps, for certain pathological cases) is not contemplated. Satisficing, moreover, is merely one manifestation of bounded rationality. It appeals to psychology and works out of an aspiration level mechanics. Incomplete contracting, by contrast, appeals to economics and employs choice mechanics of a very different kind. That satisficing has not been a very productive approach to the study of economic organization (Aumann: 35) does not therefore imply that incomplete contracting is similarly fated. To the contrary, although the study of incomplete contracting is difficult and its accomplishments to date are limited, there are reasons already to be much more optimistic.

The second behavioral assumption is that human agents are given to opportunism, which is a deep condition of self-interest seeking that contemplates guile. Promises to behave responsibly that are unsupported by credible commitments will not, therefore, be reliably discharged. Although opportunism is an unflattering behavioral assumption and is repugnant to some, H. L. A. Hart's remarks help to put the issues in perspective (193, emphasis in original):

> Neither understanding of long-term interest, nor the strength of goodness of will . . . are shared by all men alike. All are tempted at times to prefer their own immediate interests. . . . "Sanctions" are . . . required not as the normal motive for obedience, but as a *guarantee* that those who would voluntarily obey shall not be sacrificed by those who would not.

But for these two behavioral assumptions — both individually but, especially, in combination — the study of economic organization would be vastly simplified. Thus, "it is only because individual human beings are limited in knowledge, foresight, skill, and time that organizations are useful instruments for the achievement of human purpose" (Simon, 1957:199). But there is more to it than this. Given bounded rationality and opportunism, the study of economic organization needs to make allowance for both. The following imperative is therefore proposed: organize economic activity so as to economize on bounded rationality while simultaneously safeguarding the transactions in question against the hazards of opportunism. The main contractual and organizational implications of this combined behavioral orientation are summarized in table 7.1.[3]

Thus whereas behavioral assumptions are usually scanted by orthodox microtheory, transaction cost economics insists that these assumptions are vitally important — not least of all because they are the source of refutable implications. To be sure, the implications set out in table 7.1 are very general. Both parts of the following two arguments are nonetheless testable: (1a) all complex contracts will be incomplete, whence (1b) modes that support adaptive, sequential decisionmaking (as a means by which to cope with contractual incompleteness) will be observed; and (2a) "promises" that are unsupported by credible commitments will expose the parties to hazard, whence (2b) market and nonmarket safeguards will be observed to arise in support of exchange. An examination of both contract law and contract practice (including the use and nonuse of vertical integration) discloses that the data are corroborative.

1.2. Dimensionalizing

Transaction cost economics adopts John R. Commons's (1934) proposition that the transaction be made the basic unit of analysis.[4] It thereupon becomes important to identify the critical dimensions with respect to which transactions differ. The principal dimensions on which transaction cost economics presently relies for purposes of describing transactions are (1) the frequency with which they recur, (2) the degree and type of uncertainty to which they are subject, and (3) the condition of asset

Table 7.1 Organizational Implications of Behavioral Assumptions

Behavioral assumptions / Implications	Bounded rationality	Opportunism
For contractual theory	Comprehensive contacting is infeasible	Contract as promise is naive
For economic organization	Exchange will be facilitated by modes that support adaptive, sequential decisionmaking	Trading requires the support of spontaneous or crafted safeguards

specificity. Although all are important, many of the refutable implications of trans-action cost economics turn presently on this last.[5]

Asset specificity has reference to the degree to which an asset can be redeployed to alternative uses and by alternative users without sacrifice of productive value. This has a relation to the notion of sunk cost. But the pervasive organizational ramifications of asset specificity become evident only in the context of incomplete contracting. These went unrecognized in the pre-transaction cost era (Williamson, 1975, 1979; Klein, Crawford, and Alchian).[6]

The main import of the condition of asset specificity is this: whereas the identity of parties to a neoclassical transaction is irrelevant (Ben-Porath), the identi-ty of parties to a transaction that is supported by nontrivial investments in durable, transaction-specific assets is critical. In effect, parties of the latter kind are *bilater-ally dependent*. The intertemporal governance of contractual relations is greatly complicated as a consequence of this condition.

1.3. Process Analysis

The proposition that process matters is widely resisted and has attracted little concerted research attention from economists (Langlois). Although transaction cost economics is underdeveloped in process respects, process arguments neverthe-less play a prominent role.

The Fundamental Transformation, which I discuss further in section 3 below, is one illustration of the proposition that process matters. Briefly, the argument is that it does not suffice to demonstrate that a condition of large numbers competi-tion obtains at the outset. It is also necessary to examine whether this continues or if, by reason of transaction specific investments and incomplete contracting, a condition of bilateral trading *evolves* thereafter. The governance of contractual relations — which includes, but is by no means limited to, vertical integration — is massively influenced wherever ex post bilateral monopoly predictably obtains.

More generally, what I refer to as a process outcome has three common fea-tures: it is manifested intertemporally; it is an unanticipated consequence; and it is often very subtle. Usually, the unanticipated behavior in question is an unwanted outcome; but this need not always be the case.

What sociologists refer to as "dysfunctional behavior" is an illustration. As Robert Merton, Alvin Gouldner, and others have documented, the organization of work is often attended by dysfunctional consequences. This is because added "de-mands for control" within the organization have not one but two effects: the first (or intended) effect is that greater control is realized; the second (or unintended) effect is that the workers who are subject to these added controls thereafter adapt. The earlier "machine model" or organization, which made no provision for such unanticipated adaptations, thus needed to be supplanted by a richer model of organization in which effects of both kinds are appropriately taken into account.

Economists have not been deaf to this message. Indeed, agency theory has been responding precisely to such a condition for the past fifteen years. Given that agents enjoy information advantages and that they consult their own preferences when implementing incentive schemes, the design of incentives must be mindful of these "repositioning" effects. If this is the process analysis message, it has already been received and digested.

It is one thing, however, to be sensitized to secondary consequences in general. It is another to have knowledge of the particulars, some of which may be very subtle. If, moreover, all complex contracts are unavoidably incomplete, then the applicability of the mechanism design approach to economic organization is seriously called into question (Grossman and Hart, 1986; chapter 9). The study of subtle process particulars in the context of incomplete contracting is what process analysis, as herein described, is all about. A combined economics and organizations perspective is needed.[7]

2. DISCRIMINATING MATCH

2.1. General

Economic organization serves many purposes, of which transaction cost economizing is only one. Although a general theory of organization will make provision for "all significant factors," such a general theory is presently well beyond our reach. There are advantages, given our primitive understanding of these matters, in working out the ramifications of much simpler and partial models. What hypotheses have been nominated for "main case" standing, and what refutable implications are associated with each?

Note in this connection that I do not argue that refutable implications are all that matter. Rather, I subscribe to Nicholas Georgescu-Roegen's view that whereas "prediction is the touchstone of scientific knowledge . . . , the purpose of science in general is not prediction but knowledge for its own sake" (37). Especially in an area where opinions proliferate, of which the economics of organization is one, insistence upon refutable implications is needed to sort the wheat from the chaff. This is the touchstone function to which Georgescu-Roegen refers.

The main case to which transaction cost economics subscribes has been stated by Frank Knight as follows (252, emphasis added):

> Men in general, and within limits, wish to behave economically, to make their activities *and their organization* "efficient" rather than wasteful. This fact does deserve the utmost emphasis; and an adequate definition of the science of economics . . . might well make it explicit that the main relevance of the discussion is found in its relation to social policy, assumed to be directed toward the end indicated, of increasing economic efficiency, of reducing waste.

The transaction cost economics strategy for operationalizing this argument employs the following organizational imperative: align transactions (which differ in their attributes) with governance structures (the costs and competencies of which differ) in a discriminating (mainly, transaction cost economizing) way. In addition, therefore, to the heretofore mentioned effort to discover the principal dimensions with respect to which transactions differ, it is furthermore necessary to identify and describe the principal governance structures—firms, markets, hybrid modes—to which transactions might feasibly be assigned. The discriminating match between transactions and governance structures is the main source of refutable implications and plays a prominent role in both the conceptual and empirical parts of the transaction cost economics research agenda. Enunciating this purpose and thereafter working out the logic of the discriminating match describes much of what transaction cost economics has been up to.

2.2. Extant Applications

The first application of this approach, and the paradigm problem to which transaction cost economics recurrently returns, is that of vertical integration (Williamson, 1971, 1975, 1979; Klein, Crawford, and Alchian).[8] Once this issue had been worked through, it was obvious that the basic structure of the problem and its solution had general application. As Friedrich Hayek has put it, "Whenever the capacity of recognizing an abstract rule which the arrangement of these attributes follows has been acquired in one field, the same master mould will apply when the signs of those attributes are evoked by altogether different elements" (1967:52).

The study of labor organization thus turns out to have numerous parallels with, rather than be sharply different from, the study of intermediate product markets (Williamson, Wachter, and Harris; Williamson, 1985; ch. 10)—contrary opinion notwithstanding.[9] The study of public utility regulation and the feasibility of deregulation also have a contractual structure very similar to that which characterizes the make-or-buy (vertical integration) decision (Williamson, 1976; Goldberg; Joskow and Schmalensee). A wide variety of nonstandard contracting practices that were once believed to have monopoly purpose—franchising and reciprocity being examples—are likewise usefully interpreted in this way (Klein; Williamson, 1983). And even such disparate phenomena as career marriages display strong commonalities (Williamson, 1989).

The transaction cost treatment of vertical integration has proceeded in a series of stages. The first and most critical was the statement of the general verbal argument (Williamson, 1971, 1975; Klein, Crawford, and Alchian). This was then given a geometric interpretation (Williamson, 1981), was thereafter recast in a more general mathematical way (Masten, 1982; Riordan and Williamson, 1985), and has since been developed more rigorously in the context of comparative incomplete contracting (Grossman and Hart, 1986).

2.3. Debt and Equity

A recent application of transaction cost economics reasoning (that is developed more fully elsewhere, in Williamson, 1988) involves corporate finance. The object is to align investment projects (which differ in their attributes) with financial instruments (where debt and equity are viewed as alternative governance structures). Thus consider a firm that is contemplating a series of investment projects and is asking whether it makes a difference how these are financed. The conventional view is that the cost of capital is independent of the choice of financial instruments (Modigliani and Miller). Although this basic result has since been qualified — by arguing that (1) debt could be used as a signal of differential business prospects (Ross), (2) debt could be used by entrepreneurs with limited resources who were faced with new investment opportunities and did not want to dilute their equity position, thereby to avoid sacrifice of incentive intensity (Jensen and Meckling), and (3) debt could be used as an incentive bonding device (Grossman and Hart, 1982) — all of these work out of a composite capital framework. Transaction cost economics examines the issues more microanalytically. It maintains that the asset attributes of investment projects *differ* and that efficiency purposes are served by aligning projects with the governance structure competencies of debt and equity in a discriminating way.

Thus suppose that a firm wishes to build a general purpose factory, acquire inventories, install equipment, procure dies, and the like. A general purpose factory that is located in a population center is a highly redeployable asset. Lenders will be prepared to finance it at the "going rate" for real estate and take a mortgage as security. The same is true for inventories and mobile equipment (forklifts, trucks, etc.) that are unspecialized and easily redeployed or liquidated. Suppose, however, that lenders are now asked to supply funds for durable assets that are much more highly specialized. Is debt financing equally well-suited to these?

Assume, for this purpose, that debt is regarded as a governance structure that is safeguarded by prescribing (1) that fixed interest payments will be made at regular intervals, (2) that the business will continuously meet certain liquidity tests, (3) that sinking funds will be set up and principal repaid at the loan expiration date, and (4) that, in the event of default, the debt-holders will exercise preemptive claims against the assets in question. If everything goes well, interest and principal will be paid on schedule. In the event of default, however, debt-holders will realize differential recovery in the degree to which the assets in question are redeployable. Since the value of a preemptive claim declines as the degree of asset specificity deepens, the terms of debt financing will be adjusted adversely.

Confronted with the prospect that specialized investments will be financed on adverse terms, the firm might respond by sacrificing some of the specialized investment features in favor of greater redeployability. But might it be possible to invent a new governance structure to which suppliers of finance would attach added confidence? Suppose, arguendo, that a financial instrument called equity is invented and assume that equity has the following governance properties: (1) it bears a residual claimant status to the firm in both earnings and asset liquidation respects; (2) it contracts for the duration of the life of the firm; and (3) a board of directors is created and awarded to equity that (a) is elected by the pro-rata votes of those who hold tradeable shares, (b) has the power to replace the management, (c) decides on management compensation, (d) has access to internal performance measures on a timely basis, (e) can authorize audits in depth for special follow-up purposes, (f) is apprised of important investment and operating proposals before they are implemented, and (g) in other respects bears a decision review and monitoring relation to the firm's management.[10]

An *endogenous response* to the governance needs of suppliers of finance who are asked to invest in nonredeployable projects has thereby resulted. In exchange for accepting a residual claimant status to the firm, these suppliers are awarded "control" over the board of directors. Also note that equity in this scenario comes in late. It being a relatively cumbersome form of governance, equity is the financial instrument of *last resort*.

The transaction cost approach to corporate finance thus calls for the *discriminating* use of debt and equity as a function of the attributes of investment projects. Debt and equity are more than alternative sources of funds. They are alternative governance structures. This latter distinction is the key to the transaction cost economics approach to the study of economic organization in all of its forms. The discriminating use of financial instruments is merely another variation of the same underlying transaction cost economizing theme to which I referred earlier.

3. PROCESS MATTERS

The proposition that process matters enjoys widespread support throughout the social sciences,[11] economics conspicuously excepted. Economists are skeptical of process arguments for several reasons. First and foremost, appeal to process is unnecessary if the interesting action in all "properly formulated" problems is explained by ex-ante incentive alignments. To be sure, stating problems in a way that discloses the relevant incentive features is not always easy. But that is the real challenge nonetheless. Second, the incentive alignment apparatus is much more refined and fully developed than is the corresponding apparatus for assessing process. Indeed, a leading reason why the claim that "process is important" is so difficult to disprove (or even contest) is that the process mechanics are rarely displayed. Third, the analysis of process requires considerable knowledge of the nanoeconomic details to which Arrow made reference. Many economists have been loath to take this step, expressing the hope that it can be avoided (the Kreps-Spence position set out in section 1, above, is probably representative).

Transaction cost economics maintains that the comparative study of economic organization requires the discovery and explication of process features. The lack of focus to which I refer is partly rectified by studying process issues from an economizing perspective. And transaction cost economics furthermore insists that process analysis deal with specifics.

The Fundamental Transformation to which I referred earlier is examined in section 3.1. A less fully developed but, where it applies, similarly important process consequence is the need to match incentive intensities with organization form. This is examined in section 3.2. Incentive and process interpretations of takeover are contrasted in section 3.3. A brief discussion of oligarchy follows.

3.1. The Fundamental Transformation

That asset specificity was earlier regarded merely as a sunk cost is because the contracting ramifications were not wrung out. An intertemporal examination of the contracting process was needed to expose the issues. What was true of vertical integration turned out similarly to apply to franchise bidding for natural monopoly.

3.1.1. The Incentive Approach.   Harold Demsetz imaginatively reformulated the problem of natural monopoly by pushing the analysis back a stage, thereby to disclose its incentive properties. Such a reformulation led to a dramatic reinterpretation of the so-called natural monopoly dilemma: "There is unfortunately no good solution for technical monopoly. There is only a choice among three evils: private unregulated monopoly, private monopoly regulated by the state, and government operation" (Friedman: 128).

Demsetz perceptively argued that this statement of the problem omitted the possibility of conducting an ex ante bidding competition for the right to serve the market. The three-way monopoly dilemma described by Friedman could thus be relieved by inviting a large number of qualified suppliers to engage in a noncollusive "competition for the market." To be sure, an ex post monopoly condition would obtain upon awarding a franchise to the firm that offers to sell product most cheaply. But that is neither here nor there. The object is to secure the benefits of natural monopoly (economies of scale) without incurring the monopoly prices or the regulatory and bureaucratic distortions that ensue when monopoly is awarded in any of the conventional (three evil) ways. Franchise bidding for natural monopoly purportedly accomplishes the desired result.

3.1.2. The Process Approach.   Transaction cost economics fully accepts this description of ex ante bidding competition but insists that the study of contracting be extended to include ex post features. Thus initial bidding merely sets the contracting process in motion. A full assessment requires that both contract execution and ex post competition at the contract renewal interval come under scrutiny.

Contrary to earlier practice, transaction cost economics holds that a condition of large numbers bidding at the outset does not necessarily imply that a large numbers bidding condition will obtain thereafter. Whether ex post competition is fully efficacious or not depends on whether the good or service in question is supported by durable investments in transaction specific human or physical assets. Where no such specialized investments are incurred, the initial winning bidder realizes no advantage over nonwinners. Although it may continue to supply for a long period of time, this is only because, in effect, it is continuously meeting competitive bids from qualified rivals. Rivals cannot be presumed to operate on a parity, however, once substantial investments in transaction specific assets are put in place. Winners in these circumstances enjoy advantages over nonwinners, which is to say that parity at the renewal interval is upset. Accordingly, what was a large numbers bidding condition at the outset is effectively *transformed* into one of bilateral supply thereafter.

As Joskow insists, however, general arguments ought to be asked to address contractual specifics. In his case, the application of this approach to assess the purported efficacy of franchise bidding for CATV supplied the hitherto missing contractual specifics (chapter 8).

The details of the general comparative exercise and CATV specifics are set out elsewhere (Williamson, 1976; Goldberg). Suffice it to observe here that the argument is not that ex ante competition for a franchise award for natural monopoly will never work well. Rather, the argument is that whether it will work well or poorly depends on the characteristics of the assets.

Large, durable investments are not the issue. Rather, the issues are (1) whether large and durable investments are redeployable or not and, if they are not, (2) the need for and ease of adapting to changing market and technological circumstances. The initial franchise award undergoes a Fundamental Transformation if the assets in question are highly specific, in which event the efficacy of "unassisted" franchise bidding becomes highly problematic at the contract renewal intervals and when adaptations to change are attempted. Public policy toward deregulation needed (and needs) to be informed by a *discriminating* perspective in which the asset specificity attributes of investments play a key role (Joskow and Schmalensee; Levine).

3.2. Incentive Intensity

There is now widespread agreement that asset specificity and the resulting Fundamental Transformation are centrally implicated in assessing vertical integration. But this "solves" one puzzle only to pose another. If vertical integration is the source of adaptive gains and is not attended by losses, why not integrate everything?[12] More generally, why can't a large firm do everything that a collection of small firms can do and more? A different but related way of putting this query is in terms of "selective intervention" — where by selective intervention I mean that each production stage is directed to perform in the preacquisition manner except when misalignments occur and the substitution of authority for autonomy yields net gains.

Thus suppose that a procurement stage acquires a supply stage (or the reverse) and instructs the supply (procurement) stage to continue to behave in the pre-acquisition manner except on those few occasions when the aforementioned net gains from authoritarian realignment obtain. Whereas contractual misalignments previously elicited self-interested bargaining, which delayed the adjustment and itself was costly, the operating divisions in the post-merger interval simply accept hierarchical realignment decisions as determinative. Analytic processes thus supplant bargaining processes (March and Simon: 130), whence quicker and better adaptations occur after the merger has been accomplished. If the combined enterprise can never do worse and sometimes does better, then integration is everywhere the superior form.

Two very different answers have been advanced to explain wherein the costs of vertical integration arise. The first of these is an incentive argument and is due to Sanford Grossman and Oliver Hart (1986). The second invokes process considerations.

3.2.1. The Incentive Approach. The Grossman and Hart approach to vertical integration turns on ex ante investment distortions. The argument here is that the adaptive benefits of vertical integration are sometimes more than offset by induced investment distortions. Assessed comparatively, market organization will sometimes remain the preferred alternative.

This pathbreaking article works out of an incomplete contracting setup. Since a mechanism design formulation is precluded upon admitting that complex contracts are incomplete (chapter 9), new solution concepts are required (Grossman and Hart, 1986; Holmstrom and Tirole, 1988; chapter 9).

The argument expressly invokes asset specificity and implicitly turns on bounded rationality and opportunism. It also turns critically on the way in which Grossman and Hart define ownership. Whereas ownership is normally defined in terms of assets, they define ownership as ex post decision rights of control. Accordingly, they distinguish three ownership alternatives: stages A and B remain independent (nonintegration); A acquires B; B acquires A.

Each production stage in each period is assumed to make decisions of two kinds: ex ante investment decisions and, after state-of-the-world realizations obtain, ex post operating decisions. Grossman and Hart further assume that the ex ante investment decisions in each stage are made "simultaneously and independently," whatever the ownership structure, and that each stage experiences high-powered incentives — that is, each stage appropriates its net receipts — under all three ownership configurations.

An immediate consequence of this two-part decision setup, with ownership defined in terms of ex post decision rights, is that each ownership regime induces different ex ante investments. Since each stage appropriates its net receipts, investments will be "prepositioned" to reflect different ownership structures. Full optimality (which would require that investment decisions be made coordinately) being unavailable, the question is which assignment of ex post decision rights is best.

Not only will no integration sometimes be the most preferred alternative, but it furthermore matters, if integration occurs, whether A acquires B or B acquires A. The Grossman and Hart formulation thus yields a unified theory of integration *and* nonintegration. They contrast this with earlier "transaction-cost based arguments — [that] do not explain how the scope for [opportunistic] behavior changes when one of the self-interested owners becomes an *equally* self-interested employee" (Grossman and Hart, 1986:692, emphasis added). They furthermore observe that integration under their theory "does not make any new variable observable to both parties. Any audits that an employer can have done on his subsidiary are also feasible when the subsidiary is a separate company" (1986:695). Also, as Hart explains in his conference paper (chapter 9), theirs is a symmetric argument that makes no appeal to (and, indeed, denies that integration incurs) any added costs of bureaucracy.

3.2.2. The Process Approach. The process approach likewise works out of an incomplete contracting setup where bounded rationality, opportunism, and asset specificity are featured. Also, so as to implement the spirit of selective intervention, the high-powered incentives of market procurement are assumed to be replicated by vertical integration. Thus although, as discussed below, high-powered incentives are actually undone so as to secure relief from the suboptimality that integration in a high-powered incentive regime experiences, this is the operative assumption at the outset.

Ownership, however, is defined differently than Grossman and Hart. Integration places the physical assets of both stages under the unified ownership of the acquirer and awards ex post decision rights to intervene (thereby to implement a program of adaptive, sequential decisonmaking whenever ex post misalignments prospectively appear) to the acquirer.

Working through the ramifications of this statement of vertical integration is somewhat involved (Williamson, 1985: ch. 6). Suffice it to observe here that preserving high-powered incentives in both stages of the integrated firm induces distortions of three kinds: (1) the acquired stage will dissipate assets; (2) the acquiring stage will gain control over accounting and will manipulate transfer prices, overhead allocations, and the like to shift net receipts in its favor; and (3) the acquiring stage can use its control over ex post decision rights strategically.

"Promises," moreover, to eschew behavior of these kinds are lacking in credibility. Thus consider the following "modified Odysseus problem," where the issue to be evaluated is whether, as widely believed, "binding oneself is a privileged way of resolving the problem of weakness on will" (Elster, 1979:37).

Recall that Odysseus, with foreknowledge that the call of the Sirens was irresistible, commanded that he be bound to the mast when the ship came within range of the Sirens. Suppose further that Odysseus instructed the crew to "tighten and add to my bonds" should he ask for release. But suppose now that there is one exception. Should it be the case that the ship comes under attack or is otherwise in serious jeopardy, the bonds are to be relaxed if not released at his command so that he can direct the crew to take appropriate adaptive action.

The difficulty, plainly, is that the circumstances that qualify as an exception are not unproblematic. To be sure, the crew will refuse him if Odysseus signals, "Release my bonds, I must accede to the Sirens." But they are presented with a dilemma if Odysseus, whose knowledge of the seas and their perils is unsurpassed, should signal, "I perceive grave danger, loosen my bonds a little so that I may instruct the recovery." When is the latter signal to be believed and when not?[13]

Similar problems arise in conjunction with implementing the agreement between buyer and integrated supply division whereby the former "promises" to refrain from intervention except for good cause. If the supply division is awarded claims over a stream of net receipts the value of which can be altered and expropriated by asserting needs for selective intervention, and if grounds for good cause cannot be unambiguously discerned and displayed, then the supply division is exposed to hazard.

This has profound ramifications from the comparative institutional study of alternative forms of organization. If reasoned (explicit or implicit) exceptions to self-binding constraints frequently vitiate the "intended" effects, then the exercise of binding oneself may be fatuous. What applies at the individual level holds a fortiori, moreover, when attempts are made to impose constraints intraorganizationally.

One of the added complications is that internal organization experiences difficulty in using the courts to buttress the weakness of will to which Elster refers. Recall in this connection Thomas Hobbes's 1651 discussion of oaths and promises in *The Leviathan*. Upon observing that the "force of words . . . [was] too weak to hold men to the performance of their covenants" (1928:92), Hobbes went on to prescribe that "there must be some coercive power, to compel" performance (1928: 94). The state (a court system) was thus created to enforce interpersonal and interorganizational agreements.

Although I have elsewhere argued that reliance on court ordering is often exaggerated (Williamson, 1985: ch. 7), what I want here to emphasize are that (1) the courts are important for purposes of ultimate appeal, and (2) the courts are not available (either at all or in equivalent degree) to enforce intrapersonal and intraorganizational agreements. The upshot is that efforts to replicate markets within firms for all activities for which markets cannot be beat (call this the latent set) and intervene selectively only where net gains can be projected (call this the active set) are misguided. The added degrees of freedom that support intervention in the active set will extend beyond the delimited circumstances for which they are intended, which is to say that the added latitude will spill over and disturb decisions within the latent set where replication is intended. The gains of internalization (greater adaptability within the active set when the contract gets out of alignment) thus come at a cost (operating decisions within the latent set are distorted when the high-powered incentives of markets are carried over into the firm).

Selective intervention is thus defeated by the added costs to which internal organization is subject when high-powered incentives are applied within the firm. But there is more to the argument if, contrary to Grossman and Hart, internal organization is often able to exercise control instruments more effectively than the market (Williamson, 1985:154–55). The use of lower-powered internal incentives coupled with added control instruments is made more attractive as a consequence. To be sure, bureaucratic costs rise (Williamson, 1985: ch. 6). But the distortions that result when high-powered incentives are used within firms are mitigated. This shift from a high-powered incentive regime in the market to a combined lower-powered/added controls regime within the firm illustrates the microanalytic proposition to which I referred earlier: incentive intensity and organization form need to be matched.

Thus construed, the basic tradeoff is between comparative bureaucratic costs (where the market enjoys the advantage) and comparative adaptive capacity (where, under bilateral trading, internal organization enjoys the advantage). This tradeoff switches from net negative to positive as the condition of asset specificity deepens.[14] Note, moreover, that the relevant comparative institutional choice under the process approach is only two-way, market or hierarchy, since in a low-powered incentive regime, it matters little who acquires whom.[15]

More generally, the point is this: the comparative analysis of alternative modes of organization requires an examination of context. If added or different latitude exists in one contracting milieu as compared with the other, then the ramifications need to be wrung out. Microanalytic process analysis is needed.

3.2.3. Comparisons. Given bilateral dependency, the incentive and process approaches to vertical integration can be distinguished as follows:

	Integration Entails	
	Incentive	*Process*
ownership	ex post decision rights only	assets and ex post decision rights
incentives	HPI	HIP gives way to LPI
controls	unchanged by integration	extended by integration
bureaucratic costs	unchanged by integration	greater under integration
adaptation costs[16]	unchanged by integration	reduced by integration
who acquires whom	matters	negligible

Although vertical integration *in manufacturing*[17] appears to line up with the process approach, appearances are neither here nor there. The more important point is that these two approaches have different implications and can be assessed by examining the data.

3.3. Takeover

Takeover poses real puzzles for law and economics. It is plainly an anomaly if managers are assumed always and everywhere to be given to profit maximization — either because they are faithful stewards or because of the presumed efficacy of modern invisible hand arguments (von Weizsacker; Fama). The unsupported oaths of stewards lack credibility, however, while the mechanics of modern invisible hand arguments are vague. Awaiting an explication of the mechanics, it is judicious to argue that some nontrivial degree of managerial discretion survives.

The managerial discretion approach to the modern corporation assumes that managers are (within limits) in effective control of the firm and operate it with a keen view to their own interests (Baumol; Marris, 1964; Williamson, 1964; Alchian, 1965). Interestingly, the existence of managerial discretion supports two very different interpretations of contests for corporate control.

Skeptics of mergers and takeovers view these events as manifestations of managerial discretion *by the firm proposing the takeover* (the bidder or raider). The managers in the bidding firm have growth aspirations; takeover is a way of giving expression to these purposes.[18] By contrast, those who regard takeovers more favorably focus on *managerial discretion in the target firms*. Firms that are given to excesses of managerial discretion are taken over by other firms or groups whose preferences for profits, cost reduction, and the like are more nearly neoclassical. Value enhancement is thus realized by squeezing out excesses of discretion.

Whereas my earliest work emphasized the distortions that result from managerial discretion (Williamson, 1964), I am convinced that a more productive research strategy is to start from managerial discretion premises and then inquire into what means can be or have been devised to bring discretionary excesses *under control*. The basic view that informs the latter is that which informs the study of externalities quite generally: all failures to allocate resources to highest valued uses invite redress.[19]

The attenuation of managerial discretion through takeover is an application of this reasoning. But this is a two-sided phenomenon and a chronic puzzle remains. Why did takeovers appear in the 1960s rather than much earlier?

One possibility is that the invention of takeover was simply a chance event. Another possibility is that takeover appeared as a response to a change in relative prices.

3.3.1. The Incentive Argument.   Regulation is an obvious candidate for producing a change in relative prices. Takeover is thus purportedly a response to the added costs of waging proxy contests that resulted from new securities regulations in 1955 and 1964 (Jarrell and Bradley: 371). But while this hypothesis can explain recourse to a previously unused instrument for challenging incumbent managements, it is not obvious why this previously inferior instrument should have such profound effects. Proxy contests, after all, were never widely used and were rarely successful. Why should regulation-induced takeover be associated with a large number of contests for corporate control with a greater degree of success?[20]

3.3.2. Process Analysis.   A historical interpretation of takeover in which organizational innovation is featured is herein proposed. The argument proceeds in three parts. First, the organizational innovation on which I rely (multidivisionalization) is briefly described. Second, the requisites for "full functionalism" are set out and the M-form innovation is interpreted with reference to these. Differences between the M-form and rival takeover hypotheses are then briefly discussed.

3.3.2a. The Organizational Innovation.   Transaction cost economics examines alternative forms of economic organization with reference to their capacity to economize on bounded rationality while simultaneously safeguarding the transactions in question against the hazards of opportunism. I interpret the multidivisional form of organization, which first appeared in the 1920s, as having the purpose and immediate effect of relieving the pressing demands on bounded rationality that were experienced as functionally organized firms grew in size and variety. Alfred Chandler's summary of the defects of the large unitary form (U-form) enterprise, to which the multidivisional (M-form) enterprise was a response, is pertinent (1962: 382–83):

The inherent weakness in the centralized, functionally departmentalized operating company . . . became critical only when the administrative load on the senior executives increased to such an extent that they were unable to handle their entrepreneurial responsibilities efficiently. This situation arose when the operations of the enterprise became too complex and the problems of coordination, appraisal, and policy formulation too intricate for a small number of top officers to handle both long-run, entrepreneurial, and short-run operational administrative activities.

But there were (at least partly) unanticipated effects as well. In addition to relieving the communication overload in large, complex U-form firms, this same M-form structure also served (in comparison with the U-form structure which it supplanted) to attenuate subgoal pursuit (reduce opportunism). This is because the M-form structure "clearly removed the executives responsible for the destiny of the entire enterprise from the more routine operational activities, and so gave them the time, information, and even psychological commitment for long-term planning and appraisal" (Chandler, 1962:382). A strategic resource allocation orientation thus supplanted the earlier functional or operational orientation that beset the general office previously.

3.3.2b. *Full Functionalism.*   Elster maintains that a "valid functional explanation in sociology" takes the following form (1983:57):

An institution or a behavioral pattern X is explained by its function Y for group Z if and only if:

1. Y is an effect of X;

2. Y is beneficial for Z;

3. Y is unintended by the actors producing X;

4. Y — or at least the causal relation between X and Y — is unrecognized by the actors in Z;

5. Y maintains X by a causal feedback loop passing through Z.

Elster argues that full functional explanations are rarely satisfied in the social sciences. Rather, functionalism is mainly reserved for biology. This is because in biology "the theory of natural selection creates a presumption that whatever benefits reproductive capacity can also be explained by these benefits. In the social sciences there is no such theory of comparable generality, and so the actual mechanism must be specified for each particular case" (Elster, 1983:20). This being rarely possible, Elster urges that social scientists eschew functional explanation in favor of "intentional explanation [which] differs from functional in that the former can be directed to the distant future, whereas the latter is typically myopic and opportunistic" (1983:20).

Efforts to apply functional explanation in the social sciences should recognize that "condition (4) is fulfilled only if the rules are spread by takeover, not if they are spread by imitation." Also, "many purported cases of functional explanation fail because the feedback loop of criterion (5) is postulated rather than demonstrated" (Elster, 1983:58). Unlike biologists, social scientists must show in each instance how the feedback operates (Elster, 1983:61).

With reference to the organizational innovation described above, let X be the M-form structure, the appearance of which mainly had bounded rationality origins. The unanticipated consequence (in this instance a benefit) Y is that manageri-al roles have been redefined so as to favor strategic resource allocation. The general office of the firm can thus be thought of as an internal capital market. This generic competence to manage lines of business in an internal capital market mode applies, moreover, not merely to extant lines of business but includes potential lines of business as well. The acquisition of additional lines of business to which profit center standing is conferred thereby becomes feasible. The completion of full func-tionalism is thus accomplished through the spread of multidivisionalization through takeover of unadapted firms (Z), which is the *reproductive link* normally missing from functional arguments in the social sciences (Elster, 1983:58).

Indeed, there is an additional process of spreading the M-form that ought also to be mentioned: mitosis. The large and diversified M-form structure may discover that the benefits associated with new activities or acquisitions do not continue indefinitely. Acquired components or diversified parts may therefore be divested. To the extent that these are spun off or otherwise divested as discrete multidivisional units themselves, propagation through cell division may be said to exist. This quasi-biological process would also presumably qualify as a reproductive link and thereby contribute to successful functional explanation.

3.3.2c. The Data.   That the M-form explanation for takeover fulfills the requisites for full functionalism is surely to its credit. Inasmuch, however, as the M-form innovation first appeared in the 1920s, how is it that takeover was delayed until the 1960s?

Part of the answer is that imitation of the M-form occurred slowly. Prospective reorganizations were delayed, moreover, by the onset of World War II (Chandler, 1962). But more than mere imitation was needed. The conglomerate variant of the M-form needed to be evolved and thereafter applied to mergers — first of a volun-tary and then of an involuntary (takeover) kind (Williamson, 1975: ch. 9). The experience with conglomerates in the 1950s was thus the last of a series of organiza-tional developments — innovation, imitation, conglomeration — antecedent to take-over in the 1960s.

To rest here, however, is merely ex post rationalization. How can this explana-tion for takeover be distinguished from alternative plausible explanations for these events? Specifically, what are the attributes of takeover that are distinctively asso-ciated with this organizational rationale that would not be predicted by rival theo-ries of takeover?

The first is that the firms that attempt takeover will come predominantly from the universe of those that have previously adopted the M-form structure. The second is that M-form firms will have greater success in managing disparate lines of takeover-acquired assets than will similar takeovers by non–M-forms firms (the so-called go-go conglomerates of the 1960s). A differential success rate is therefore predicted. A third is that M-form firms will engage in voluntary divestiture more readily than U-form firms. And finally, M-form firms will divest with reference to a value enhancement criterion — which will sometimes entail divesting the "crown jewels" — whereas U-form firms will divest the troublesome parts.

None of this is to say that managerial discretion vanishes upon the appearance of the M-form. Both the immediate and secondary effects of the M-form nevertheless favor incentive attenuation.

3.4. Oligarchy

Robert Michel's statement of the iron law of oligarchy is a classic example of the proposition that organization has a life of its own or, more generally, that process matters: "It is organization which gives birth to the dominion of the elected over the electors, of the mandataries over the mandators, of the delegates over the delegators. Who says organization, says oligarchy" (Michels, 1962:365). But what is the comparative institutional significance of this condition?

3.4.1. Incentive Assessment. The incentive literature makes no provision whatsoever for the possibility that oligarchy is a predictable process outcome. Such neglect comes at a slight cost if oligarchy affects all forms of organization equally. In that event, only older and younger firms need to be distinguished. But conceivably there is more to it than this.

3.4.2. Process Analysis. Process analysis has been neglectful of oligarchy as well. The evolution of oligarchy is, however, a matter with which process analysis can and should be engaged. What are the factors that contribute to oligarchy, what can be done to delay or deflect these developments, and what are the comparative institutional ramifications? Explicating these matters is a microanalytic undertaking.

Note that if, as seems plausible, larger and more complex organizations are more given to oligarchy than smaller and simpler firms, then the decision to integrate should make allowance for the differential costs of oligarchy that are associated with integrated and nonintegrated forms of supply. Also, voluntary divestiture may sometimes be a means by which to relieve oligarchical outcomes.

4. CONCLUSIONS

A three-stage program for operationalizing transaction cost economics has been described. The first entails comparative contractual analysis of a microanalytic kind. This is implemented by (1) making the transaction the basic unit of analysis, (2) identifying the relevant behavioral assumptions for assessing contract, and (3) naming and explicating the critical dimensions with respect to which transactions differ. The second stage entails a concerted effort to develop refutable implications based on the logic of discriminating alignment. With respect to each distinct class of transactions, the object is to assess the comparative efficacy of alternative forms of governance—market, hybrid, and hierarchy—with reference to (1) how well does each implement a program of adaptive, sequential decisionmaking, and (2) what are the associated costs? An examination of intertemporal process differences among modes, which is the third stage, is an integral part of the effort to ascertain the relevant tradeoffs.

Although the study of process has long been of interest to Austrian economists (Langlois), evolutionary economists (Nelson and Winter), and sociologists (Granovetter), this often proceeds at a very high level of abstraction. Transaction cost economics insists that the process features of organization be examined in the context of specific contractual relationships. Greater knowledge of and attention to microanalytic detail is thus required.

Transaction cost economics argues that process effects are much more subtle and pervasive than most economists (and economic models) currently admit. Thus although economic models can always be amended or extended to make allowance for all regularities of whatever kind, it is first necessary to be apprised of what these regularities are. Vague arguments that process matters are unhelpful. What is needed is to identify and explicate process particulars. To be sure, use of a comparative, microanalytic, transaction cost economizing perspective is not the only way to address these issues. It is nonetheless instructive that intertemporal contractual issues are ones to which transaction cost economics easily relates. That this approach has already helped to unpack puzzles that had hitherto gone unsolved and even undetected augurs well for the future.

NOTES

1. Coase remarks that his 1937 paper was "much cited and little used" over the interval 1937–1972 (Coase, 1972:63).

2. William McNeill's remarks about Chinese history are apposite. He observes that an understanding of markets and command in medieval China is impaired not by a failure to study this period but because "historians of China have yet to work through the voluminous records . . . *with the appropriate questions in mind*" (1982:25, emphasis added). The study of business history in the United States has benefited from Alfred D. Chandler's perceptive research (1962; 1977), but Chandler is the exception who proves the rule. Much the same can be said of Chester Barnard (1938) in the organization theory area. Most business historians, organization theory specialists, sociologists, and the like simply do not examine the microanalytics of organization from an economizing (or even quasi-economizing) point of view. Power, more often, is the congenial perspective.

3. I have argued elsewhere (Williamson, 1985:30–32, 66–67) that contractual problems vanish if *either* bounded rationality or opportunism can be presumed to be absent. The dashed vertical line in the table is intended as a reminder that the indicated contractual implications and organizational responses are joint responses to a combined condition of bounded rationality and opportunism.

4. Note that Simon advised that the "decision premise" be made the basic unit of analysis (1946; 1957:201). The transaction cost ramifications of working out of such a highly microanalytic framework have yet to be displayed. I conjecture that the decision premise is *too* microanalytic for the purpose of doing "middle range" analysis of the kind discussed here. Choice of the unit of analysis really matters.

5. Although asset specificity can be and sometimes has been overworked, it has played a key role in the progressive operationalization of transaction cost economics from the outset (Williamson, 1971, 1975, 1979, 1985; Klein, Crawford, and Alchian; Teece, 1981; Stuckey; Alchian, 1984; Monteverde and Teece; Masten, 1984; Palay, 1985; Crocker and Masten;

Joskow, 1985, 1987, chapter 8 of this volume; Joskow and Schmalensee; Anderson and Schmittlein; Spiller; Grossman and Hart, 1986; Bjuggren; Weaklium). Interestingly, Coase states in his third conference lecture (chapter 5) that he considered and then rejected the possibility that asset specificity played a key contractual role when he was studying the U.S. automobile industry in the 1930s. Having rejected asset specificity, however, he has since proposed no alternative key contractual dimension (or set of dimensions) for assessing the comparative efficacy of contract. As Thomas Kuhn reminds us, it takes a concept to beat a concept.

Coase evidently rejects asset specificity as a key dimension because he observed that A. O. Smith was supplying body frames to the major automobile firms by contract. The fact, therefore, that General Motors had acquired Fisher Body, purportedly for asset specificity reasons (Klein, Crawford, and Alchian: 308–10), was unpersuasive.

I conjecture, however, that there were real differences between these two transactions for which greater microanalytic detail is needed. Thomas Palay's study (1981) of transportation transactions is apposite.

Thus Palay examined the ownership of "high cube" railroad cars that are specialized to automobile parts shipment. The cars, larger and more expensive than standard box cars, are, however, transferable among automobile manufacturers without sacrifice of value. He also examined the racks used to secure automobile parts in transit. These racks are not only specialized to the automobile industry but they are nonredeployable among automobile firms. Although initially the carriers owned both the high cube cars and the racks, problems developed with respect to the latter. Racks are now mainly owned, therefore, by the shippers.

Industry specificity, even in a concentrated market, thus needs to be distinguished from firm specificity. Like Klein (chapter 13), I conjecture that the manufacture of automobile frames (A. O. Smith) entails a lesser investment in firm-specific assets than does the manufacture of automobile body panels (Fisher Body), especially when the latter is located cheek-by-jowl to GM assembly. Thus whereas Coase seems implicitly to assume that frames and bodies are on a parity in asset specificity respects—whence, upon observing different organizational responses to what he believed to be an identical condition of asset specificity, he concluded that the explanation for the differences must reside elsewhere—Klein argues otherwise.

Note, moreover, that transaction cost economics maintains that added contractual safeguards will appear as the condition of asset specificity deepens and that vertical integration is the organizational mode of *last resort*. Hybrid forms of contract—those for which private ordering safeguards have been crafted—are often able to cope effectively with intermediate degrees of asset specificity (Williamson, 1985; Joskow, 1987). Coase makes no reference to the possibility that the A. O. Smith contract was of a hybrid kind.

Thus although the earlier literature, mine included (1975), worked out of a binary firm or market framework, later work has disclosed the need to make prominent provision for the intermediate (hybrid) contracting category (Macneil; Williamson, 1979, 1985; Klein, 1980; Palay, 1981, 1985; Joskow, 1987).

6. My initial effort to break out of the Coasian tautology and offer a predictive theory of economic organization in which transaction cost differences were featured was in 1971, when my paper "The Vertical Integration of Production: Market Failure Considerations" was published. I expressly appeal to idiosyncratic trading relations (which have their origins in asset specificity) in this article. Armen Alchian and Harold Demsetz (1972) offer an alternative hypothesis: firms supplant markets so as more effectively to deal with a condition of technological nonseparability.

7. The question might be posed, how do we train students to bring a combined economics and organization perspective to bear? I conjecture that experience with and/or training in the area of business administration is important if not essential. Coase's own unusual educational training (see lecture 1, above) is pertinent.

8. Benjamin Klein (chapter 13, n. 3) points to a significant difference between their treatment and mine. Thus whereas Klein, Crawford, and Alchian rely entirely on the *existence* of a potentially appropriable quasi-rent, which is a static measure, I have continuously emphasized the differential competence of firm and market to implement a program of adaptive, sequential decisionmaking. Contractual incompleteness and uncertainty give rise to contractual misalignments, the costs of adaptation to which varies with asset specificity — markets having the advantage when asset specificity is low, the advantage shifting to internal organization as asset specificity deepens. Process analysis is needed to explicate this condition.

9. Martin Weitzman maintains that the labor market is unique and is flawed by rigidities. By contrast, I argue that labor and intermediate product markets display strong commonalities and that the rigidities observed in each often serve value-enhancing contractual purposes (Williamson, 1986).

10. See Eugene Fama and Michael Jensen (1983).

11. For recent research that advocates or illustrates process analysis, see Mark Granovetter, who is a sociologist, Robert Axelrod, a political scientist, and Mary Douglas, an anthropologist.

12. Coase perceptively posed the issues as follows: "Why does the entrepreneur not organize one less transaction or one more?"; and "Why is not all production carried on in one big firm?" (chapter 2: 21).

13. One possibility is for Odysseus to delegate this judgment to a trusted subordinate (maybe to a committee). But this poses further difficulties. First, the ship is deprived of Odysseus's superior powers of inference during the period that he is bound. Second there is a concern that the individual to whom responsibility is delegated may exercise it not in Odysseus's interests but instead look to his own situation. And third, there are delays of getting composite judgments if, to deter defection by any single individual, a committee is charged to make the decision. Thus a better decision may be reached, but to what avail if it sometimes comes too late.

14. The transaction cost story of vertical integration thus comes down to this: (1) although markets support high-powered incentives, such incentives impair adaptability when bilateral dependency is great; (2) moving a transaction out of the market into the firm is attended by a weakening of incentives and the appearance of added control instruments, with the result that adaptability under bilateral trading is facilitated; whence (3) integration is reserved for those transactions where bilateral adaptability needs are great (namely, those where asset specificity and uncertainty are substantial), but market organization is elsewhere favored (being less subject, as it is, to the bureaucratic distortions that attend internal organization).

15. This is not to say that the perceived benefits of integration will be equally evident ex ante to both parties. Assume, however, in the Grossman and Hart setup, that A's decisions are "much more important" than B's. Then whereas the acquisition of B by A is apt to lead to net grains, their model predicts that a "wrong way" acquisition (of A by B) could well be worse than for the two to remain independent.

Transaction cost economics maintains that, since low-powered incentives supplant high-powered incentives in the integrated state, the matter of who acquires whom is relatively unimportant. Thus if A has limited resources, B has many, and the capital market cannot easily be persuaded of the idiosyncratic gains, then the acquisition of A by B will occur with substantially the same net gains as would have been realized had A acquired B.

16. Because Grossman and Hart "do not want to get into the details of contract renegotiation" (1986:702), they assume that renegotiation is costless under all ownership conditions. By contrast, I argue that high-powered incentives not only give rise to operating distortions under vertical integration but are an obstacle to ex post adaptation under all ownership configurations. That vertical integration experiences reduced adaptation costs is because high-powered (market) incentives are supplanted by lower-powered (internal) incentives under the process analysis scenario.

17. Manufacturing is the context out of which Grossman and Hart and I all work. A recent acquisition in which an unusual effort was made to preserve high-powered incentives is the merger of EDS into General Motors. This acquisition has led to protracted disputes and has been reformed. Among other things, EDS was dissatisfied with the transfer prices proposed by GM.

18. This is the orientation of Robin Marris and Dennis Mueller (1980), and John Coffee.

19. The collision of strategic purposes and efficiency purposes sometimes prevents this from going through, although strategic purposes themselves then need to be unpacked. What prevents value-enhancing deals from being reached whereby strategic distortions are eliminated?

20. A different argument has recently been advanced to explain timing: takeover purportedly has technological origins. The requisite technological precondition was that it be "possible to trade millions of shares of stock instantly," whence takeover awaited computer developments in the 1960s (Labaton: 8).

REFERENCES

Alchian, Armen. 1965. "The Basis of Some Recent Advances in the Theory of Management of the Firm," 14 *Journal of Industrial Economics* 30–41.

———. 1984. "Specificity, Specialization, and Coalitions," 140 *Journal of Economic Theory and Institutions* 34–49.

———, and Harold Demsetz. 1972. "Production, Information Costs, and Economic Organization," 62 *American Economic Review* 777–95.

Anderson, Erin, and David Schmittlein. 1984. "Integration of the Sales Force: An Empirical Examination," 15 *Rand Journal of Economics* 385–95.

Aoki, Masahiko. 1984. *The Cooperative Game Theory of the Firm*. London: Oxford University Press.

Arrow, Kenneth J. 1969. "The Organization of Economic Activity: Issues Pertinent to the Choice of Market versus Nonmarket Allocation." In *The Analysis and Evaluation of Public Expenditure: The PPB System*. Vol. 1. U.S. Joint Economic Committee, 91st Congress, 1st Session. Washington, D.C.: U.S. Government Printing Office.

———. 1987. "Reflections on the Essays." In George Feiwel, ed., *Arrow and the Foundations of the Theory of Economic Policy*. New York: New York University Press.

Aumann, Robert. 1985. "What Is Game Theory Trying to Accomplish?" In K. Arrow and S. Honkapohja, eds., *Frontiers of Economics*. Oxford, England: Basil Blackwell.

Axelrod, Robert. 1984. *The Evolution of Cooperation*. New York: Basic Books.

Barnard, Chester. 1938. *The Functions of the Executive*. Cambridge: Harvard University Press.

Baumol, William. 1959. *Business Behavior, Value and Growth*. New York: Macmillan.

———, John Panzer, and Robert Willis. 1982. *Contestable Markets and the Theory of Industry Structure*. New York: Harcourt Brace Jovanovich.

Ben-Porath, Yoram. 1980. "The F-Connection: Families, Friends and Firms and the Organization of Exchange," 6 *Population and Development Review* 1–30.

Bjuggren, Per-Olof. 1987. "Vertical Integration in the Swedish Pulp and Paper Industry," 1 *Skandinaviska Euskida Banken Quarterly Review* 23–31.

Chandler, Alfred, Jr. 1962. *Strategy and Structure*. Cambridge: MIT Press; New York: Doubleday, 1966.

———. 1977. *The Visible Hand: The Managerial Revolution in American Business*. Cambridge: Harvard University Press.

Coase, Ronald. 1937. "The Nature of the Firm," 4 *Economica* n.s. 386–405 [chapter 2 of this volume].

———. 1960. "The Problem of Social Cost," 3 *Journal of Law and Economics* 1–44.

———. 1964. "The Regulated Industries: Discussion," 54 *American Economic Review* 194–97.

———. 1972. "Industrial Organization: A Proposal for Research." In V. R. Fuchs, ed., *Policy Issues and Research Opportunities in Industrial Organization*. New York: National Bureau of Economic Research.

———. 1984. "The New Institutional Economics," 140 *Journal of Institutional and Theoretical Economics* 229–31.

———. 1988. "The Nature of the Firm: Origin, Meaning, Influence," 4 *Journal of Law, Economics, and Organization* 3–47 [chapters 3–5 of this volume].

Coffee, John. 1988. "Shareholders versus Managers." In J. Coffee, S. Rose-Ackerman, and L. Lowenstein, eds., *Knights, Raiders, and Targets*. New York: Columbia University Press.

Commons, John R. 1934. *Institutional Economics*. Madison: University of Wisconsin Press.

Crocker, Keith, and Scott Masten. 1986. "Mitigating Contractual Hazards: Unilateral Options and Contract Length." Unpublished manuscript.

Demsetz, Harold. 1978. "Why Regulate Utilities?" 11 *Journal of Law and Economics* 55–56.

Douglas, Mary. 1986. *How Institutions Think*. Syracuse: Syracuse University Press.

Elster, John. 1979. *Ulysses and the Sirens*. Cambridge: Cambridge University Press.

———. 1983. *Explaining Technical Change*. Cambridge: Cambridge University Press.

Fama, Eugene. 1980. "Agency Problems and the Theory of the Firm," 88 *Journal of Political Economy* 288–307.

———, and Michael Jensen. 1983. "Separation of Ownership and Control," 26 *Journal of Law and Economics* 301–26.

Fischer, Stanley. 1977. "Long-Term Contracting, Sticky Prices, and Monetary Policy: Comment." 3 *Journal of Monetary Economics* 317–24.

Friedman, Milton. 1962. *Capitalism and Freedom*. Chicago: University of Chicago Press.

Georgescu-Roegen, Nicholas. 1971. *The Entropy Law and Economic Process*. Cambridge: Harvard University Press.

Goldberg, Victor. 1976. "Regulation and Administered Contracts," 7 *Bell Journal of Economics* 426–52.

Gouldner, Alvin. 1954. *Industrial Democracy*. Glencoe, Ill.: The Free Press.

Granovetter, Mark. 1985. "Economic Action and Social Structure: The Problem of Embeddedness," 91 *American Journal of Sociology* 481–510.

Grossman, Sanford. 1981. "An Introduction to the Theory of Rational Expectations under Asymmetric Information," 48 *Review of Economic Studies* 541–59.

_____, and Oliver Hart. 1982. "Corporate Financial Structure and Managerial Incentives." In J. McCall, ed., *The Economics of Information and Uncertainty*. Chicago: University of Chicago Press.

_____. 1986. "The Costs and Benefits of Ownership: A Theory of Vertical and Lateral Integration," 94 *Journal of Political Economy* 691–719.

Hart, H. L. A. 1961. *The Concept of Law*. Oxford: Oxford University Press.

Hart, Oliver. 1988. "Incomplete Contracts and the Theory of the Firm," 4 *Journal of Law, Economics, and Organization*.

_____, and Bengt Holmstrom. 1987. "The Theory of Contracts." In T. Bewley, ed., *Advances in Economic Theory*. Cambridge: Cambridge University Press.

Hayek, Friedrich. 1945. "The Use of Knowledge in Society," 35 *American Economic Review* 519–30.

_____. 1967. *Studies in Philosophy, Politics, and Economics*. London: Routledge & Kegan Paul.

Hobbes, Thomas. [1651] 1928. *Leviathan, or the Matter, Forme, and Power of Commonwealth Ecclesiastical and Civil*. Oxford: Basil Blackwell.

Holmstrom, Bengt. 1982. "Managerial Incentive Problems—A Dynamic Perspective." In B. Wahlroos, ed., *Essays in Economics and Management in Honor of Lars Wahlbeck*. Helsinki: Swedish School of Economics.

_____, and Jean Tirole. 1988. "The Theory of the Firm." In Richard Schmalensee and Robert Willig, eds., *Handbook of Industrial Organization*. Amsterdam: North-Holland.

Jarrell, Gregory, and Michael Bradley. 1980. "The Economic Effect of Federal and State Regulation of Cash Tender Offers," 23 *Journal of Law and Economics* 371–94.

Jensen, Michael, and William Meckling. 1976. "Theory of the Firm: Managerial Behavior, Agency Costs, and Capital Structure," 3 *Journal of Financial Economics* 305–60.

Joskow, Paul. 1985. "Vertical Integration and Long-Term Contracts," 1 *Journal of Law, Economics, and Organization* 33–80.

_____. 1987. "Contract Duration and Relationship-Specific Investments," 77 *American Economic Review* 168–85.

_____. 1988. "Asset Specificity and the Structure of Vertical Relationships: Empirical Evidence," 4 *Journal of Law, Economics, and Organization* 95–117 [chapter 8 of this volume].

_____, and Richard Schmalensee. 1983. *Markets for Power*. Cambridge: MIT Press.

Klein, Benjamin. 1980. "Transaction Cost Determinants of 'Unfair' Contractual Arrangements," 70 *American Economic Review* 356–62.

_____. 1988. "Vertical Integration as Organizational Ownership," 4 *Journal of Law, Economics, and Organization* 199–213 [chapter 13 of this volume].

_____, Robert Crawford, and Armen Alchian. 1978. "Vertical Integration, Appropriable Rents, and the Competitive Contracting Process," 21 *Journal of Law and Economics* 297–326.

Knight, Frank. 1941. "Anthropology and Economics," 53 *Journal of Political Economy* 247–68.

Koopmans, Tjalig. 1957. *Three Essays on the State of Economic Science*. New York: McGraw-Hill.

Kreps, David, and Michael Spence. 1985. "Modelling the Role of History in Industrial Organization and Competition." In George Feiwel, ed., *Issues in Contemporary Microeconomics and Welfare*. London: Macmillan.

Kuhn, Thomas. 1970. *The Structure of Scientific Revolutions*. Chicago: University of Chicago Press.

Labaton, Stephen. 1987. "For the State, a Starring Role in the Takeover Game," *New York Times* (May 3): F-8.

Langlois, Richard. 1986. *Economics as a Process*. Cambridge: Cambridge University Press.

Levine, Michael. 1987. "Airline Competition in Deregulated Markets: Theory, Firm Strategy, and Public Policy," 4 *Yale Journal on Regulation* 393–494.

Macneil, Ian. 1978. "Contracts: Adjustments of Long-term Economic Relations under Classical, Neoclassical and Relational Contract Law," 47 *Northwestern University Law Review* 697–816.

McNeill, William. 1982. *The Pursuit of Power*. Chicago: University of Chicago Press.

March, James, and Herbert Simon. 1958. *Organizations*. New York: John Wiley.

Marris, Robin. 1964. *The Economic Theory of Managerial Capitalism*. New York: Free Press.

———, and Dennis Mueller. 1980. "The Corporation and Competition," 18 *Journal of Economic Literature* 32–63.

Masten, Scott. 1982. *Transaction Costs, Institutional Choice, and the Theory of the Firm*. Unpublished Ph.D. dissertation, University of Pennsylvania.

———. 1984. "The Organization of Production: Evidence from the Aerospace Industry," 27 *Journal of Law and Economics* 403–18.

———, and Keith Crocker. 1985. "Efficient Adaptation in Long-Term Contracts: Take-or-Play Provisions for Natural Gas," 75 *American Economic Review* 1083–97.

Merton, Robert. 1936. "The Unanticipated Consequences of Purposive Social Action," 1 *American Sociological Review* 894–904.

Michels, Robert. 1962. *Political Parties*. Glencoe, Ill.: Free Press.

Modigliani, Franco, and Merton Miller. 1958. "The Cost of Capital, Corporation Finance, and the Theory of Investment," 48 *American Economic Review* 261–97.

Monteverde, Kirk, and David Teece. 1982. "Supplier Switching Costs and Vertical Integration in the Automobile Industry," 13 *Bell Journal of Economics* 206–13.

Nelson, Richard, and Sidney Winter. 1982. *An Evolutionary Theory of Economic Change*. Cambridge: Harvard University Press.

Palay, Thomas. 1981. "The Governance of Rail-Freight Contracts: A Comparative Institutional Approach." Unpublished Ph.D. dissertation, University of Pennsylvania.

———. 1985. "The Avoidance of Regulatory Constraints: The Use of Informal Contracts," 1 *Journal of Law, Economics, and Organization* 155–75.

Radner, Roy. 1987. "The Internal Economy of Large Firms," 46 *Economic Journal–Conference Papers* 1–22.

Riordan, Michael, and Oliver Williamson. 1985. "Asset Specificity and Economic Organization," 3 *International Journal of Industrial Organization* 365–78.

Ross, Stephen. 1977. "The Determination of Financial Structure: The Incentive Signaling Approach," 8 *Bell Journal of Economics* 23–40.

Simon, Herbert. 1946. "The Proverbs of Administration," 6 *Public Administration Review* 53–67.

———. 1957. *Models of Man*. New York: John Wiley and Sons.

———. [1947] 1961. *Administrative Behavior*, 2nd ed. New York: Macmillan.

———. 1984. "On the Behavioral and Rational Foundations of Economic Dynamics," 5 *Journal of Economic Behavior and Organization* 35–56.

Spiller, Pablo. 1985. "On Vertical Mergers," 1 *Journal of Law, Economics, and Organization* 285–312.

Stuckey, John. 1983. *Vertical Integration and Joint Ventures in the Aluminum Industry*. Cambridge: Harvard University Press.

Teece, David. 1981. "Internal Organization and Economic Performance: An Empirical Analysis of the Profitability of Principal Firms," 30 *Journal of Industrial Economics* 173–200.

———. 1986. "Profiting from Technological Innovation," 15 *Research Policy* 285–305.

Weaklium, David. 1987. "Explaining the Outcome of Collective Bargaining: Transaction Cost and Power Approaches." Unpublished manuscript. Madison, Wisconsin.

Weitzman, Martin. 1984. *The Share Economy*. Cambridge: Harvard University Press.

Weizsacker, C. C. von. 1984. "The Costs of Substitution," 52 *Econometrica* 1085–116.

Williamson, Oliver. 1964. *The Economics of Discretionary Behavior: Managerial Objectives in a Theory of the Firm*. Englewood Cliffs, N.J.: Prentice-Hall.

———. 1971. "The Vertical Integration of Production: Market Failure Considerations," 61 *American Economic Review* 112–23.

———. 1975. *Markets and Hierarchies: Analysis and Antitrust Implications*. New York: Free Press.

———. 1976. "Franchise Bidding for Natural Monopoly — in General and with Respect to CATV," 7 *Bell Journal of Economics* 73–104.

———. 1979. "Transaction-Cost Economics: The Governance of Contractual Relations," 22 *Journal of Law and Economics* 3–61.

———. 1981. "The Economics of Organization: The Transaction Cost Approach," 87 *American Journal of Sociology* 548–77.

———. 1983. "Organizational Innovation: The Transaction Cost Approach." In J. Ronen, ed., *Entrepreneurship*. Lexington, Mass.: Heath Lexington.

———. 1985. *The Economic Institutions of Capitalism*. New York: Free Press.

———. 1986. "A Microanalytic Assessment of 'The Share Economy,'" 95 *Yale Law Journal* 627–37.

———. 1988. "Corporate Governance and Corporate Finance," 43 *Journal of Finance* 567–91.

———. 1989. "Transaction Cost Economics." In Richard Schmalensee and Robert Willig, eds., *Handbook of Industrial Organization*. Amsterdam: North Holland 136–84.

———, Michael Wachter, and Jeffrey Harris. 1975. "Understanding the Employment Relation: The Analysis of Idiosyncratic Exchange," 6 *Bell Journal of Economics* 250–80.

8

Asset Specificity and the Structure
of Vertical Relationships: Empirical Evidence

PAUL L. JOSKOW

A meeting to celebrate the fiftieth anniversary of "The Nature of the Firm" could not take place at a more appropriate time. Theoretical and empirical research into the kinds of issues raised by Professor Coase in his 1937 paper has increased substantially in recent years. It is a good time to take stock of where we are, how we got here, and where we are going in this area.

I have been asked to do two things in this paper. First, to discuss the theoretical research that has had an important influence on my own thinking and research on issues related to the nature of the firm. I will use this opportunity to reminisce about my own intellectual enlightenment to provide a historical survey of the conceptual developments that I feel have been of most importance. Second, to review recent empirical research that has been stimulated by this theoretical work. Since my recent research interests in this area have focused primarily on issues associated with the structure of vertical relationships, and, in particular, the role of asset specificity, transactions costs, and incomplete contracts, it is this strand of the literature that I will focus on here.

1. TRANSACTIONS COSTS, INCOMPLETE CONTRACTS, AND ASSET SPECIFICITY

I first read the paper whose anniversary we are here to celebrate when I was in my first year of graduate school at Yale. When I arrived at Yale in the fall of 1968, I chose the industrial organization course (140a) as my one free elective. The course was taught by Richard Nelson, who had recently returned to Yale from Rand. I recall arriving early for the first meeting of the course along with a couple of other students. Dick Nelson arrived early too. We chatted with Dick in the nervous way that first-year students are apt to do, and it soon became clear that our professor had never taught an industrial organization course before. We were lucky. Rather than concentration ratios, profit rates, measurement of scale economies, and inter-industry regressions of these variables on one another, the course focused on the structure and behavior of firms and related organizations. It was a very exciting course.

In a more recent paper Professor Coase (1972) discussed the state of industrial organization at that time. While his characterization and criticisms of what the field was like then reflects my own views very well, Dick Nelson's course was nothing like that at all. We read papers by Coase, Alchian, Simon, Cyert and March, Marschak and Radner, Chandler, Williamson, Winter, Arrow, Downs, Niskanen, and others. The industrial organization field to which we were introduced included discussions of manufacturing firms and nonmanufacturing firms, for-profit and nonprofit firms, government bureaucracies and other political institutions. We were asked to explore questions about the boundaries between firms and markets, the internal organization of firms, the costs of obtaining, processing, and communicating information, information flows and decisionmaking within firms, organizational objectives, and organizational behavior. I am fairly sure that we never learned what a concentration ratio was or why it might be of interest.

My interest in the nature of firms and other organizations can be traced directly to Economics 140a at Yale. This exposure to the literature on firm and organizational structure and behavior, combined with my interests in empirical applications and public policy that brought me to Yale, have largely defined the kinds of problems that I find interesting to work on as well as my approach to these problems.

At that time I had not yet focused on "transactions costs" as being of central importance to my understanding of the boundary between firms and markets, the structure of firms, and the nature of contractual relationships between firms at different levels of the production chain. As a new Ph.D. in 1972 I was still very much influenced by the psychological and sociological perspective developed by Herbert Simon and his students. Indeed, I think that it is fair to say that I was suspicious of the use of vague notions of transactions costs for explaining economic institutions that did not fit neatly into the model of perfect competition. I did not find a clear and consistent body of theoretical work that carefully identified what the relevant transactions costs were, why they were important in some contexts but not in others, and how institutional arrangements should be expected to respond to them. My concern was that one could always invent a specification of transactions costs that could rationalize almost anything.[1] By rationalizing everything we might really be explaining nothing.

My interest in transactions costs was stimulated considerably by the work that Oliver Williamson was doing about the time that I began teaching at MIT. After I came to MIT in 1972, Williamson sent me drafts of a manuscript that was to be published as *Markets and Hierarchies* in 1975. I still remember reading those drafts. It was hard going. I was confronted with a whole new language plus an older language used in new ways; information impactedness, opportunism, small-numbers bargaining, bounded rationality, etc.[2] I felt that there was something important there, however, and worked hard to understand what Williamson was saying. I understood that uncertainty, adverse selection problems, moral hazard problems, the costs of writing, monitoring, and enforcing contracts, sequential bargaining over the distribution of benefits associated with sunk investments, and so on were all somehow important. However, I don't think that I understood how it all fit together or how these considerations could be related systematically to variations in institutional arrangements.

The most important thing that I took away from *Markets and Hierarchies* was the "comparative institutional" perspective. That is, a general recognition that there is a wide range of institutional arrangements that can be used to govern transactions between economic agents. Specific institutional arrangements emerge in response to various transactional considerations in order to minimize the total cost of making transactions. The boundary between a firm and a market provides a very rough distinction between the two primary institutional mechanisms for allocating resources, but this is the beginning, not the end, of the inquiry. Firms can take on many different organization structures. Market transactions can take many different forms ranging from simple spot market transactions to complex long-term contracts. The specific set of institutional arrangements chosen would represent the governance structure that minimized the total cost of consummating the transactions of interest.

Markets and Hierarchies also had important implications for antitrust policy, around which so much of contemporary industrial organization had evolved. Many of the institutional arrangements that conventional economic theory could not explain as natural outcomes of a model of perfect competition—vertical integration, contractual vertical restraints, joint ventures, and certain other horizontal agreements—were viewed as being suspect within the Bain-Mason branch of industrial organization and were often presumed to be a consequence of monopoly power or efforts to obtain it. This view provided the intellectual basis for antitrust policies that are now in disrepute and have, to a great extent, been reversed.[3]

One can of course find these same themes in Coase's 1937 paper and certainly in his 1972 paper. And of course, the Chicago branch of industrial organization had a very different perspective on antitrust policy. But for me, it is *Markets and Hierarchies* that put needed structure on this perspective. It provided the foundation for a theory of institutional choice and design that had the prospect of yielding clear causal relationships between transactional characteristics and institutional arrangements. This in turn began to give us a theoretical framework that could be subjected to empirical verification. However, as of 1975 I think that it is fair to say that I found what was now the Coase/Williamson view in my own mind to be interesting, but I did not know what to do with it or have much interest in doing something with it myself.

Several papers that appeared after 1975 helped to improve my understanding of the transactions cost framework and how it could be used to explain the choice and structure of institutional arrangements designed to minimize the costs of transacting. The first paper was Williamson's (1976) paper on franchise bidding for monopoly franchises. This paper included a case study of the franchising process for the cable television franchise in Oakland, California. The paper is in a sense a reply to the franchise bidding solution to the natural monopoly problems advanced by Demsetz (1968). Williamson uses the transactions cost framework to provide an alternative analysis of bidding for monopoly franchises.[4] He argues quite convincingly that in the real world characterized by uncertainty, changing input prices, changing technology, multiple products, long-lived investments specific to a particular buyer/seller relationship, there are significant costs associated with writing, monitoring, and enforcing the different types of contracts between a supplier and a municipality that are the outcome of a franchise bidding scheme. The characteristics of the product at issue—a cable television system offering a variety of service—led Williamson to conclude that the least cost governance structure emerging from a franchise bidding process in this case will be an incomplete long-term contract that has adaptive properties with many similarities to public utility regulation.

The analysis of franchise bidding through the transactions cost lens does not necessarily mean that franchise bidding is inferior to state commission regulation of franchised monopolies either in general or with regard to cable television circa 1970, but rather that the two modes of control may not be as different as first meets the eye.[5] Williamson (1976:74) argues that both modes of organization must confront a variety of command and control problems because of the characteristics of the transaction, both are imperfect compared to some abstract ideal, and that they differ "mainly in degree, rather than in kind." The comparative institutional perspective comes out very clearly. What is the best that we can do in an imperfect world? The analysis can usefully be guided by theory, but the answer to the public policy question is inherently an empirical matter. It cannot be resolved "in theory."

Victor Goldberg's (1976) paper further develops the relational contracting paradigm contained in Williamson's paper and applies it more broadly to the economic analysis of public utility regulation.[6] Goldberg's primary point is that traditional economic analysis of the benefits and costs of regulation implicitly assumes that the alternative to regulation is a perfectly competitive market or a frictionless, transactions-cost-free franchise bidding system. This type of comparison will necessarily make administrative regulation look bad because it necessarily has imperfections. But Goldberg argues convincingly, as does Williamson, that this is the wrong comparison to make. "Many of the problems associated with regulation lie in what is being regulated, not in the act of regulation itself" (Goldberg, 1976:426). Public utility regulation is an administrative contract that must be compared to contractual arrangements that are realistic alternatives to the regulatory status quo. Williamson and Goldberg make it clear that we must start our analysis of institutional choice, whether the analysis is normative or positive, with a complete understanding of the characteristics of the transactions that buyers and sellers are seeking to consummate. We can then identify the problems that must be confronted to provide for an efficient trading relationship and compare alternative institutional arrangements in terms of their ability to cope efficiently with these problems. Thus, in evaluating traditional public utility regulation we must carefully and completely articulate the nature and expected performance of the institutions that we anticipate will replace it given the characteristics of the services being regulated and the transactional problems associated with these characteristics that must be confronted.

The Williamson and Goldberg papers had an important effect on my own understanding of the importance of the economic characteristics that characterize specific buyer and seller relationships and the role of transactions costs in determining the cost-minimizing governance structure for exchange. My thinking is always stimulated by a concrete example and Williamson provided one. Furthermore, my general interests in regulation meant that these papers had focused transactions cost considerations on issues of central concern to me. The combination of durable relationship-specific investments, uncertainty about future demand and cost realizations, and contractual incompleteness arising from the costs of writing, monitoring, and enforcing full contingent claims contracts began to emerge as the key elements of this theoretical approach to understanding institutional choice and design.

Two additional papers helped to crystallize these ideas for me. Klein, Crawford, and Alchian's (1978) paper was certainly very influential in clarifying my thinking on the broad challenge raised by Coase and advanced by Williamson. They focus very clearly on the importance of relationship-specific investments, combined with incomplete contracts, as the critical factors that lead simple spot market transactions to be plagued by transactional difficulties. Klein, Crawford, and Alchian argue that more complex long-term contracts may be an attractive alternative to spot markets, but that incomplete long-term contracts can run into performance problems as well. They argue that coordination problems arising from specific investments will be less severe if the transaction is internalized. As a result, they hypothesize that internal organization (vertical integration) is more likely to become the preferred governance structure the more important are specific investments by the buyer and/or the seller. The exposition in this paper was clear and it was backed up with several interesting examples, the relationship between General Motors and Fisher Auto Body being the one that I found most interesting.[7]

Williamson's (1979) contemporaneous paper focuses much more attention on the importance of asset specificity and idiosyncratic investments than does his early book and papers.[8] It also focuses more on the structure of vertical relationships between firms, independent of the internal structure of the organization, internal labor markets, and so forth. The paper develops a clear mapping between three dimensions of transactions—the degree of asset specificity, the importance of uncertainty,[9] and the frequency of transactions—and the cost-minimizing governance structure for transactions between different levels in the supply chain. The paper also concludes with some concrete predictions about the nature of the institutional arrangements that are likely to emerge with different combinations of these three variables. For example, as investments become more specific to the buyer/seller relationship, Williamson anticipates that cost-minimizing institutional choice will respond by moving from simple anonymous (spot) market contracting (classical contract law), to more complex long-term contractual arrangements with protective provisions (neoclassical contract law), and ultimately to internal organization. Williamson defines transaction- or relationship-specific investments more completely in a subsequent paper (Williamson, 1983).

By 1980, this body of research had moved us from a general understanding of the importance of transactions costs in explaining the choice between firms and markets and issues associated with the internal organization of the firm, to a fairly

specific theory for explaining the structure of vertical relationships based on variations in the importance of asset specificity, uncertainty, product complexity, and the
constraints of repeat purchase activity.[10] Asset specificity means that hold-up or
opportunism problems must be confronted by the transacting parties at the contract execution stage. Full contingent claims contracts become more costly to write,
monitor, and enforce when uncertainty and complexity increase (that is, there are
more contingencies). Incomplete long-term contracts are a potentially attractive
alternative to sequential spot market trade, but such contracts will necessarily be
imperfect governance mechanisms. The most costly it is to contract on all contingencies and the greater the ex ante incentive effects of potential ex post hold-ups,
the more imperfect long-term contracts are likely to be. Internal organization has
costs, but as the costs of incomplete long-term contracts increase, internal control is
likely to become more attractive. This suggests that if we can find a way to measure
variations in the choice of governance structure and can match these choices with
measures of the associated degree of asset specificity, uncertainty, and complexity,
we are on our way to being able to test this theory empirically.

I do not want to suggest that by 1980 this theory of the determinants of the
structure of vertical relationships was all neatly tied down. The theory did not have
a rigorous mathematical foundation and, it is my perception, was not taken very
seriously at that time by those who call themselves theorists.[11] How this all related
to the evolving theory of agency which relied so heavily on information asymmetries and risk aversion was elusive (and still is).[12] Of more concern, exactly why
internal organization should be expected to yield outcomes superior to imperfect
market transactions was not, in my mind, developed very well. Rather, there was an
implicit reliance on the power of the master-servant relationship to resolve disputes
that would otherwise arise when independent firms deal with each other through a
market. Many of these gaps have been explored in more depth since then, as
theorists have come to recognize the importance of the ideas advanced by Coase,
Williamson, Goldberg, Klein, and others and have turned their attention to the
development of a more complete theoretical structure.[13] In any event, things had
moved far enough by 1980 or so that the stage was set for more systematic empirical
work, going beyond individual examples, aimed at testing the causal relationships
suggested by this theoretical framework.

2. VERTICAL INTEGRATION
IN THE ELECTRIC POWER INDUSTRY

Before proceeding with a discussion of this recent empirical work and my own
efforts to contribute to it, I would like to detour slightly to discuss my first effort to
apply what I had learned from this body of research to a particular problem.
Beginning in 1978 or so, several sectors of the economy that had been subject to
pervasive price and entry regulation for many years were fully or partially deregulated. These sectors included airlines, trucking, railroads, telecommunications, cable television, etc. After President Reagan took office, the pressure to extend the

deregulation movement to other industries and aspects of economic activity increased. Sometime in late 1981 or early 1982, Richard Schmalensee and I were asked by the Department of Energy to do a study of the prospects and problems associated with deregulation for the electric utility industry. This study eventually became a book entitled *Markets for Power: An Analysis of Electric Utility Deregulation* (Joskow and Schmalensee, 1983).

I will not go into the details of our analysis of the many proposals for restructuring and deregulation that were being discussed, but I do want to emphasize the contribution of what we had learned from the transactions cost research that was maturing at about that time. The traditional analysis of restructuring and partial deregulation of the electric utility industry assumed implicitly that there were no benefits from vertical integration. Indeed it implicity took the posture that vertical integration, long-term requirements contracts, and the like were sinister instruments to monopolize the business. The "irrelevant complications" that Williamson (1976) and Goldberg (1976) found to be so important for comparing alternative control mechanisms were ignored. The books called certain functions (for example, generation, transmission, distribution) by different names so it was simply assumed that they could be costlessly separated into independent firms and that "the market" could be relied upon to govern efficiently exchange relationships between them. There were many generating plants, so "in theory" a competitive generation market which relied on simple spot market transactions to govern trade would result.

Schmalensee and I observed that the nature of generation, transmission, and distribution technology and the physical operating characteristics of an integrated AC electric power system suggested that the "irrelevant complications" that were being ignored were likely to be of considerable potential importance. Long-lived investments specific to individual geographical areas, transmission nodes, fuel supply, and transportation opportunities were the norm. Planning of generation and transmission were intimately related to one another and were as much substitutes as complements. Power flowed according to the laws of physics, not according to the terms of contracts, and it moved very fast. The efficient and reliable operation of the system was quite complex. Following Williamson and Goldberg, we recognized that these realities had important implications for the structure of electricity supply entities and the kinds of governance structure that would emerge in the absence of vertical integration. We went on to discuss the kinds of contractual relationships that might emerge with different degrees of government-mandated vertical disintegration and with different assumptions about the nature of electric power technology.

The purpose of our analysis was not to show that restructuring and deregulation was necessarily a bad idea. Indeed, we concluded that some restructuring and deregulation of certain aspects of electricity supply might be a very good idea. What we did try to show was that the model against which the existing system was being compared was unrealistic and would not work well if it were imposed. Many of the problems perceived with the electric power industry were inherent problems associated with the characteristics of electricity supply, not problems that were simply a consequence of public utility regulation. These problems would have to be confronted by any institutional alternative to the status quo. As a result, we argued that the analysis of alternative public policies toward competition and regulation in the electric power industry should carefully incorporate the important transactional characteristics associated with the efficient production of electricity.

I think that we succeeded in elevating the discussion of restructuring, deregulation, and competition to a higher plain. Gradual restructuring is now taking place in this industry, and more reliance on competition in just those areas we identified as being most conducive to it is taking place today (Joskow, 1986). The role of long-term contracts and the benefits and costs of vertical integration have become central to the debate.

3. ASSET SPECIFICITY, VERTICAL INTEGRATION, AND LONG-TERM CONTRACTS: EMPIRICAL EVIDENCE

I think that Schmalensee and I would have been much happier with our analysis if there had been more (any!) empirical support available for the transactions cost perspective that we found so intuitively appealing and so consistent with the historical evolution of the electric power industry. At about the time we finished our book more empirical analysis of and support for the transactions cost perspective to vertical integration and long-term contracts finally began to emerge. I will now proceed to discuss this recent empirical work. I start with work that focuses on vertical integration and then go on to discuss empirical work that examines "nonstandard" contractual relationships between buyers and sellers.

3.1. Vertical Integration

As I suggested above, by roughly 1980 the theoretical discussion of the role of transactions costs in determining the nature of the firm and the structure of "nonstandard" market relationships between firms had been refined considerably. From the broad set of issues regarding the structure of firms and markets raised by Coase (1937, 1972) and Williamson (1975), the discussion had come to focus on the determinants of vertical integration (internal organization) and the nature of contractual relationships between firms at different levels of the production process.[14] The importance of asset specificity had become the key factor used to explain departures from governance by simple spot market transactions. Indeed, things had moved far enough along that we had a theory that was conducive to empirical verification.

For useful empirical work to proceed several conditions must be satisfied. First, we need a theory that provides us with clear structural relationship between a set of dependent variables and a set of independent variables. Second, we need to be able to measure empirically variations in the key independent and dependent variables. Finally, ideally, we should have one or more alternative and observationally distinct theories that explain variations in the independent variables of interest so that the competing theories can be compared to one another.[15]

The bare-bones theory that has evolved from this literature appears to be something like the following: when specific investments represent a significant fraction of the costs of consummating an efficient vertical supply arrangement, the reliance on simple anonymous spot market transactions is likely to be an unsatisfactory governance mechanism for inducing the parties to make the specific investments necessary to yield a least-cost supply relationship. Anonymous spot markets fail because the sinking of relationship-specific investments transforms a large-numbers bargaining situation ex ante into a small-numbers bargaining situation ex post in which one or both parties have an opportunity to extract a portion of the quasi-rent stream associated with the specific investments. To induce the parties to make optimal investments ex ante, some method must be found to constrain the ex post hold-up and haggling problems that would emerge if the parties relied on repeated bargaining over the terms of trade ex post. In principle this can be accomplished if the parties can costlessly contract on the specific investments that they agree to make, the quantities they agree to deliver, and the prices that they agree to pay when various contingencies arise as the contractual relationship plays out over time.[16] They are likely to be able to do so only imperfectly, however. This is because there are costs associated with writing, monitoring, and enforcing contracts and because there are likely to be information asymmetries. Furthermore, long-term contracts themselves may introduce costs and performance problems of their own. Internal organization or vertical integration is viewed as a method for overcoming some of the problems associated with imperfect long-term contracts, although vertical integration may confront costs of its own as well. The ultimate choice of governance structure requires balancing the costs and benefits of these alternative governance systems.

The theory suggests that we think of the primary dependent variable here as being a limited dependent variable that indicates what mode of organization will be chosen by the parties to the transactions: vertical integration, long-term contracts, or spot market trade. Finer distinctions within each of these three categories could also be made. Other things equal, we expect the parties more frequently to choose vertical integration or a long-term contract as the quasi-rents associated with specific investments become more important and the associated benefits of precommitment increase. Some measure of asset specificity is therefore a necessary independent variable to consider in any empirical analysis. There are likely to be different transactions and organization costs associated with vertical integration and long-term contracts that are not present with simple spot markets. Difficulties in writing, monitoring, and enforcing a long-term contract that can respond efficiently to changing market conditions over time may impose costs that tip the balance toward vertical integration. Internal organization costs, scale economies, experience, and so forth may tip the balance back toward contract or spot market mechanisms. Ideally, we should also include independent variables measuring these costs as well.[17]

Given this structural framework, we are left with the task of measuring the choices among alternative vertical structures (the dependent variables), measuring variations in the importance of asset specificity, and measuring the transactions costs of the various alternatives to simple spot market transactions. These measurement tasks are not trivial. At least in principle we should be able to determine whether specific types of transactions involve internal production, long-term contracts, or simple spot market transactions. We can in principle distinguish important differences between long-term contracts such as the extent of precommitment, the use of financial hostages (Williamson, 1983), and various other protective measures. In practice, this kind of very disaggregated firm and input-specific data can be very difficult to obtain. Relying on industry level data and inter-industry comparisons, as has been typical in empirical work in industrial organization (Schmalensee, 1987), is not likely to be at all satisfactory.

Even if we can get satisfactory measures of variations in the structure of vertical relationships, we must, at the very least, find some way to measure variations in the importance of asset specificity. This is even a more difficult task. How do we know whether a particular investment has the specificity characteristics of interest? How do we measure how important the ex post performance problems would be if repeated bargaining were relied upon? How do we measure the nature and costs of the agents' production decisions if denied the opportunity to rely on nonstandard arrangements to minimize ex post performance problems? We are certainly not going to find these numbers written down neatly in a book of industry statistics. The best that we can hope for is more qualitative information on variations in the importance of asset specificity.

Williamson's (1983) discussion of four distinct types of relationship-specific investment is very helpful for identifying and measuring variations in the importance of asset specificity. Very briefly, they are:

A. Site specificity: The buyer and seller are in a "cheek-by-jowl" relationship with one another, reflecting ex ante decisions to minimize inventory and transportation costs. Once sited, the assets in place are highly immobile.

B. Physical asset specificity: When one or both parties to the transaction make investments in equipment and machinery that involves design characteristics specific to the transaction and which have lower values in alternative uses.

C. Human asset specificity: Investments in relationship-specific human capital that often arise through a learning-by-doing process.

D. Dedicated assets: General investments by a supplier that would not otherwise be made but for the prospect of selling a significant amount of product to a particular customer. If the contract were terminated prematurely it would leave the supplier with significant excess capacity.

With this framework in mind, let me turn to a discussion of the empirical evidence.[18]

Monteverde and Teece (1982) (henceforth, M-T) is the first systematic effort to try to examine empirically the role of asset specificity in determining the structure of vertical relationships. They focus on the choice between internal production (vertical integration) and market procurement of automobile components by Ford and General Motors (GM). They work with a list of 133 automotive components and determine whether each is produced internally or purchased through the market.[19] In this way, they measure variations in the choice of vertical integration or market procurement using a dichotomous dependent variable that takes on a value of one if the component is manufactured internally and zero otherwise. They are concerned only about the choice between vertical integration and market procurement and not about intermediate contractual forms.

The focus of the M-T paper is on applications engineering effort as a measure of the degree of asset specificity. This would appear to fall into Williamson's (1983) category of "human asset specificity." They state their hypothesis as follows: "The greater is the application engineering effort associated with the development of any given automobile component, the higher are the expected appropriable quasi rents, and therefore, the greater is the likelihood of vertical integration of production for that component" (Monteverde and Teece, 1982:207). To measure variations in applications engineering effort an index of its importance was developed with the help of an automobile design engineer. The expectation is that where applications engineering is more important, vertical integration will be more prevalent. A dummy variable is also used to identify components as either "specific" to a particular company or "generic" to all auto companies. M-T expect to find that "specific" components will have a higher probability of being vertically integrated. Finally, a dummy variable is used to distinguish between observations for GM and Ford. This variable may pick up idiosyncratic differences between Ford and GM or serve as a very imperfect proxy for the role of scale economies as a potential cost of vertical integration. In the latter case we would expect GM to be more integrated than Ford, other things equal.[20]

A natural question that arises at this point is: What is the alternative explanation for variations in make or buy decisions? An alternative theory is not provided here. Furthermore, the simultaneous comparison of many models can be methodologically very difficult. Instead, as is quite common in this line of work and economics more generally, hypothesis testing pertains to a single model which is either consistent or inconsistent with the data. If it is inconsistent with the data it is rejected. If it is consistent with the data it is implicitly accepted until new hypotheses or data can be examined. In M-T, the null hypothesis is simply that asset specificity is not important for explaining variations in vertical integration. The alternative hypothesis is that vertical integration is more likely when asset specificity is more important.

M-T's results lead to the rejection of this null hypothesis. The coefficient estimates obtained are consistent with the predictions of the asset specificity/transactions cost theory. More applications effort, more specificity, and a large firm (GM) make vertical integration more likely. This empirical work therefore provides support for the view that variations in asset specificity affect the choice between vertical integration and market procurement as hypothesized.

Scott Masten (1984) provides a related empirical analysis of make or buy decisions by an aerospace firm for the components of a large system that it had contracted to provide to the government. Masten's analysis takes more explicit account of the comparative institutional choice aspect of the problem, by explicitly setting up the empirical analysis as an expected cost-minimizing problem involving the choice between two alternative governance mechanisms, and by attempting to incorporate directly considerations reflecting the costs of internalization versus market procurement.

The empirical analysis proceeds in the following way. A sample of components is drawn and a dichotomous variable indicating whether the component is produced internally or purchased in the market is the dependent variable. A questionnaire was given to the firm's procurement team to obtain their rankings of the various components in terms of their "specificity" and "complexity." Two measures of specificity are utilized. One is a measure of design specificity based on questionnaire responses as to whether the components were "specific," "somewhat specific," or "standard" vis-à-vis this system.[21] The second is a measure of site specificity or colocation. A third variable measures the complexity of the component and is designed to capture the costs of writing complete contracts. The more important are these variables, Masten hypothesizes, the higher are the costs of market contracting compared to internal organization. Masten, following Williamson, assumes that as complete contracting becomes more costly, vertical integration is more likely. A maximum likelihood model is specified in which the probability of the firm choosing vertical integration is equal to the probability that the costs of governance through vertical integration are lower than the costs of trading through the market.

Masten finds that variations in the importance of asset specificity affect the choice between vertical integration and market procurement as hypothesized. The specificity and complexity variables have the expected signs and are very significant, while the other variables generally have the expected signs. This is further evidence that asset specificity considerations are important for understanding the structure of vertical relationships. It also suggests that contractual "complexity" as well as asset specificity leads vertical integration to be chosen over contracting.

· Anderson and Schmittlein look at a different dimension of internalization. They examine firm decisions to integrate the marketing function as measured by their reliance on employee sales personnel (direct sales people) or independent sales agents (manufacturer's representatives) to market products to customers. Direct sales people are employees of a single firm and are paid a salary or salary plus incentive payment. Manufacturer's representatives are organized as separate firms and represent many manufacturers. The use of direct sales people is the integrated governance structure. The focus of the analysis is on the role of asset specificity, the difficulty in monitoring the performance of sales personnel (as a measure of asymmetric information problems), and scale economies (a potential source of internalization costs), in the choice between organizational modes. The asset specificity in question here is related to Williamson's notion of "human asset specificity."

Anderson and Schmittlein make use of a data base they develop for firms in the electronic components industry. The unit of analysis is the product line of individual firms sold into specific sales territories. An index of asset specificity based on the results of a questionnaire is developed which takes account of variations in service territory characteristics and company size. The authors find that as asset specificity becomes more important, vertical integration is more likely. They also find that vertical integration is more likely when it is more difficult to evaluate the performance of sales personnel. Finally, larger firms are more likely to utilize employees to market their products. The results are quite consistent with the predictions of transactions cost theory.

Stuckey (1983) provides a very interesting, though rarely cited, study of vertical integration in the aluminum industry. Unlike the previous studies, this is a more traditional empirical industry study that does not rely extensively on econometric analysis. Nevertheless, Stuckey has put together a great deal of information on vertical integration, contractual relationships, and the characteristics of the firms and products involved at all stages of the aluminum industry. He argues quite convincingly that the extensive reliance on vertical integration between bauxite mines and alumina refineries is a consequence of physical asset specificity and site specificity considerations. These considerations are also important for transactions between alumina refineries and smelters, although they are less important and have declined over time. Stuckey argues that integration between smelting and fabrication is likely to be more a consequence of the desire of aluminum firms to engage in downstream price discrimination (Perry) than a consequence of transactions cost considerations. These results serve to remind us that there are many possible reasons for vertical integration rather than a single one which will necessarily apply in all circumstances.[22]

My paper (Joskow, 1985) on vertical integration by electric utilities into coal production takes a similar approach to Stuckey's.[23] My interest in doing some empirical work in this area was stimulated by Williamson's discussion of "site-specificity." An example of site specificity near and dear to my heart is a mine-mouth coal burning generating plant. I thought that it would be interesting to see whether there were significant organizational and contractual differences for coal supply between mine-mouth plants and other types of electric generating plants burning coal.

I decided to examine the extent of vertical integration between electric utilities and coal suppliers, as well as the reliance on long-term contracts and spot market purchases. I discovered that there are wide variations in coal supply relationships. Roughly 15 percent of utility coal is supplied by utility subsidiaries. Another 15 percent is purchased in a spot market. The rest is purchased under contracts that vary in duration from one year to fifty years. Unlike aluminum, where upstream vertical integration is pervasive, the variations in the structure of vertical relationships between electric utilities and coal suppliers provide an opportunity to see if intra-industry variations in asset specificity and transactions costs could explain variations in the vertical governance structure chosen.

I proceeded to identify a set of mine-mouth plants and put together detailed information on coal supply arrangements for each of them. In those cases where long-term contracts are used to govern coal trade, I was generally able to obtain the actual contracts. If Williamson's site specificity story was correct, I hypothesized that I would find vertical integration to be much more prevalent for mine-mouth plants than for other plants. If market procurement was relied upon by a mine-mouth plant, I hypothesized that long-term contracts would be used and that they would carefully specify the terms of future trade when various contingencies arose and contain protective provisions to guard against opportunistic behavior. This is just what I found. Vertical integration is much more likely for a mine-mouth plant than other coal-burning plants. When vertical integration is not chosen, unusually long detailed contracts are used to support exchange. These contracts usually involve thirty-five-year commitments by the buyer and the seller to the terms of future trade.

The studies that I have discussed so far all focus on a specific industry and use firm level, plant level, and transaction level data to examine empirically the factors that determine intra-industry variations in the structure of vertical relationships. An alternative approach is to use inter-industry data to try to explain variations in the structure of vertical relationships across industries. This approach would require finding some meaningful way to measure differences in the extent of vertical integration across industries, to measure variations in asset specificity across industries, and control for other inter-industry characteristics that might be correlated with these independent variables.

The use of inter-industry data has a long tradition in industrial organization (Schmalensee, 1987). As Schmalensee suggests, it is an approach for testing hypotheses in industrial organization that has significant limitations. I believe that good empirical work aimed at testing theories such as those I have been discussing here *requires* that we know a lot about the characteristics of the firms and products that we are relying on in the empirical work. The use of industry-level aggregate values for the relevant variables, drawn for hundreds of industries, precludes doing so. Measurement of the degree of vertical integration, using the kinds of inter-industry data that are readily available, is itself a very difficult problem. The traditional use of the ratio of value added to sales seems to me to have too many problems to be used with great credibility (Scherer: 79). More meaningful measures of vertical integration can be developed for a cross-section of industries (Scherer: 79; Bradburd and Caves), but it is a lot of work. In any case, I am not aware of any contemporary studies that have taken the inter-industry approach to examine the role of asset specificity or transactions costs more generally in explaining variations in the extent of vertical integration.[24]

3.2. Long-term Contracts

Whereas the earliest empirical work focused on the choice between vertical integration and market procurement, there is now a growing body of empirical evidence which examines the structure of contractual relationships from a transactions cost perspective. This work focuses on the role of asset specificity and contracting hazards in explaining variations in the use and structure of long-term contracts. Most of this work has either been published in the last few years or is still unpublished.

Goldberg and Erickson (1987) analyze the characteristics of ninety contracts for petroleum coke written between 1946 and 1973. The contracts were produced in the course of a Federal Trade Commission investigation which charged that the long-term contracts between eight oil refiners and Great Lakes Carbon Corporation violated the antitrust laws. Goldberg and Erickson compile and analyze the provisions of the contracts and certain characteristics of the transactions. They argue that the price and quantity provisions of the contracts are best understood from a "relational contracting" perspective. The provisions of the contracts reflect the interest of the parties in guarding against the expropriation of idiosyncratic investments and contain provisions to mitigate contracting hazards.

Mulhern (1986) examines the relationship between specific "protective" features and price adjustment provisions contained in a large sample of pre–regulatory era natural gas contracts and variables that measure variations in ex post bargaining problems.[25] He also discusses and analyzes alternatives to the transactions cost explanations for the use of these provisions. The empirical results suggest that transactions cost considerations play a significant role in explaining variations in contractual provisions. Furthermore, the transactions cost approach explains these variations better than the competing hypotheses that Mulhern examines.[26]

Palay (1984, 1985) has done an extremely interesting study of the evolution of informal contracts between railroads and shippers. During the period he studied, railroad rates were regulated by the Interstate Commerce Commission. However, the provisions of the regulated tariffs available to shippers were not sensitive to the desire of certain shippers to have "specialized services" made available to them that would require the railroads to make idiosyncratic investments.

Regulated firms typically are subject to a broad but vague "obligation to service" all demand at prevailing regulated rates. Exactly how far these obligations to provide service on demand extend is not always clear, but generally they do not extend to specialized and nonstandard services. These same tariffs impose no explicit long-term obligations on shippers to take or pay for service. As a result, the railroads were reluctant to make durable investments specific to a particular service pursuant to a traditional tariff which did not protect these investments.[27] Palay demonstrates how a system of informal contracts between railroads and shippers emerged "underneath" the standard regulated tariffs, to support relationship-specific investments.[28]

Palay's study has important implications for the growing trend in some regulated industries to increase the opportunities buyers have to switch suppliers while continuing to regulate rates using generally available tariffs that do not recognize the importance of specific investments, and which place no long-run obligations on buyers. Informal contracts may emerge to fill in the gaps created by imperfect regulation, but a formal contract negotiation system is likely to be superior to simplistic regulated tariffs. Providing for more opportunities for buyers to search among competing regulated suppliers while continuing to regulate rates and service obligations is bound to lead to inefficiencies.

Stuckey's study of vertical relationships in the aluminum industry also examines the use and structure of long-term contracts. He focuses his discussion on examples of contracting problems and contractual failures that have emerged between smelters and upstream mining and refining operations in the relatively rare circumstances when they relied on contracts rather than vertical integration. The contractual failures he discusses are associated with ex post coordination and haggling problems that arise when relationship-specific investments are important. The prevalence of contracting problems is probably why vertical integration is so pervasive at these levels in the aluminum industry. Gallick performs a similar type of analysis of contracts and vertical integration between the fishing and processing segments of the U.S. tuna industry. Complex contracts appear to emerge to cope with a variety of vertical coordination problems identified in the transactions cost literature. Co-ownership of vessels (vertical integration) is also a factor in some cases. Contracts seem to deal with contracting hazards better in the tuna industry than in the upstream segments of the aluminum industry.

In a recent paper (Joskow, 1987) I analyze the relationship between the duration of contracts between electric utilities and coal suppliers, agreed to by the parties at the contract execution stage, and several variables designed to capture variations in the importance of relationship-specific investments associated with each contract. The empirical work relies on a sample of about 300 coal contracts written between 1960 and 1979. Contract duration is used to measure the extent to which the parties to the contract are willing to precommit to the terms of future trade ex ante rather than relying on repeated negotiation. I argue that when relationship-specific investments are more important the parties will be more likely to tie down the terms of future trade ex ante by specifying contracts with longer durations. I use several variables to serve as proxies for physical asset specificity, dedicated assets, and site specificity (Williamson, 1983) measured on a contract-by-contract basis. I find that these variables explain variations in contract duration quite well.[29]

In a subsequent paper (Joskow, 1988), I went on to examine price adjustment provisions and actual price adjustment behavior in long-term coal contracts. The average duration of the contracts in my sample (adjusted for truncation bias) is about fifteen years. How does one go about setting prices in advance for deliveries over such a long period of time which will not lead to ex post adaptation problems? Since long-term contracts are used extensively to govern transactions between coal suppliers and electric utilities the parties have presumably found a way to adjust prices over time that does not seriously distort the incentives of either party to perform as promised under the agreement. How well have these contractual provisions worked? I found that the vast majority of contracts rely on a pricing *formula* that adjusts prices for changes in input prices and certain other contingencies. I argue that this approach is designed to track changes in prevailing market conditions arising from general changes in the costs of producing coal, although they can do so only imperfectly. These provisions are likely to track changes in prevailing market conditions due to market demand shocks, compared to cost-side shocks, much less well.

The paper examines the determinants of the initial base prices in these contracts as well as the subsequent prices that are observed for deliveries in 1979, 1980, and 1981. By looking at the prices charged in 1979, 1980, and 1981 pursuant to contracts written in many different years, we can determine whether there are any significant systematic ex post price rigidities associated with the economic conditions prevailing at the time the contracts were written. Base prices (controlling for coal characteristics and production region) appear generally to reflect prevailing average market prices at the time the contract is written. There is no evidence of hostages or front-loading of payments for other reasons. The basic structure of the price equation is similar for subsequent transactions prices to that observed for base prices. Transactions prices pursuant to these long-term contracts move along reasonably closely with changes in prevailing market conditions during the period studied. However, I do find some price rigidities that are associated with differences in economic conditions at the time the contracts were signed. At least for the period studied, the rigidities are not so large, *on average*, as to suggest that they would lead to serious performance failures.[30] Some contracts do very poorly at tracking prevailing market conditions, however, and serious contracting disputes have arisen as a result.

4. CONCLUSIONS

We have come a long way since 1937. The nature of the firm and the nature of market relationships between firms has attracted a lot of recent theoretical interest. Relationship-specific investments, asymmetric information, and the costs of writing, monitoring, and enforcing contractual relationships have emerged as the key factors explaining "nonstandard" vertical relationships. The development of more specific theories of the firm and contractual relationships between firms is now being followed by more and more empirical work. This work generally provides strong empirical support for the importance of transactions cost considerations, especially the importance of asset specificity, in explaining variations in vertical relationships. Clearly there is more theoretical and empirical work to be done. I hope that theoretical and empirical work will continue to have a closer relationship to one another in this area than is typical in industrial organization. Both the theoretical and empirical analysis can go forward with greater assurance that there is indeed a pot of gold to be found at the end of the rainbow if we continue to look for it.

NOTES

1. This concern was shared by my colleague Stanley Fischer (1977).

2. I think that I am the anonymous colleague expressing some difficulty with the exposition whom Williamson (1975:xii) quotes in the preface. Alas, my correspondence files are not nearly as complete as are Professor Coase's.

3. It should be recalled that the full title of Williamson's 1975 book is *Markets and Hierarchies: Analysis and Antitrust Implications*.

4. As Demsetz (57, n. 7) recognizes, the franchise bidding approach can be traced back

at least to a paper by Chadwick published in 1859. Municipal franchising and regulation also characterized the provision of electricity, telephone, and gas service in the United States prior to the rapid diffusion of state commission regulation after 1907.

5. Indeed, two recent MIT Ph.D. theses have examined the performance of cable TV franchising using comprehensive data bases (Prager and Zupan). They find that, with some exceptions, reneging on franchise agreements and renegotiation problems at the refranchising stage have not been a serious problem in practice. There are other inefficiencies associated with franchise bidding for cable TV franchises, however.

6. While Goldberg's paper appeared after Williamson's, I believe that the two papers were written at about the same time.

7. Coase's lectures indicate that he identified asset specificity as being of potential importance in an unpublished letter more than forty years earlier. He also studied the GM/Fisher Body relationship at that time. His third lecture suggests, however, that he no longer believes that asset specificity is of great importance for understanding vertical integration and long-term contracts.

8. *Markets and Hierarchies* focuses much more on ex ante and ex post information asymmetries, although the opportunism problem is developed clearly in this context. Long-lived assets specific to the relationship play a more important role in Williamson's 1976 paper.

9. Uncertainty is treated in the text (253–54), but not in the tables and figures included in the paper.

10. I have not emphasized the role of reputation in this discussion, but it plays a role in both Williamson's and Klein's work.

11. This never concerned me too much since so much of what passes as "theory" is little more than toy models with no obvious value in explaining real economic phenomena. Really good theory is too rare but is of fundamental importance to our understanding of these phenomena.

12. It should be emphasized, however, the information asymmetries, moral hazard, and adverse selection problems were central to Williamson's discussion in *Markets and Hierarchies*.

13. See, for example, Hart and Holmstrom and the references they cite, and Grossman and Hart.

14. This is not to suggest that issues associated with horizontal integration and the internal organization of firms are not important. Transactions cost theory has just not developed as far in exploring these issues.

15. Let me emphasize that I do not believe that there is a single general theory that will ever provide a unified explanation of vertical integration and the structure of long-term contracts. There are a variety of economic characteristics that will influence firm decisions to organize and contract in different ways. At least some of the alternative theories need to be developed further so that they can yield hypotheses that can be subjected to empirical verification. Stigler, Warren-Boulton, and Perry offer theories that are not necessarily in conflict with transactions cost theories, but rather suggest that there are situations where vertical integration will be relied upon even in the absence of asset specificity and the like.

16. The implication of Fudenberg, Holmstrom, and Milgrom appears to be that if we assume that there is no private information (common knowledge), only the ability to contract on the specific investments is necessary. If the parties can contract on the specific investments and there is common knowledge, then the parties can rely on sequential renegotiation to determine prices and quantities at each point in time. These are strong assumptions.

17. Leaving these variables out may not be a serious problem in certain circumstances. See the approach taken by Masten (1984).

18. It is not my intention to survey all of the empirical evidence. I will discuss my favorite papers.

19. In fact this is not an all-or-nothing decision. Internal production *and* market procurement take place for many components. M-T choose an arbitrary cutoff value for the proportion of each component's supply that is attributable to internal production to define whether it is "integrated" or "not integrated" based on this cutoff value. The results are not sensitive to certain variations in the cutoff, however. It is not clear why a continuous variable measuring the proportion of production attributed to vertical integration was not used, perhaps in conjunction with a switching regressions technique.

20. M-T also group components into systems, using system-specific dummy variables, but have no prior expectations about which systems are characterized by greater asset specificity.

21. Two dummy variables are used. The first indicates whether the component is highly specific or not. The second indicates whether the component is standard or not. The "somewhat specialized" category is the comparison group.

22. Stuckey also examines Stigler's "life-cycle" theory of vertical integration and finds, at best, only limited support for it in the time series patterns of vertical integration.

23. I had not read his book until I prepared the present paper.

24. Many of these same problems emerge if we rely on a cross-section of *firms* drawn from different industries.

25. He also examines the relationship between the ownership of gathering lines which are durable, site-specific investments, and potential ex post bargaining problems associated with asset specificity.

26. Masten and Crocker (1985) examine take-or-pay provisions in post–regulatory era natural gas contracts. They obtain results similar to those reported by Mulhern but also find that price regulation has a significant effect on variations in take-or-pay obligations.

27. In theory of course regulators could design the terms and conditions of suitable contracts to match variations in transactional characteristics, but this is asking much more of regulators than even the best-intentioned are likely to be able to deliver.

28. In my work on coal supply relationships I have found that utilities requiring specialized rail cars to transport coal purchased under a long-term contract sometimes own or lease the cars themselves, rather than relying on the railroad to provide them on an as-available basis.

29. Crocker and Masten (1986) have written a related paper that looks at the duration of natural gas contracts, making use of the data in Masten and Crocker (1985). My paper emphasizes the benefits of long-term contracts. Their paper tries to capture both the costs and the benefits.

30. Remember the parties always can rely on vertical integration or spot market transactions (or very short contracts), if performance problems are likely to be associated with long-term contracts. Further research on pricing behavior when coal markets became very soft in 1984 and 1985 is ongoing.

REFERENCES

Anderson, Erin, and David Schmittlein. 1984. "Integration of the Sales Force: An Empirical Examination," 15 *Rand Journal of Economics* 385.

Bradburd, Ralph E., and Richard Caves. 1986. "Transactional Influences on the Adjustment of Industries' Prices and Outputs." Unpublished mimeo.

Coase, Ronald H. 1937. "The Nature of the Firm," 4 *Economica* n.s. 386.

_____. 1972. "Industrial Organization: A Proposal for Research." In V. R. Fuchs, ed., *Policy Issues and Research Opportunities in Industrial Organization*. New York: National Bureau of Economic Research.

Crocker, Keith J., and Scott E. Masten. 1986. "Mitigating Contractual Hazards: Unilateral Options and Contract Length," Working paper no. 449, Graduate School of Business Administration, University of Michigan, March 1986 (revised June 1986, April 1987).

Demsetz, Harold. 1968. "Why Regulate Utilities," 11 *Journal of Law and Economics* 55.

Fischer, Stanley. 1977. "Long-term Contracting, Sticky Prices, and Monetary Policy: Comment," 3 *Journal of Monetary Economics* 317.

Fudenberg, Drew, Bengt Holmstrom, and Paul Milgrom. 1987. "Short-term Contracts and Long-term Agency Relationships." Unpublished mimeo.

Gallick, Edward C. 1984. "Exclusive Dealing and Vertical Integration: The Efficiency of Contracts in the Tuna Industry." Washington, D.C.: Bureau of Economics Staff Report, U.S. Federal Trade Commission.

Goldberg, Victor. 1976. "Regulation and Administered Contracts," 7 *Bell Journal of Economics* 426.

_____, and John R. Erickson. 1987. "Quantity and Price Adjustment in Long-term Contracts: A Case Study of Petroleum Coke," 30 *Journal of Law and Economics* 369.

Grossman, Sanford J., and Oliver D. Hart. 1986. "The Costs and Benefits of Ownership: A Theory of Vertical Integration," 76 *Journal of Political Economy* 691.

Hart, Oliver, and Bengt Holmstrom. 1987. "The Theory of Contracts." In T. Bewley, ed., *Advances in Economic Theory*, Fifth World Congress. Cambridge: Cambridge University Press.

Joskow, Paul L. 1985. "Vertical Integration and Long-term Contracts: The Case of Coal-Burning Electric Generating Plants," 1 *Journal of Law, Economics, and Organization* 33.

_____. 1986. "Competition and Deregulation in the Electric Power Industry." Paper presented to the International Association for Energy Economists, October 1986.

_____. 1987. "Contract Duration and Transactions Specific Investment: Empirical Evidence from Coal Markets," 77 *American Economic Review* 168.

_____. 1988. "Price Adjustment in Long-term Contracts: The Case of Coal." MIT Department of Economics Working paper no. 444, March 1987(b). 31 *Journal of Law and Economics* 47–83.

_____, and Richard Schmalensee. 1983. *Markets for Power: An Analysis of Electric Utility Deregulation*. Cambridge: MIT Press.

Klein, Benjamin, Robert A. Crawford, and Armen A. Alchian. 1978. "Vertical Integration, Appropriable Rents, and the Competitive Contracting Process," 21 *Journal of Law and Economics* 297.

Masten, Scott. 1984. "The Organization of Production: Evidence from the Aerospace Industry," 27 *Journal of Law and Economics* 403.

_____, and Keith J. Crocker. 1985. "Efficient Adaptation in Long-term Contracts: Take-or-Pay Provisions for Natural Gas," 75 *American Economic Review* 1083.

Monteverde, Kirk, and David Teece. 1982. "Supplier Switching Costs and Vertical Integration in the Automobile Industry," 13 *Bell Journal of Economics* 206.

Mulhern, J. Harold. 1986. "Complexity in Long-term Contracts: An Analysis of Natural Gas Contract Provisions," 2 *Journal of Law, Economics, and Organization* 105.

Palay, Thomas. 1984. "Comparative Institutional Economics: The Governance of Rail Freight Contracting," 13 *Journal of Legal Studies* 265.

———. 1985. "Avoiding Regulatory Constraints: Contracting Safeguards and the Role of Informal Agreements," 1 *Journal of Law, Economics, and Organization* 155–76.

Perry, Martin K. 1978. "Price Discrimination and Forward Integration," 9 *Bell Journal of Economics* 209.

Prager, Robin Ann. 1986. "Firm Behavior in Franchise Monopoly Markets: The Case of Cable Television." Unpublished Ph.D. dissertation, MIT.

Scherer, F. M. 1980. *Industrial Market Structure and Economic Performance*. Chicago: Rand McNally.

Schmalensee, Richard. 1987. "Interindustry Studies of Structure and Performance." Sloan School of Management, Working paper no. 1874–87.

Stigler, George. 1951. "The Division of Labor Is Limited by the Extent of the Market," 59 *Journal of Political Economy* 185.

Stuckey, John. 1983. *Vertical Integration and Joint Ventures in the Aluminum Industry*. Cambridge: Harvard University Press.

Warren-Boulton, Frederick R. 1967. "Vertical Control with Variable Proportions," 75 *Journal of Political Economy* 123.

Williamson, Oliver. 1975. *Markets and Hierarchies: Analysis and Antitrust Implications*. New York: Free Press.

———. 1976. "Franchise Bidding for Natural Monopolies—In General and with Regard to CATV," 7 *Bell Journal of Economics* 73.

———. 1979. "Transactions-Cost Economics: The Governance of Contractual Relations," 22 *Journal of Law and Economics* 3.

———. 1983. "Credible Commitments: Using Hostages to Support Exchange," 73 *American Economic Review* 519.

———. 1985. *The Economic Institutions of Capitalism*. New York: Free Press.

Zupan, Mark. 1987. "Three Essays on the Efficacy of Cable Franchise Bidding Schemes." Unpublished Ph.D. dissertation, MIT.

9

Incomplete Contracts
and the Theory of the Firm

OLIVER D. HART

1. INTRODUCTION

"The Nature of the Firm" (together with Coase's later paper, "The Problem of Social Cost") has had an enormous influence on the development of research in the theory of organization, even if for a long time it was, in Coase's words, "much cited and little used." The situation has changed in the last ten to fifteen years, however, with the publication of a number of contributions which have refined and extended Coase's ideas about the firm. My plan in this paper is to reflect on recent developments and to offer a perspective on where the field stands and also where it may be going. I will begin with a brief summary of the main ideas and issues as they have grown out of Coase's work.[1] I will then discuss how the firm as an institution can be thought of as arising from the incompleteness of contracts and the need to allocate residual control rights. Finally, I will return to a comparison of this view of the firm with others that have been advanced in the literature.

2. A BRIEF SUMMARY OF THE MAIN IDEAS

As many people have noted, standard neoclassical theory treats the firm as a black box. The firm is taken as given; no attention is paid to how it came into existence, the nature of its internal organization, or whether anything would change if two firms merged and called themselves a single firm.

Given this background, Coase's 1937 paper was a very refreshing development. Coase began to deal with the very questions that neoclassical theory had ignored. What is a firm? Where do the boundaries of one firm cease and those of another firm begin? What are the costs and benefits of integration? As is well known, Coase's answers are based on the idea that the benefit from firm A merging with firm B comes from the fact that the manager of firm A will have authority over the manager of firm B. That is, if B is an employee of A, A can (within limits) give B

138

orders. In contrast, if firms *A* and *B* are separate entities, manager *A* must resort to persuading or enticing *B* to do what he wants by the use of prices (more generally, via a contract). In other words, integration effectively shifts the terms of the relationship from a price mode to a quantity mode. Coase's point is that in certain circumstances the quantity mode may be more efficient. Under these conditions, integration will occur.[2]

Put this way, the argument seems symmetric: we would also expect there to be cases where the quantity mode is *less* efficient than the price mode. That is, integration might be *un*desirable. Interestingly, however, Coase did not take this route. Rather he argued that the costs of integration come from increased bureaucracy and also from the greater likelihood of managerial error. That is, managers of large firms are simply likely to be less efficient than managers of small firms.

Perhaps one of the reasons it took time for Coase's work to catch on is that it is not at all obvious how to formalize or operationalize the benefits from being in the quantity mode. Moreover, as Alchian and Demsetz (1972) have pointed out, the quantity mode is not peculiar to transactions within the firm. In particular, given that most employment contracts are "at will," usually the most extreme penalty a boss can impose on an employee is to fire him. However, this option may also be available in an ordinary contractual relationship. For example, as Alchian and Demsetz (1972) note, a customer who decides to abandon his grocer and shop elsewhere may be interpreted to have "fired" him. That is, it is not clear that the benefit of moving to the quantity mode can only be achieved through integration.[3]

The work which followed Coase has taken a rather different approach to the benefits of integration. A major development, due to Williamson (1975, 1979, 1985) and Klein, Crawford, and Alchian (1978), is the idea that integration is likely to be important in situations where relationship-specific investments are large, that is, where the investments the parties make have a much greater use inside the relationship than outside.[4] Once such a relationship-specific investments have been made the parties are (at least partially) "locked in," and hence they are at each other's mercy and opportunistic behavior may rule.[5] Such behavior may cause an ex post division of surplus which does not appropriately reflect ex ante investment decisions, and, as a consequence, these decisions may be distorted. In the eyes of Williamson and Klein, Crawford, and Alchian, a benefit of integration is that the scope for opportunistic behavior may be reduced. For example, the ability of the supplier of an input to "hold up" a would-be purchaser may be lessened if the supplier is part of the same enterprise. This may be either because the buyer has greater control over the seller (for example, because of the shift to Coase's quantity mode) or because he is more informed about the seller's behavior; or because the seller's monetary incentives are different under integration.[6] Like Coase, however, Williamson and Klein, Crawford, and Alchian do not use the same theory to explain the costs of integration.[7] Rather the costs of integration are ascribed by Williamson to increased bureaucracy and are not discussed at any length by Klein, Crawford, and Alchian.

3. INCOMPLETE CONTRACTS AND RESIDUAL RIGHTS OF CONTROL

The work of Coase, Williamson, and Klein, Crawford, and Alchian is based on the idea that there are transaction costs of writing contracts. In a world where it was costless to think about, plan for, and write down provisions for future events, parties engaged in trade would write a "comprehensive" contract which specifies precisely what each of their obligations is in every conceivable state of the world. Under these conditions, there would never be any reason for the parties to modify or update their contract since everything would be anticipated and planned for in advance. Nor would any disputes ever occur since an outsider (for instance, a court) could (costlessly) determine whether one of the parties has been in breach of contract and impose an appropriate penalty.

In such a world, it is hard to see what the benefits (or costs) of integration could be. Take, for example, Coase's distinction between the price mode and the quantity mode. If there are no transaction costs, the quantity mode can be achieved directly by a contract: B can simply agree to take orders from A (within limits perhaps), while remaining a separate firm. There is no need for A to buy up B or make manager B an employee to achieve this outcome. Equally the price mode can be achieved, should this be desirable, even when A and B are part of the same firm (the parties can simply agree that A *cannot* give B orders). The general point is that with zero transaction costs, any rights that ownership may confer can be undone through a contract. Hence an optimal outcome can be achieved whether A and B are separate firms or part of the same firm: in an important sense, ownership is simply irrelevant.

Now it could, of course, be argued that ownership is a shorthand for a certain sort of contractual arrangement, and the fact that the same outcome can be achieved without ownership is just a matter of semantics. This argument is sometimes made for the case where it is efficient for moral hazard reasons, say, for one party to receive the residual income stream from an asset; it seems natural to call that person the asset owner. The problem with this point of view is that only rarely would we expect one person to receive 100 percent of a profit stream. In general we would predict that the parties will engage in profit sharing. But this means that this approach predicts *joint* ownership for most assets — a conclusion which is not only too vague to be useful but is also unrealistic.

Note that the argument that ownership is irrelevant under comprehensive contracting is robust to the introduction of asymmetric information, for example, in the form of moral hazard or adverse selection. Asymmetric information leads to departures from Arrow-Debreu contingent contracting, but it does not provide a role for ownership unless the limits to contracting are themselves sensitive to who owns what. In particular, under asymmetric information optimal contracts will still be "complete" in the sense that each party's obligations are fully specified in all eventualities; and hence it will be possible for any rights that ownership confers again to be contracted away. For example, if a seller S of an input has private information about his costs, then an optimal contract between S and a purchaser P will make the quantity of input to be traded and the price to be paid a function of

S's announced costs. In order to encourage truth-telling by S, the contract will typically involve some production inefficiency, that is, it will be "second-best."[8] However, the point is that this production inefficiency will be present whether S and P are separate firms or are integrated — it is a function of the asymmetry of information, not of who owns what. The only exception to this is if the asymmetry of information itself depends on the ownership structure; that is, a change in ownership affects what contingencies can be included in the contract and what cannot. However, it is a strong assumption to suppose that the simple act of transferring the legal title of S's assets to P allows P to observe S's costs, which he could not observe as a separate entity.[9]

The above comments cover situations where transaction costs are zero and the parties can write a comprehensive contract. As Coase, Williamson, and Klein, Crawford, and Alchian have emphasized, however, this is very unrealistic: in practice, transaction costs are pervasive and large. A consequence of the presence of such costs is that the parties to a relationship will *not* write a contract that anticipates all the events that may occur and the various actions that are appropriate in these events. Rather they will write a contract that is *incomplete*, in the sense that it contains gaps or missing provisions; that is, the contract will specify some actions the parties must take but not others; it will mention what should happen in some states of the world, but not in others. A result of this incompleteness is that events will occur which make it desirable for the parties to act differently from the way specified in the contract.[10] As a consequence the parties will want to *revise* the contract. In addition the parties may sometimes disagree about what the contract really means; disputes may occur and third parties may be brought in to resolve them.

Incompleteness of contracts opens the door to a theory of ownership. In particular, when contracts are incomplete, it is no longer the case that any rights conferred by ownership can necessarily be contracted away — except by undoing the ownership itself — since it may be impossible to describe these rights unambiguously. This observation, of course, does not tell us what the rights of ownership *are*; however, it does reassure us that we may be able to develop a theory where ownership plays a non-trivial role.

In order to understand what the rights of ownership might be, it is useful to introduce the notion of *residual rights of control*. The idea is that if the contract the parties write is incomplete, there must be some mechanism by which the gaps are filled in as time passes. For example, suppose that I contract with you to supply a certain number of car bodies for my automobile manufacturing plant. Imagine that demand rises and I want to increase the quantity you supply. It seems reasonable that to the extent that the contract was silent about this (the increase in demand was a state that we did not plan for or at least did not explicitly include in the contract), I need to get your agreement. That is, the status quo point in any contract renegotiation will be where you do *not* provide the extra supply; in other words you possess the residual rights of control in this case. As another example, suppose that you rent my house, and that a friend of yours moves in who hates the color of the bedroom. The decision to repaint would presumably be mine, not yours. That is, you would have to persuade me to repaint the room; you could not force me to do so (so in this example, I possess the residual rights of control). On the other hand, if the paint began to peel or an effluent of a neighboring factory reacted with it, it would probably be within your rights to insist that I repaint the room.

These examples suggest that residual rights of control may be closely connected to the issue of *ownership*. The reason I cannot force you to supply extra car bodies is that the body factory belongs to you and it is up to you how to operate it, except to the extent that you have explicitly contracted certain rights away. If I owned your body factory as well as my automobile plant, the story might well be different: I could insist that the extra bodies be supplied since I can decide how your factory is used. (Of course, you could quit, but I could then hire another manager to run the factory.) In the case of the house, the reason that you need to persuade me to repaint the room that is unattractive to your friend is because it is my house, not yours. However, as the last example shows, ownership is not absolute: sometimes a non-owner has some residual rights of control (these rights might be his under common or statutory law).

The idea that ownership is linked with residual rights of control forms the basis of a theory of integration developed in Grossman and Hart (1986). In fact this paper identifies ownership of an asset with the possession of residual rights of control over that asset, that is, the rights to use the asset in any way except to the extent that specific rights have been given away in an initial contract. The paper argues that in a world of incomplete contracts there is an optimal allocation of residual rights of control; to the extent that ownership goes together with residual rights of control, there is therefore an optimal allocation of asset ownership. The paper builds on the work of Williamson and Klein, Crawford, and Alchian in emphasizing asset specificity, quasi-rents, and hold-up problems as the key issues in an incomplete contracting relationship. That is, residual rights of control are important in influencing ex ante specific investment decisions. There are two important differences from previous work, however. First, the theory focuses on residual rights of control over *physical assets* (as opposed, say, to other aspects of the firm, such as employee decisions). Secondly, the theory uses the same concept of residual rights of control to explain the *costs* of integration as well as the benefits. That is, in contrast to (most) previous work, the disadvantages of integration are explained without resort to such notions as bureaucracy costs.

In the next section I will illustrate the way residual rights of control can explain asset ownership with a few examples. These examples are in the spirit of the model presented in Grossman and Hart (1986); however, they are in some respects simpler (although they are also special). Then in section 5 I will return to a comparison of the residual rights of control approach with others in the literature.

4. EXAMPLES OF THE COSTS AND BENEFITS OF ASSET OWNERSHIP

4.1. Example 1: Ownership of a Single Asset

It is useful to begin with an extremely simple case. Consider a machine which requires one operator or manager. If operated appropriately, the machine generates a perfectly certain profit. Assume that the operations of the machine impose no externality on anyone else—either positive or negative. Also suppose there are no other inputs apart from managerial effort. The question is, who should own the machine?

The answer seems intuitively clear: the manager should own the machine (assuming he can afford to buy it). While this seems trivial, it is not. Furthermore, any theory of integration *must* be able to explain this, since a simpler example of the advantages of ownership would be hard to find.

Note that the question being asked is *not* (at least directly) who should own the machine's profit stream. Standard moral hazard ideas tell us that the operator's incentives will be dulled if he does not earn the return from his activities. There is a distinction between asset ownership and return ownership, however. For example, it is frequently the case that workers or managers are put on an incentive scheme, so that they have an interest in their firm's performance. This does not automatically make them *owners* of the firm, however. (The net income of the CEO of GM is sensitive to GM's performance, but that does not make him a significant owner of GM.) In the case in question, for example, the machine could belong to an outsider who hires the manager as his employee and gives him a salary compensation package equal to the firm's profit. Would such an arrangement be as good as the one where the manager is the owner?

To see that it might not be, consider a two-period model where the manager must choose an action x at date 0 (which might represent an investment or effort level), and let this yield a total return $B(x)$ at date 1. Assume that the manager incurs a private cost (for example, a disutility of effort) equal to x. The action x is supposed to be observed only by the manager (so this is a classic case of moral hazard). We shall take $B(x)$ to be deterministic, although the analysis would easily generalize to the case where it is a random variable as long as the manager is risk neutral.[11]

I will suppose that there is some action involving the asset which can be taken ex post at date 1 but which cannot be specified in the initial contract, for instance, because it is too complex.[12] Because of this incompleteness, residual rights of control will be important. It will not be necessary to model the ex post action in detail; it will be enough to assume that the right to control the asset in an unspecified way allows one to "cream off" a fraction $(1-\lambda)$ of the return $B(x)$, where $0 < \lambda < 1$.[13] An example of this would be where the machine is used in such a way as to benefit some other activity the controller is engaged in. For instance, if the controller is an outsider, he may employ the machine to increase the profit of another firm he owns; this other firm might be in a related business or might be an upstream supplier or downstream purchaser of the original asset's output.[14]

I will assume that the creamed-off component of return, $(1-\lambda) B(x)$, is *not* verifiable, but that the remaining return $\lambda B(x)$ *is*, so that contracts can be written on the latter. Finally, I assume that the manager has access to financial resources which he can use to boost the machine's profit on a dollar-for-dollar basis if this should suit him (and this boosting cannot be verified; moreover, no part of this boosted profit is subject to creaming off by the asset owner). In equilibrium, no boosting will occur but the possibility of it will put constraints on the form of the contract.

We have set things up so that the only variable that the parties can contract on is the asset's verifiable profit, $\pi = \lambda B(x)$. Thus a contract consists simply of a division rule $I = I(\pi)$, where I is the operator's remuneration as a function of π. We now argue that in the case where the manager owns the machine, an optimal contract can be devised to achieve the first-best, but this is impossible if an outsider owns the machine.

The first-best allocation consists of a level of x, x^* say, which maximizes social surplus, $B(x) - x$. If the manager owns the machine, this value x^* can be induced by giving the manager at the margin 100 percent of the firm's profit stream, that is, $I(\pi) = \pi - E = \lambda B(x) - E$, where E can be interpreted as an entry fee. Since the manager, as owner, receives the creamed-off portion of profit $(1-\lambda)B(x)$, his total return net of effort cost is

$$R = \lambda B(x) - E + (1-\lambda)B(x) - x = B(x) - E - x.$$

Maximization of this therefore yields the solution $x = x^*$.[15]

Consider next the case where an outsider owns the machine and receives the unverifiable component $(1-\lambda)B(x)$. Then the manager will maximize:

$$I(\pi) - x = I(\lambda B(x)) - x.$$

The first order conditions for this are

$$I'\lambda B'(x) = 1. \tag{1}$$

Note, however, that $I' \leq 1$, since otherwise the manager will have an incentive to boost profit by pumping in extra financial resources (if $I' > 1$, for each dollar that π goes up, the manager's income will increase by more than a dollar). Hence (1) implies that $B'(x) \geq 1/\lambda > 1$, from which it follows that $x = x^*$ cannot be sustained (since $B'(x^*) = 1$). The conclusion is that it is impossible to achieve the first-best in the case where there is outside ownership.[16]

The moral of this story is that in an externality-free world the person whose actions determine the profitability of an asset (assuming there is one such person) should also own the asset. Giving this person entitlement to the asset's profit stream will not be enough since an outside owner may be able to divert some of the asset's return for his own uses, thus dulling the manager's incentives. Note again the importance of contractual incompleteness for this conclusion.[17] Under complete contracting, it would be possible to achieve the first-best even with outside ownership by including a clause in the contract which explicitly rules out any profit-diverting uses of the asset.[18]

4.2. Example 2: Complementary Activities

The case of an asset operated in a vacuum is obviously extreme. We consider now how our results change if we introduce a second asset, whose activities are complementary with those of the first. Examples might be the furniture department and hardware department in a department store, the compact car division and subcompact car division of an automobile manufacturer, and (to take a far-fetched but nonetheless illuminating example suggested by Klein, Crawford, and Alchian, 1978) the windows of the building and the rest of the building.

Let the return on asset 1's activities be $B_1(x,y)$ and that on asset 2's activities be $B_2(y)$, where x,y represent the date 0 actions (for example, effort levels or investment decisions) of the operators of assets 1 and 2 respectively. The presence of y in B_1 captures the idea of an externality: asset 1's return depends on manager 2's action as well as manager 1's (in this sense, the activities are complementary).[19]

As in example 1, we assume that the owner of each asset can siphon off a fraction $(1-\lambda)$ of the asset's return for himself in the form of unverifiable profit. Therefore the verifiable profits from the activities are given by

$$\pi_1 = \lambda B_1(x,y),$$
$$\pi_2 = \lambda B_2(y). \tag{2}$$

As above, a contract consists of an agreed-upon division of the surplus, that is, a pair of functions $I_1(\pi_1,\pi_2)$, $I_2(\pi_1,\pi_2)$ where I_1, I_2 are the remunerations of the two operators and $I_1 + I_2 = \pi_1 + \pi_2$. We also make one additional assumption now: profit can be freely disposed of, that is, each manager can, if it suits him, reduce profit in an unverifiable way (the reduced profit is thrown away, however; it does not go to the manager). We continue to assume that a manager can boost profit (this applies to manager 2 as well as manager 1 now).[20]

We will be concerned with two situations. In the first, each manager owns his own asset (this can be interpreted as nonintegration). In the second, manager 2 owns both assets (which can be interpreted as integration).[21]

Under separate asset ownership, the net returns of the two managers are given by

$$R_1 = I_1(\pi_1,\pi_2) + (1-\lambda)B_1 - x$$
$$R_2 = I_2(\pi_1,\pi_2) + (1-\lambda)B_2 - y, \tag{3}$$

since the creamed-off profits go to the respective operators. On the other hand, if manager 2 owns both assets, he gets both sets of the creamed-off returns, and so we have

$$R_1 = I_1(\pi_1,\pi_2) - x,$$
$$R_2 = I_2(\pi_1,\pi_2) + (1-\lambda)B_1 + (1-\lambda)B_2 - y. \tag{4}$$

To illustrate that integration may be superior to nonintegration, consider the case where the marginal return to 1's effort is very small—in fact zero, that is, $B_1(x,y) = \gamma(y)$. The first-best allocation consists of $x = x^*$, $y = y^*$, where

x^* maximizes $\gamma(y) + B_2(y) - x$, i.e., $x^* = 0$
y^* maximizes $\gamma(y) + B_2(y) - y$.

This first-best allocation can be achieved in the case where manager 2 owns both assets by giving him (at the margin) 100 percent of both profit streams, that is, $I_2 = \pi_1 + \pi_2 - E$, $I_1 = E$. It is clear from (4) that 2 will then maximize $B_1 + B_2 - y$, which leads to the outcome $y = y^*$. On the other hand, manager 1 will set $x^* = 0$ since he gets no benefit from his asset.

In contrast, the first-best cannot be achieved under nonintegration. In this case, 2 maximizes:

$$I_2(\pi_1, \pi_2) + (1 - \lambda)B_2(y) = I_2(\lambda\gamma(y), \lambda B_2(y)) + (1 - \lambda)B_2(y) - y.$$

The first order conditions are:

$$\frac{\lambda\partial I_2}{\partial p_1}\gamma'(y) + \lambda\frac{\partial I_2}{\partial p_2}B'_2(y) + (1 - \lambda)B'_2(y) = 1. \tag{5}$$

We know, however, that

$$\frac{\partial I_1}{\partial \pi_1} \geq 0$$

and

$$\frac{\partial I_2}{\partial p_2} \leq 1$$

since manager 1 can freely dispose of profit and manager 2 can, if it suits him, boost profit. Therefore

$$\frac{\partial I_2}{\partial p_1} \equiv 1 - \frac{\partial I_1}{\partial p_1} \leq 1.$$

It follows that the left-hand side of (5) is strictly less than $\gamma'(y) + B'_2(y)$ and hence $y = y^*$ cannot be a solution of (5) (y^* satisfies $\gamma'(y) + B_2'(y) = 1$). We may conclude that $x = x^*$, $y = y^*$ cannot be implemented under nonintegration.[22/23]

The intuition behind this example is simple. Given the positive externality that manager 2 imposes on manager 1, manager 2 must be given a large fraction of asset 1's return in order to encourage him to exert appropriate effort. Providing 2 with a substantial part of 1's profit stream is not enough, however: without control of the activity (via ownership of the asset), the profit stream lacks "integrity."

The principle which operates here is exactly the same as in the first example. There manager 1's effort was important and so it was optimal for manager 1 to own asset 1, so that he could be assigned asset 1's return stream. In the present example, it is manager 2's effort that is important, and so he is made owner of asset 1 and is assigned its return stream. Note that the conclusion that 2 should own both assets generalizes to the case where 1's marginal product of effort is small (but positive), namely, $B_1(x,y) = \gamma(y) + \epsilon_1 \partial(x)$, $B_2(x,y) = \eta(y) + \epsilon_2 \zeta(x)$, where ϵ_1, ϵ_2 are small.

Of course, the example has been "fixed" to give the result. In general, 1's actions will be important as well as 2's. The choice between integration and noninte-gration then involves a trade-off: giving 2 ownership dulls 1's incentives, while giving 1 ownership dulls 2's incentives. Which arrangement is optimal will depend on the parameters. The main point of the analysis remains true, however: the set of feasible allocations under integration is different from that under nonintegration.

4.3. Example 3: A Vertical Relationship

So far we have considered the case of an asset operated in isolation and two assets whose operations are complementary (they might be regarded as "lateral" activi-ties). For our last example we consider a vertical relationship between the upstream supplier of an input and a downstream purchaser who uses this input in his own production process. As Williamson and Klein, Crawford, and Alchian have em-phasized, contractual problems may be particularly severe in such situations, and it is important to know whether integration will provide an appropriate form of relief.

Let the manager of asset U (the upstream firm) produce the input (one unit of it) which is then supplied to the manager of asset D (the downstream firm). As above we consider a two-period model. At date 0, the managers take actions, while, at date 1, trade occurs and profit is realized. We suppose that after date 0 the two managers are locked into each other, that is, neither has an alternative trading partner.

The issue which we will focus on is the quality of the input. We suppose that this is determined by manager U at date 0, and denote it by x; hence, assuming that delivery of the input occurs (which it always will in equilibrium), 2's return depends on x, as well as on manager D's effort y: $B = B(x,y)$. We now ignore U's effort cost but assume that U faces a variable (dollar) cost of production at date 1, $C(x)$, which is increasing in quality (higher quality might require more labor or raw materials). Hence in the absence of a contract the net returns of the managers are $B(x,y) - y$, and $-C(x)$, respectively.

We suppose that quality is observable only to manager U. Hence the contract price cannot be conditional on quality; nor can a take-it-or-leave-it offer be used (since manager D doesn't observe quality). The only way to induce U to produce high-quality input is to reward him according to D's ultimate return, B.

We will not need to assume in this example that the owner of asset D can siphon off a fraction $(1 - \lambda)$ of B for his own use. However, we *will* suppose that the owner of asset U has the ability to increase the variable costs attributable to asset U by an arbitrary amount and receive a fraction $0 < \mu < 1$ of those extra costs as an (unverifiable) private benefit. (In equilibrium, such cost manipulation will not occur, but, as in the previous examples, it constrains the form of the incentive contract.) For example, the owner may be able to use extra labor or raw materials to increase the profits of other projects he's engaged in rather than for the purpose of supplying manager D.[24]

An optimal contract rewards the two managers according to the verifiable returns $B(x,y)$, $C(x)$, that is, $I_U = I_U(B(x,y), C(x))$, $I_D = I_D(B(x,y), C(x))$, where $I_U + I_D*B(x,y) - C(x)$. The net returns of the two managers are then, respectively:

$$R_U = I_U(B(x,y), C(x)),$$
$$R_D = I_D(B(x,y), C(x)) - y. \tag{6}$$

Note that (6), which excludes the return from cost manipulation, applies whether the assets are integrated or not. There is an important difference between the two cases, however. If manager U owns asset U, then in equilibrium it must be that

$$\frac{\partial I_U}{\partial C} \leq -\mu$$

since manager U will have access to the cost manipulation technology (if

$$\frac{\partial I_U}{\partial C} > -\mu,$$

manager U can make himself better of by raising costs by η and increasing his income by

$$\mu\eta + \frac{\partial I_U}{\partial C}\eta).$$

On the other hand, if manager D owns asset U, the corresponding condition is

$$\frac{\partial I_D}{\partial C} \leq -\mu.$$

To see why ownership of both assets by D may be desirable, note that the first-best allocation consists of $x = x^*$, $y = y^*$, where

$$x^*, y^* \text{ maximize } B(x,y) - C(x) - y. \tag{7}$$

This can be achieved when D owns both assets by setting $I_U = 0$, $I_D = (B(x,y) - C(x))$, that is, U is recompensed for his variable costs and D receives the residual. The point is that this makes the objective function of manager D, $B(x,y) - C(x) - y$, while U is indifferent about his action; and thus, from (7), private and social incentives are aligned (U can be provided with a positive incentive to choose x^* by giving him a small fraction of net surplus, $B(x,y) - C(x)$).[25] Moreover,

$$\frac{\partial I_D}{\partial C} = -1 \leq -\mu,$$

that is, owner D will not have an incentive to manipulate costs.

However, such an arrangement is not feasible under nonintegration since $(\partial I_U / \partial C) = 0 > -\mu$, and so U *will* have an incentive to manipulate costs. To put it slightly differently, the first-order conditions corresponding to (6) are

$$\frac{\partial I_U}{\partial B} \frac{\partial B}{\partial x} + \frac{\partial I_U}{\partial C} C'(x) = 0,$$

$$\frac{\partial I_D}{\partial B} \frac{\partial B}{\partial y} = 1. \tag{8}$$

However, at $x = x^*$, $y = y^*$,

$$\frac{\partial B}{\partial x} = C'(x)$$

and

$$\frac{\partial B}{\partial y} = 1.$$

Hence, from (8),

$$\frac{\partial I_U}{\partial B} \equiv 1 - \frac{\partial I_D}{\partial B} = 0,$$

and so

$$\frac{\partial I_U}{\partial C} = 0;$$

in particular

$$\frac{\partial I_U}{\partial C} \leq -\mu$$

is not satisfied.

What drives this example is the following. Getting U to choose efficient quality is not a problem as long as U's production cost $C(x)$ can be assigned to D. Such an arrangement is possible when D owns both assets since U's costs can be transferred to D without distortion (their "integrity" is preserved). However, such a transfer is impossible under nonintegration since if manager D agrees to pay manager U's costs, manager U will have an incentive to manipulate his costs at D's expense.

The principle here is no different from that in examples 1 and 2. In all three cases it is desirable for incentive reasons for some part of the overall return stream to be borne by one party. This can be achieved by transferring one asset's returns to that party (in the first two examples an asset's profits were transferred; in the last example its costs were). We saw, however, that if the transfer is attempted without a corresponding change in ownership or control rights, it will not be fully effective: some of the returns will be diverted by the owner, and the incentive effect will be diminished. Thus to resolve incentive problems, it is necessary not only to assign the various parts of the return scheme to the different managers efficiently, but also to allocate ownership and control rights to support this assignment.

5. DISCUSSION

I want to consider now how the notion of residual rights of control explored in the last section fits in with other ideas in the literature. I will argue that it is broadly consistent with other theories and that it provides a useful organizing framework. In addition, as I have mentioned above, it allows the costs and benefits of ownership to be addressed within the same theory.

Before embarking on this, however, let me remark that any theory of ownership worth its salt should be consistent with the following basic observations:

A. If one individual is entirely responsible for the return of an asset, he should own it.

B. If there are increasing returns to management, so that one person can manage two firms, then these firms should have a common owner—that is, we should see integration.

C. If firm D wishes to be supplied by firm U, but firm D's business with U is only a small fraction of both U's and D's total business, then we would expect to see D sign a (long-term) contract with U rather than D buy U up or U buy D up. (We are assuming here that the spot market solution is infeasible.)

D. If an industry is declining we would expect to see firms merge so as to save on overheads (their headquarters, advertising division, and so on), rather than stay independent and share these overhead activities via a long-term contract.

The theory described in the last section (more generally, that set out in Grossman and Hart, 1986) is consistent with all of the above (by the way, I am not suggesting that other theories are *inconsistent* with these observations). Observation (A) has already been discussed with reference to example 1; (B) is just an extension of the idea that a person who is responsible for the return of an asset should own it; now one manager is responsible for the returns of two assets. To understand (C), note that, while there can be benefits from D owning U and thereby controlling its operations, there will also be costs in the form of reduced incentives for U; these costs may result from D's ability to divert some of U's earnings in other activities to himself. The larger U's outside business is, the bigger these costs are likely to be. Hence if D's activities with U are a small fraction of U's total operations, we would expect the costs to outweigh the benefits and nonintegration to be superior. The same argument applies to U owning D if D's activities with U are a small fraction of D's total operations.

In (D), we have in mind a situation where two firms initially set up, each with a headquarters (or advertising division or marketing division), but now in a shrinking market there is a need for only one headquarters. The parties could stay independent, with one renting headquarter services from the other. However, the owner of the headquarters would then be in a good position to hold up his contractual partner by supplying low-quality services (or failing to supply at all), and so the costs of this arrangement might be large. One way to reduce such opportunistic behavior is to transfer to the firm with the headquarters the profit of its partner, an arrangement which, as we saw in section 4, is more easily accomplished under integration than under nonintegration. Hence we would expect to see the firms take advantage of the cost savings by merging.

Having drawn out some implications of the residual rights of control approach, let us turn to its relationship to the rest of the literature. As noted earlier, one difference with previous work is the emphasis on how integration changes control over physical assets. This is in contrast to Coase's 1937 paper which focuses on the way integration changes an ordinary contractual relationship into one where an employee accepts the authority of an employer (within limits). Note that these approaches are not contradictory. Authority and residual rights of control are very close and there is no reason why our analysis of the costs and benefits of allocating residual rights of control could not be extended to cover human, as well as physical, assets. In fact, residual rights of control over employees and over physical assets are likely to be related. In particular, an important difference between an employment contract and a contract between independent parties is that the former allows the employer to retain the use of assets used by the employee in the event of a separation (he can hire another employee to operate them). In contrast, an independent contractor would typically own some of these assets and would be able to decide how they should be used if the relationship terminates.

The emphasis on control rights over assets also distinguishes the approach outlined here from that of Klein, Crawford, and Alchian, and Williamson. It would be impossible to do justice to the many writings of Williamson here. We can note, however, that for Williamson (and Klein, Crawford, and Alchian too), control over assets is only one aspect of the benefits of integration. Others which are important (see Williamson, 1975, 1979, 1985) include the ability of a party with authority to resolve disputes by fiat (as opposed to the parties going through litigation); the fact that asymmetries of information (which are a cause of contractual imperfection) can be reduced to the extent that it is easier for a firm to monitor or audit one of its subdivisions than to monitor or audit an independent contractor; and the fact that a merger between firms A and B is likely to change the atmosphere and feelings of loyalty; for instance, now that the employees of B owe their allegiance to the enterprise as a whole they may be less likely to engage in opportunistic behavior against A.

Note that the first of these ideas seems consistent with the notion of residual rights of control (over human assets), as does the second (having residual rights of control over physical assets—such as an employee's office, files, etc.—may allow an employer to obtain information that would otherwise be unavailable). The last, however, may involve other considerations.[26]

In more recent work, Williamson has argued that a further benefit of integration comes from the increased ability to control accounting procedures (see

Williamson, 1985, ch. 6). In particular, Williamson distinguishes between "high-powered" incentives provided by the market (in the form, for example, of a compensation system which rewards parties according to performance and makes each party the residual claimant to its profit stream) and "low-powered" incentives which are used more frequently within a firm (for example, in the form of a cost-plus arrangement). Williamson's point is that the use of these different incentive arrangements inside and outside the firm is not coincidental. In particular, it may be unattractive for a firm to sign a cost-plus arrangement with an independent supplier if the firm has no control over the supplier's accounting procedures. Equally a subsidiary may be unwilling to accept an arrangement in which it is compensated according to its profit given that it has little control over transfer prices. Note that example 3 in the last section is very much in the spirit of this idea, and in fact can be regarded as a formalization of it (for another formalization, see Holmstrom and Tirole, 1989). One difference is that in this example the ability to manipulate the accounts is traced to the residual rights of control over physical assets, rather than being taken as a primitive.

In chapter 5 of his 1985 book, Williamson explores another interesting aspect of ownership. He presents a number of examples showing that ownership of an asset will often be assigned in order to minimize "lock-in" effects. For instance, consider a buyer who must make an investment in order to be supplied by a seller. Suppose that this investment is transferable by the buyer in the sense that it can be used in the event that this buyer switches to another seller. However, suppose that the investment is useless to the seller in the event of a separation. Then Williamson argues (and produces supporting evidence) that the buyer will own the investment. The idea is that this returns the relationship to a spot market one where lock-in is absent and contracts work well. Note that this is also consistent with the broad perspective provided by the notion of residual rights of control (although more with the model of Grossman and Hart, 1986, than with the examples presented here). If the seller owns the investment, his incentive to provide good service to the buyer will be diminished since the buyer cannot easily switch to another seller (he's locked in). This will allow the seller in effect to "hold up" the buyer and will distort the buyer's investment decision in the manner described in section 4. In contrast, if the buyer owns the investment, his ability to switch (costlessly) will keep the seller "honest," and he will realize the full return from his activities. Thus the buyer's investment is protected and an efficient outcome can be achieved. (To tell this story properly would require a model of a repeated relationship where, for some reason, perhaps reputation, the supplier's performance today is positively related to performance tomorrow.)

Up to now, when we have referred to the assets of the firm, we have had in mind its *physical* assets. However, a firm may also have intangible assets, such as good will or reputation. A recent attempt to get at the role of these intangibles can be found in the work of Kreps. Kreps models the firm as a hierarchical structure where an individual who enters into an employment relationship with the firm accepts (within broad limits) the firm's right (as expressed by the employee's supervisor) to specify how the employee's time will be used as contingencies arise. This view is reminiscent of Coase's. The difference is that what makes the employee prepared to grant this authority to the firm is that the firm is long-lived and wishes to maintain its reputation for fair dealing; to put it in Krep's terms, the firm has an incentive to promote a particular "corporate culture."

Kreps, like Coase, stresses residual rights of control over employee actions rather than over physical assets as the key feature of ownership. One reason for doing this is that Kreps wants to explain how a firm can be a meaningful entity even if its ownership of physical capital is quite limited. The idea is that reputation can be a substitute for physical assets. Kreps in fact considers the extreme case where the firm consists entirely of reputational capital: the firm is neither more nor less than its reputation for dealing with unanticipated (or at least uncontracted for) contingencies.

The view of the firm as a repository of reputation has some appeal and may be relevant for understanding the nature of investment banking or law firms (or some economics departments for that matter), whose physical assets are hard to identify. However, a satisfactory formalization requires an explanation of how the firm's reputational capital is sustained and what is distinctive about the firm as a carrier of reputation. One problem is that, while the firm may be long-lived, individual managers are not (or at least they have finite lives). Hence even if we can explain how one manager builds up a reputation for decent (and honest and competent) behavior, it is far from clear what is the process by which a firm acquires a reputation for decency, that is, one set of decent managers is succeeded by another. Kreps argues that one way to understand this is to suppose that the characteristic of decency in a manager is associated with a desire also to choose a decent successor. This seems a strong assumption on which to base the theory, however. A second problem is that it is unclear why a new institution – the firm – needs to be created as a repository of reputation. That is, given that individuals engaged in standard contractual relationships acquire reputations, what is distinctive about a firm as a carrier of reputation? To put it somewhat differently, the view that a firm is solely a repository of reputation does not seem consistent with the fact that a firm's reputation is often not homogeneous – a firm can have units or subdivisions with different reputations, and the question is why these do not count as separate firms. (An example would be Stanford Business School and Stanford Economics Department – both subdivisions of Stanford University – which are arguably different repositories of reputation.)

In conclusion, while Krep's view of the firm is an interesting one, it leaves some questions unanswered. In particular, the issue of what it means for reputation to be embodied in an organization as opposed to an individual – and the extent to which an organization can be said to be characterized by its reputation – has still to be resolved.

6. CONCLUDING REMARKS

Coase's 1937 paper has unquestionably been a key development in the theory of organizations. As a result of his work and the more recent work of Williamson and others, we now have some answers to the question of what is a firm. In this paper I have argued that incomplete contracts and residual rights of control provide a useful organizing framework for thinking about the firm. Among other things, they permit the costs and benefits of integration to be examined in a unified manner; one does not require one theory to understand the benefits and another to understand the costs.

There is an enormous amount of work still to be done, however. A major limitation of the analysis presented here is that financial resource constraints are ignored and the owner of an asset is assumed to be a single individual. In particular, we supposed that if it is efficient for a manager to own an asset, he will purchase it; the possibility that he does not have the funds to do so was not considered. In reality, of course, managers or entrepreneurs often do not have the resources to finance projects themselves and they approach investors for assistance (another possibility is that they have the funds but do not wish to bear all the risk from the project themselves). External financing, however, introduces a further class of interested parties into the transaction: creditors or equity holders. This complicates the ownership puzzle greatly. Who should now have control rights in the firm? Should it be the firm's manager? Its investors? Some combination of the two? And if, say, equity holders have control rights, how are these to be exercised given that the shareholders may be a widely dispersed group?

Questions like these are just beginning to be addressed in the theoretical literature.[27] The answers should help us to gain a deeper understanding of the nature of organizations. There is every reason to be excited about the next fifty years.

NOTES

Research support from the National Science Foundation and the Center for Energy Policy Research at MIT is gratefully acknowledged. I would like to thank Bengt Holmstrom, Paul Joskow, and Jean Tirole for useful conversations. I have also benefited from seeing an early version of Holmstrom-Tirole (1989).

1. For an excellent review of the literature which has followed Coase, see Joskow. The reader is also referred to the recent general survey of vertical integration by Perry. One very important topic considered by Perry (but ignored here) is the role of integration in permitting the exploitation of monopoly power in upstream or downstream markets.

2. The discussion of price and quantity modes is suggestive of the later work of Weitzman, although the latter is not explicitly concerned with the structure of firms. See also Simon for an early formalization of the two modes.

3. Coase might well respond that the rights and duties that two parties have in an employment relation differ from those in a standard contractual relation by more than just the right to fire. This idea has been elaborated on recently by Masten, who argues that an employee has a duty of loyalty and a responsibility to disclose relevant information to an employer in a way that an independent contractor does not. Coase's current view appears to be that the emphasis on the employee relationship as the archetype of the firm is a *weakness* of his 1937 paper. In chapters 3–5, he argues that an essential aspect of the firm relationship is the multiplicity of contracts with different individuals who cooperate with each other.

4. Williamson has also emphasized the role of impacted information, bounded ration-

ality, and opportunism. It is now apparent from Coase's correspondence that Coase considered the importance of specific investments as early as 1932. However, Coase was not persuaded of their significance and did not mention specific investments in his 1937 paper.

5. The link between relationship-specific investments and opportunistic behavior is stressed in Goldberg.

6. Or it could even be that the seller's feelings of loyalty change.

7. An exception is Williamson (1985, ch. 6). This will be discussed at greater length below.

8. See, e.g., Hart and Holmstrom.

9. Two papers which do make this assumption are Arrow and Crocker. It should be noted that there may be indirect mechanisms by which change in ownership lead to changes in information structure; see Grossman and Hart (1986, n. 3) and below.

10. These events may have been unanticipated by the parties, or they may have been anticipated, but the parties may have been unable to provide for them in advance in a clear (and enforceable) manner.

11. $B(x)$ is assumed to have the usual neoclassical properties (e.g., strict concavity).

12. For more on this, see Grossman and Hart (1986).

13. We'll take λ to be deterministic, but again the analysis would easily generalize to the case where λ is stochastic.

14. An extreme case of an outsider creaming off profit at the expense of the manager is if he sells the machine and pockets the profit (to the extent that the original contract does not restrict this).

15. The equilibrium value of E will depend on the relative bargaining strength of the two parties at the time the contract is written, which in turn will depend on how competitive the ex ante market for contracts is. Our results are independent of how the ex ante surplus is divided, and so we will not need to deal with the determination of E in what follows.

16. The argument generalizes to the case where I is not differentiable. The manager chooses his effort level, x, and the amount by which to boost profit, u, so as to maximize $I(\lambda B(x) + u) - x - u$. The solution to this *cannot* be $x = x^*$. To see this note that if the manager reduces x from x^* to $(x^* - \epsilon)$, and increases u to keep $\lambda B(x) + u$ constant, then I will remain constant while, for ϵ small, $(x + u)$ will fall (since $(d/d\epsilon)(x + u) = -1 + \lambda B'(x^*) = -1 + \lambda < 0$); hence the manager is better off.

17. The conclusion of this example should be contrasted with the standard result in the property rights literature that in an externality-free world private property is efficient (see, e.g., Demsetz). What drives the latter result is the idea that only if a property is privately owned, will a user get the full return from his activities and hence take socially efficient actions. In this literature, efficiency is achieved *whoever* owns the property—as long as the property right is well-defined and not too widely dispersed (so that negotiation costs between different owners are avoided). In contrast the present model takes as given the idea that assets are privately owned, and asks what the optimal ex post allocation of assets is in a world of incomplete contracting. In spite of the difference between the approaches, the intellectual debt of the present study to the property rights literature should be apparent.

18. It is worth relating this example to the model presented in Grossman and Hart (1986). The creaming-off activity which the asset owner can engage in in the above example corresponds to the ex ante noncontractible, ex post contractible variable q in Grossman and Hart (1986). In that paper the owner of the asset did not generally have an incentive to choose q in an ex post efficient manner, and so it was supposed that the parties negotiated an efficient choice of q at date 1 via a new contract. In the present example (and those that follow), residual rights of control are always used efficiently by the person who exercises them

(these rights affect only the distribution of ex post surplus, not its size). There is therefore no role for any renegotiation or new contract at date 1.

19. A more general model would have a two-way externality.

20. The precise timing is that the managers choose their effort levels x, y and the amounts by which to boost profit u, v simultaneously and noncooperatively at date 0. At date 1, each is assumed to know the choice of his counterpart, and to have the chance to dispose of some of the profit on the asset he operates before π_1, π_2 are realized. The model is reminiscent of Alchian and Demsetz's theory of complementary production. See also Holmstrom.

21. There is also the possibility that manager 1 owns both assets. Given our specification, this case is uninteresting.

22. As before, we do not require the differentiability of I_1, I_2 to reach this conclusion. Manager 2 chooses y and the amount by which he boosts profit, v, to maximize $R_2 = I_2(\lambda B_1(x,y) + u, \lambda B_2(y) + v) + (1 - \lambda)B_2(y) - y - \text{Max}(v,0)$. (If v is negative, the manager is throwing away profit instead of adding to it.) Suppose $x = x^*$, $y = y^*$ is an equilibrium. Let manager 2 reduce y from $y^* + \Delta y$, where Δy is small and negative, and increase v by Δv to keep $\lambda B_2(y) + v$ constant. Then B_1 falls, but

$$
\begin{aligned}
\Delta R_2 &\geq I_2(\lambda B_1 + \lambda \Delta B_1 + u, \lambda B_2(y^*) + v) - I_2(\lambda B_1 + u, \lambda B_2(y^*) + v) \\
&\quad + (1 - \lambda)\Delta B_2 - \Delta y - \Delta v \\
&= \lambda \Delta B_1 - (I_1(\lambda B_1 + \lambda \Delta B_1 + u, \lambda B_2(y^*) + v) - I_1(\lambda B_1 + u, \lambda B_2(y^*) + v)) \\
&\quad + (1 - \lambda)\Delta B_2 - \Delta y - \Delta v \\
&\geq \lambda \Delta B_1 + (1 - \lambda)\Delta B_2 - \Delta y - \Delta v,
\end{aligned}
$$

since $I_1(\lambda B_1 + \lambda \Delta B_1 + u, \lambda B_2(y^*) + v) \leq I_1(\lambda B_1 + u, \lambda B_2(y^*) + v)$ (otherwise manager 1 would have disposed of ΔB_1 himself by reducing u). However, the last expression is approximated by $(\lambda \gamma'(y^*) + B'_2(y^*) - 1)\Delta y$ when Δy is small, and this is positive (since $\Delta y < 0$). Hence $\Delta R_2 > 0$, i.e., manager 2 is better off. This contradicts the hypothesis that $x = x^*$, $y = y^*$ is an equilibrium.

23. As in Holmstrom, a third party would be useful; in fact, the first-best could then be achieved under nonintegration by setting

$$
I_1 = \pi_1 + \frac{\pi_2}{\lambda}, \ I_2 = \frac{\pi_1}{\lambda} + \pi_2.
$$

Standard collusion arguments can be used to justify the absence of a third party, however.

24. The idea that the owner of an asset can manipulate the costs assigned to that asset has been emphasized by Williamson (1985, ch. 6). This idea is also the basis of the model of vertical integration in Holmstrom and Tirole.

25. This assumes that the objective function $B(x,y) - C(x) - y$ is concave.

26. Milgrom has argued that a further cost of integration is that an employee may spend too much time trying to influence an employer who has control over him. This effect can also be understood in terms of residual rights of control.

27. See, e.g., Aghion and Bolton, Grossman and Hart (1988), and Harris and Raviv. Note that giving managers or investors control is not the only possibility. Others include worker control (as in worker-managed firms) and consumer control (as in consumer cooperatives). For an interesting discussion of some of these possibilities, see Fama and Jensen, and Hansmann.

REFERENCES

Aghion, P., and P. Bolton. 1987. "An 'Incomplete Contracts' Approach to Bankruptcy and the Optimal Financial Structure of the Firm." Unpublished mimeo.

Alchian, A., and H. Demsetz. 1972. "Production, Information Costs and Economic Organization," 62 *American Economic Review* 777–95.

Arrow, K. J. 1975. "Vertical Integration and Communication," 6 *Bell Journal of Economics* 173–83.

Coase, R. 1937. "The Nature of the Firm," 4 *Economica* n.s. 386–405; repr. (1952) in G. Stigler and K. Boulding, eds., *Readings in Price Theory*. Homewood, Ill.: Richard D. Irwin.

———. 1960. "The Problem of Social Cost," 3 *Journal of Law and Economics* 1–44.

———. 1988. "The Nature of the Firm: Origin, Meaning, Influence," 4 *Journal of Law, Economics, and Organization* 3–47 [chapters 3–5 this volume].

Crocker, K. J. 1983. "Vertical Integration and the Strategic Use of Private Information," 14 *Bell Journal of Economics* 236–48.

Demsetz, H. 1967. "Toward a Theory of Property Rights," 57 *American Economic Review* 347–58.

Fama, E. F., and M. C. Jensen. 1983. "Separation of Ownership and Control," 26 *Journal of Law and Economics* 301–25.

Goldberg, V. 1976. "Regulation and Administered Contracts," 7 *Bell Journal of Economics* 426–48.

Grossman, S., and O. Hart. 1986. "The Costs and Benefits of Ownership: A Theory of Vertical and Lateral Integration," 94 *Journal of Political Economy* 691–719.

———. 1988. "One Share/One Vote and the Market for Corporate Control," 20 *Journal of Financial Economics* 175–202.

Hansmann, H. 1986. "A General Theory of Corporate Ownership." Unpublished mimeo, Yale University.

Harris, M., and A. Raviv. 1988. "Corporate Governance: Voting Rights and Majority Rules." Forthcoming, 20 *Journal of Financial Economics* 203–35.

Hart, O., and B. Holmstrom. 1987. "The Theory of Contracts." In T. Bewley, ed., *Advances in Economic Theory*, Fifth World Congress (Cambridge: Cambridge University Press).

Holmstrom, B. 1982. "Moral Hazard in Teams," 13 *Bell Journal of Economics* 324–40.

———, and J. Tirole. 1989. "The Theory of the Firm." In R. Schmalensee and R. Willig, eds., *Handbook of Industrial Organization*, forthcoming.

Joskow, P. 1985. "Vertical Integration and Long-Term Contracts," 1 *Journal of Law, Economics, and Organization* 33–80.

Klein, B., R. Crawford, and A. Alchian. 1978. "Vertical Integration, Appropriable Rents and the Competitive Contracting Process," 21 *Journal of Law and Economics* 297–326.

Kreps, D. 1984. "Corporate Culture and Economic Theory." Unpublished mimeo, Stanford University.

Masten, S. 1988. "A Legal Basis for the Firm," 4 *Journal of Law, Economics and Organization* [chapter 12 of this volume].

Milgrom, P. 1988. "Employment Contracts, Influence Activities, and Efficient Organization Design," 96 *Journal of Political Economy*, 42–60.

Perry, M. 1989. "Vertical Integration: Determinants and Effects." In R. Schmalensee and R. Willig, eds., *Handbook of Industrial Organization*, 183–255.

Simon, H. 1951. "A Formal Theory of the Employment Relation." 19 *Econometrica* 293–305.

Weitzman, M. 1974. "Prices versus Quantities," 41 *Review of Economic Studies* 477–91.

Williamson, O. 1975. *Markets and Hierarchies: Analysis and Antitrust Implications*. New York: Free Press.

———. 1979. "Transaction-Cost Economics: The Governance of Contractual Relations," 22 *Journal of Law and Economics* 3–61.

———. 1985. *The Economic Institutions of Capitalism*. New York: Free Press.

10

The Theory of the Firm Revisited

HAROLD DEMSETZ

From the birth of modern economics in 1776 to 1970, a span of almost 200 years, only two works seem to have been written about the theory of the firm that have altered the perspectives of the profession—Knight's *Risk, Uncertainty, and Profit* (1921) and Coase's "The Nature of the Firm" (1937). This neglect is attributable fundamentally to the preoccupation of economists with the price system; the study of the price system, characterized as it is by Marshall's representative firm and Walras's auctioneer, undermines serious consideration of the firm as a problem solving institution.

Coase's contribution is seminal for several reasons, but certainly for calling attention to the absence of a theory of the existence of the firm and to the importance (to this theory) of the fact that markets do not operate costlessly. Nonetheless, the theory of the firm is still incomplete and unclear in ways that are discussed in the middle part of this paper. A more complete theory of the firm must give greater weight to information cost than is given either in Coase's theory or in theories based on shirking and opportunism. This is discussed in the last part of this paper. Information cost figures importantly in transaction cost theory because information cost is an important component of transaction cost. It also figures importantly in Knight's risk-sharing and in agency theories of the firm. Its importance, however, is more fundamental than even these theories contemplate. It is useful therefore to begin this paper with a discussion of why the costless information that is assumed in the perfect competition model renders the model ineffective for studying the firm.

1. PERFECT DECENTRALIZATION

What parades as perfect competition is a model that has much to say about the price system, but little to say about competition or the organization of firms. This probably is due to its intellectual origins in the eighteenth-century debate between mercantilists and free traders. The debate was not about competition per se, and it certainly was not about the organization of the firm. It was about the proper scope of government in the economic affairs of England and Europe. Is central economic planning necessary to avoid chaotic economic conditions? Smith's answer, though preserving a limited role for the state, was persuasively in the negative. The subsequent conflict between "Smithian" and dissenting views led to a closer examination of the conditions necessary for the price system to function in a manner that substantiates Smith's arguments. Almost 200 years later, these conditions became formalized in the perfect competition model.

The intellectual achievement of this model is its complete abstraction from centralized control of the economy (Demsetz, 1982). What is modeled is not competition but extreme decentralization, and one can assess through its use whether extreme decentralization leads to chaotic resource allocation. The actors in this model maximize utility or wealth, and they do so in complete disregard of the decisions of others or, indeed, of even the existence of others. The same decisions follow from the same prices (and technology) whether or not anyone else is "out there" reacting to these parameters. If such impersonal maximizing behavior is competition, it is a very restricted variety. As Knight points out, doing better than others is not involved. No small amount of mischief has resulted from identifying this model with competition. Its appropriate name is perfect *decentralization*.

Perfect decentralization is realized theoretically through assumptions guaranteeing that authority, or command, plays no role in coordinating resources. The only parameters guiding choice are those that are given — tastes and technologies — and those that are determined impersonally on markets — prices. All parameters are beyond the control of any of the model's actors or institutions, so these assumptions effectively deprive authority of any role in allocation. They are fully justified by the theory's remarkable yield — a compact, coherent, subtle yet simple model for deducing the equilibrium consequences of extreme decentralization of resource ownership. The model is not only a powerful tool for understanding how prices guide decisions in a decentralized economy, but also for assessing the impact of exogenous changes in the parameters that are taken as given by the model. The impact of changes in tax rates or tariffs, or the consequences of price supports, can be deduced with comparative ease.

The model contributes little to our understanding of the workings of a command economy or of political processes that might be structured around authority. Its use in public finance, for example, is to understand how the price system "digests" taxes, not to understand the behavior of political parties. The model also casts little light on legal institutions. Exchange is viewed as taking place without regard to problems of theft or fraud. The property right system, so important to the functioning of the price system, is implicitly assumed to operate costlessly in matters of exchange. These abstractions are defensible because the real objective of the model is to study allocation in the absence of authority.

More to the point of this paper, the model sets the maximizing tasks of the firm in a context in which decisions are made with full and free knowledge of production possibilities and prices. The worldly roles of management, being to explore uncertain possibilities and to control resources consciously, where owners of resources have a penchant for pursuing their own interests, are not easily analyzed in a model in which knowledge is full and free. "Firm" in the theory of price is simply a rhetorical device adopted to facilitate discussion of the price system. Tasks normally to be expected of management are given only the most superficial, formal discussion; they are performed without error and costlessly, as if by a free and perfect computer. The real tasks of management, to devise or discover markets, products, and production techniques, and actively to manage the actions of employees, have no place in the perfect decentralization model because it assumes that all products, markets, production techniques, and prices are fully known at zero cost.

The only management task that seems to remain, and which is the focus of attention in the firm of traditional price theory, is the selection of profit-maximizing quantities of outputs and inputs. But, since the required information for doing this is also freely in hand, and the required calculations are costless to make, the model strips management of any meaningful productivity in the performance of even these tasks. The *cost of maximizing* is ignored or implicitly assumed to be zero. De facto, the resources that might be required to make maximizing decisions are treated as if they are not scarce.[1]

The sole (seeming) exception to this generalization is the rationale sometimes adopted to justify U-shaped average cost curves — diminishing returns to "entrepreneurial capacity." Entrepreneurial decision capacity is assumed to be limited and, therefore, costly. Because this capacity cannot be increased in proportion to increases in other inputs, cost curves ultimately turn up. However, this rationale is inconsistent with the model's assumptions, and it must be thought of as ad-hoc and exogenous. The model assumes free and full information about technical relationships and prices, thus making it difficult to rationalize why size of the firm should affect the owner/entrepreneur's decisionmaking capacities.[2]

The absence of substantive managed coordination is the sine qua non of the perfect decentralization model. This is its intellectual achievement and its source of strength in providing an understanding of the price system in a situation of extreme decentralization. It is its source of weakness in analyzing managed coordination. Clearly our understanding of firms can be improved by recognizing that management is a scarce resource employed in a world in which knowledge is incomplete and costly to obtain. This is explicitly recognized by Knight and Coase, and it is an important component of theories based on monitoring cost. Knight's analysis of the firm as an institution for efficient risk-sharing is based on risk aversion and costly knowledge; Coase's theory, known as the transaction cost theory of the firm, has as its central theme the relevance of costly managing and exchanging, which certainly contain important components of information cost.

2. THE TRANSACTION COST THEORY OF THE FIRM: SOME PROBLEMS

Before turning to a discussion of transaction cost theory, it is desirable to clarify terminology. Throughout this paper, I use transaction cost and management cost to refer to the costs of organizing resources, respectively, across markets and within firms. This accords with Coase's terminology. Recent writings on the theory of the firm sometimes use transaction cost to refer indiscriminately to organizational costs whether these arise from within the firm or across the market. This rather inept language forces textual discussion to make distinctions that would be better left to single-word labels. For example, Williamson frequently is forced to use phrases such as "the governance costs of internal organization exceed those of market organization." If the reader feels more comfortable with the newer terminology, although I cannot see why he should, he may translate my use of management and transaction costs for the governance costs, respectively, of organization achieved through firms and organization achieved across markets.

The early development of the transaction cost paradigm deals with the question of the existence of firms. Why do firms emerge as viable institutions when the perfect decentralization model amply demonstrates the allocative proficiency of the prices that emerge from impersonal markets? The question is asked and answered by Coase. Profit maximization (or efficiency) requires the substitution of firms for markets if the cost of using markets becomes large relative to the cost of managing. With compelling skill, he plays transaction cost against management cost to arrive at the formal condition that defines the extent of the firm. Equality between the marginal values of these costs, with respect to extending the tasks undertaken by the firm, defines a boundary on one side of which resources are managed within the firm and on the other side of which they are price-directed across markets. This comparison of transaction and management costs has become the focusing conceptualization of the transaction cost theory in all applications to the theory of the firm of which I am aware. Difficulties with it have gone unrecognized. Some of these are discussed next.

It is not so easy to distinguish purchase across a market from in-house production because in-house production involves the use of inputs that are *purchased*. Purchasing inputs (across markets) is substituted for purchasing goods that are more nearly complete (across markets). Hence, in-house production does not constitute a clear elimination of transaction cost. Similarly, purchasing goods from another firm, rather than producing these in-house, involves an implicit purchase of the management services undertaken by the other firm, so management cost is not eliminated by purchasing more nearly complete goods across markets. The correct question to ask if we remain within the Coasian framework is not whether management cost is more or less than transaction cost, but whether the sum of management and transaction cost incurred through in-house production is more or less than the sum of management and transaction cost incurred through purchase across markets, since either option entails expenditures on both cost categories.

This problem can be considered from a slightly different angle. If transaction cost is zero, yet management cost is positive, the transaction cost theory predicts the demise of the firm. But what can this mean? It can mean only that each individual acts as a firm, selling the output of his efforts to other individuals acting in similar fashion. But it is a mistaken belief of the transaction cost theory that this organization of production eliminates management cost. Management is not eliminated except, perhaps, by definition. It is functioning in more diffuse fashion across very many firms since management cost is incurred by each such individual as he plans and executes his production activities unless the meaning of management is restricted to dealing with others.

Moreover, the inference drawn, that all production is individualized if transaction cost is zero, is wrong. Whether individuals act independently, as just described, or cooperate through a multiperson firm, depends on the extent of scale economies to management. Multiperson firms are fully consistent with zero transaction cost if management is subject to scale economies. Zero transaction cost informs us only that these cooperating efforts will be organized with greater reliance on explicit negotiations than would be true if transaction cost were positive. Greater reliance on explicit negotiations may be of importance in some contexts, but not others. The difference between these organizing techniques does not carry substantive consequences if the cooperating individuals would perform essentially the same actions, with the same continuity of association over time, when they rely on a series of explicit transitory negotiations as when they rely on an "employment contract." In either case, the substance of the firm is reflected in the style of cooperative behavior that obtains. This may be the same with both organizing techniques.

Another informative way to view the problem is to recognize that the output of another firm can be purchased, or, in substitution for this, the other firm can be purchased. Purchasing the other firm is in-house production because it amounts to the purchase of the inputs required to produce the good. If transaction cost is assumed to be zero, while management cost is assumed to be positive, the answer given by transaction cost theory is to purchase the good, for it will cost something to manage in-house production. But there is a cost to managing the other firm when it stands independently, and this cost must factor into the price of the good that is to be purchased. This implicit management cost must be paid whether the firm or its output is purchased. Hence, the decision rests on a traditional consideration—is management subject to economies of scale? And, in the more realistic context in which management, transaction, and production costs are all assumed to be positive, the correct decision is reached by assessing whether merger or independent production yields the lowest unit cost, taking all these costs into account, over the relevant range of output. Transaction cost is relevant to this judgment, but so are the other costs.

The degree to which coordination is vertically decentralized is no longer simply a matter of transaction cost, or even of transaction cost relative to management cost. Firms purchase inputs when they can secure them more cheaply than by producing them. The cost of transacting is one element of the cost of purchasing from others, but only one. There are a variety of others, including what we ordinarily call production costs. A firm purchases an input if the price asked for the input, which reflects the production cost of prospective sellers, when added to the costs of transacting and transporting, comes to less than the cost of making the input in-house. Thus, to say that firms produce their own inputs when it is cheaper to do so is *not* equivalent to saying that firms will purchase from others if the cost of transacting is less than the cost of managing. The decision also hinges on the internal costs of production that burden the potential purchaser and supplier. Quite simply, it depends on a comparison of *all* the gains and losses that attach to external procurement relative to in-house production. Indeed, an increase in the cost of transacting leads not to a substitution of managed coordination for market coordination, as users of the transaction cost theory assert, but to a substitution of managed coordination within fewer, larger firms for managed coordination in more numerous, smaller firms. *Managed* transfer of inputs between the departments of (a now larger) firm is substituted for *managed* buying and selling. One type of management substitutes for another.

It is with respect to the above points that new terminology is especially confusing. By using governance or transaction costs to refer to all costs, whether they be within the firm or across markets, it is easy to assert that the newer writings utilizing transaction cost theory refer to the necessity for taking account of all costs (at least of all costs of organizing). If so, have we come to the point of saying that firms are used when they are cheaper, all costs considered, but not when markets are cheaper? I am quite prepared to accept this position for what it is worth, but my point is that it deprives transaction cost theory of any predictive content. Moreover, the broader considerations that occupy some of the newer writings about the firm put them at some distance from the transaction cost theory being discussed here. For example, Williamson uses the first part of his book about the institutions of capitalism to claim that its foundation lies in transaction cost considerations, but he fails to make substantive use of transaction cost throughout the remainder of the book. The only link to predictive content that remains is to be found in asset specificity, which he interprets to imply higher cost of using market governance of activities. But, as I argue later, and as Coase himself argues in the present lectures, the linkage is weak.

The emphasis that has been given to transaction cost (or that has been claimed to be given) dims our view of the full picture by implicitly assuming that all firms can produce goods or services equally well. "Implicitly," because the "other" firm is represented by the "market," and the market is treated as a perfect substitute in production for a firm. The only comparison sought is between the cost of transacting across this market and the cost of in-house managing. Since firms may not be perfect substitutes in the production of goods and services, and since they generally will not be if information cost is positive, it might be in the interest of a firm to produce its own inputs even if transaction costs were zero and management costs were positive. The production cost of other firms might simply be so high as to make in-house production superior to relying on these other firms. Or, if the production cost incurred by other firms is sufficiently low, it might serve the firm to purchase its inputs even though the cost of managing in-house production is zero.[3]

The confusion that exists in the literature derives from a hidden presumption that we are still guided by the perfect decentralization model, and that, in some respects, information remains full and free. Although information is treated as being costly for transaction or management control purposes, it is implicitly presumed to be free for production purposes. What one firm can produce, another can produce equally well, so the make-or-buy decision is not allowed to turn on differences in production cost. The only choice criterion that remains is that which compares transaction and in-house management costs, or, more correctly, the sum of these costs in each alternative offered by the make-or-buy choice. In this manner, the transaction cost theory of the firm ignores differences between firms when these lie outside the control function and discourages a search for such differences. Merged firms may be unable to duplicate the sum of what independently standing firms can accomplish for a variety of reasons, and many of these may be resistant to an analysis that is guided by the management and transaction cost categories. Productivity may be affected by considerations that are not plausibly included in these cost categories. Each firm is a bundle of commitments to technology, personnel, and methods, all contained and constrained by an insulating layer of information that is specific to the firm, and this bundle cannot be altered or imitated easily or quickly. The components of this bundle that are emphasized by transaction cost theory are important, but not exclusively so.

In a brief general critique of transaction cost theory, such as this, there is bound to be some oversimplification and some neglect of more subtle uses of the theory. Justice cannot be done to everyone who has used the theory in a broader sense than the interpretation given to it here. Nonetheless, the main emphasis and usage of transaction cost theory surely is to compare transaction and management costs so that conclusions may be drawn about organization. This emphasis has led to the neglect of other determinants of economic organization (one of which is discussed below) even though some of these are mentioned in passing, as it were, by those who make (or claim to make) transaction cost theory their paradigm of institutional organization. It is the paradigmatic use of transaction cost theory that is at issue here.[4]

Beyond considerations of production functions and the total cost of organization, the power of transaction cost theory turns on our ability to make it operational and to bring it to bear on substantive issues. This is not so easily done. It is difficult to discuss the relevance of transaction, management, and production costs without a clear distinction between these, and none is provided. One person phones another and directs him to purchase specific assets by a certain time if they can be acquired for less than a stipulated price. Is this activity transacting or managing? Knowing the answer would allow us to determine if an increase in the cost of this activity is expected to lead to the substitution of one firm for two or two for one. Since the call might be from an owner/manager of a firm to his employee in the purchasing department or from a customer/investor to the brokerage house whose services he purchases, it is hard to know whether we are dealing with a transaction or management cost until we *already know* whether we are discussing a firm or a market. This is true for the general case even though it might be possible in a specific instance, such as in the case of a tax on transactions, to be certain that we are dealing with only one of these costs. This makes it difficult to use the magnitude of "transaction" cost relative to "management" cost to predict how changed circumstances affect economic organization. The inherent difficulty is that the same organizing activities often characterize exchange *and* management.

Assuming that the problem of disentangling these costs is somehow resolved, there is still the problem of being able to stipulate the conditions that tend to make the relative magnitude of these costs high or low. This is necessary if we are to apply the theory of transacting positively to explain the structure of economic organization. Does an increase in the size of the market decrease transaction cost relative to management cost? Does dealing in services rather than products? Does dealing across national boundaries? Questions such as these must have answers about which we are confident if the transaction cost theory of the firm is to be applicable to the study of firms. As of now, we know very little about the forces that might influence the relative magnitude of these costs.

Klein, Crawford, and Alchian (1978), Riordan and Williamson (1985), and Williamson (1985) adopt the view that asset specificity is one such force. Asset specificity raises the prospect for opportunism. This heightened prospect is presumed to raise the cost of transacting. I am not sure that it costs (much) more to detail the terms of a contract when asset specificity is involved than when it is not. Even if it does, the change in the cost of contracting is unlikely to be very great. Asset specificity problems may be almost as easy to resolve through contract as through vertical integration, the latter being the option preferred by these authors. Truth is, it is not a predictably significant variation in transaction cost that motivates the vertical integration solution offered by these authors. It is the presumption that losses are greater if an agreement fails when asset specificity is involved than when it is not. This can be the case (although I am not sure that it is) even if transaction cost is unaffected by the presence or absence of asset specificity. It is simpler and less misleading to state that asset specificity increases the loss attendant on failure of agreement than that it increases the cost of transacting.

If we suppose that activities which increase transaction cost are distinguishable from those that increase management cost, there remains a problem of understanding just which issues are illuminated by using transaction cost theory. Consider the long-term contract that Coase identifies with the employment relationship. From Coase's perspective, costly transactions lead to greater reliance on longer-term contracts. The firm hires an employee for a duration rather than for each day or for each instant. There is much truth to this but, in principle at least, since employees can quit at any instant, or be fired, we have a long-term arrangement only because it is in the interest of both parties to continue in association. The avoidance of costly transacting is part of the motivation for this interest, but our focus on this has led us to ignore other, possibly more important, reasons for continued association. If these other reasons exist, and some are discussed below, then a durable association replicating that achievable through a long-term contract would be sought even if transaction cost were zero. A series of costless transitory market negotiations would bring the same employers and employees together, so that, de facto, the firm that is characterized in terms of employment contracts would be achieved through repeated market negotiations. The same behavioral interrelationship might arise when transaction cost is zero as when it is positive. If we conceive of "the" firm as a set of particular behavioral interactions guided by agreements of one sort or another, transaction cost would then determine only how the firm is achieved, not whether it exists. How the firm is achieved is of interest in some contexts, but the behavior that characterizes the firm, which may be achieved through a variety of contractual arrangements, would seem to be a substantive issue determined by considerations that go beyond those highlighted by the transaction cost theory of the firm.

3. MORAL HAZARD, SHIRKING, AND OPPORTUNISM

Writings about the theory of the firm began to diverge from the simple transaction cost format during the decade of the 1970s. Increasing attention was given to the problem of achieving incentive alignment. Attention began turning toward the issue raised by Berle and Means in *The Modern Corporation and Private Property* (1932) — the alleged separation between ownership and control — with the important difference that, unlike Berle and Means, the task became one of understanding how firms organize to resolve the problem. The recent investigation of the ownership structure of the firm undertaken by Ken Lehn and myself (1985) is a continuation of this line of development.

This issue does not permit one to ignore the task of understanding the inner organization of the firm, whereas the transaction cost approach encourages one to dwell on questions like "Why do firms exist?" or "Why is there vertical integration?" Moral hazard analysis, shirking, and opportunism — the problems of incentive compatibility — yield explanations of the internal organization of the firm that are difficult to derive from only transaction cost considerations. It is true that transaction cost is involved in the existence of these problems, at least for a (too) broad definition of transaction cost.[5] They presuppose a positive cost of negotiating them completely out of existence. However, the role of transaction cost in explaining the manner in which organization responds to these problems is like the role of gravity in explaining chemical reactions; gravity influences chemical reactions, but seldom is it the key variable whose behavior importantly explains variations in the reactions observed.

Thus, Alchian and Demsetz (1972) rely on differences in shirking opportunities to understand the organization of the firm, not differences in transaction cost. Their focus is on how the organization of the firm can be accounted for by the differences in the monitoring needs that result.[6] Similarly, as discussed above, the literature on opportunism really relies on a presumed correlation between asset specificity and the loss to be expected from contract failure, and not on variations in transaction cost. The organizations selected and the incentive systems brought into play to moderate incentive incompatibilities are analyzed through variations in the nature of the monitoring problem that is faced, not through variations in the cost of transacting. It is because of this that incentive incompatibilities offer an alternative to transaction cost analysis in the developing theory of the firm, even though transaction cost is embedded in the organization problem. However, the shirking-opportunism alternative has shortcomings of its own. These are now outlined briefly.

Alchian and Demsetz view shirking as an activity to which firm-like organization (to be discussed more fully below) is particularly susceptible. This is because the revenues of the firm must be shared by the various owners of inputs used by the firm without the full guidance or protection normally offered by intervening competitive markets. These markets would exist if the firm purchased goods from other firms rather than producing them in-house. The centralization of production in firm-like (team) organization therefore is more productive under particular conditions if it survives in the face of the greater shirking costs it must bear. The reason for firm-like production is to be found in the special productivity it offers in some circumstances. Alas, although Alchian and Demsetz make this clear, they fail to discuss the sources of this special productivity. Abating the cost of shirking helps explain the firm's inner organization but provides no rationale for the firm's existence. The extension of this analysis to general agency problems (Jensen and Meckling) fails to remedy this defect.

The literature on post-contractual opportunistic behavior extends the notion of shirking to contractual exchange, but it takes a position that is different than, and possibly contrary to, Alchian and Demsetz. Thus, Klein, Crawford, and Alchian (and Riordan and Williamson also) lean toward a position in which firm-like production, through vertical integration, reduces the severity of opportunism in the presence of asset specificity. This position implicitly views market contracting as bearing the special costs of opportunism (shirking across markets), but then an explanation is needed as to why markets exist if firm-like organization reduces the cost of opportunism more than does the market. The existence of markets is rationalized by the belief that they offer "high-powered" incentives not provided by the firm, but Alchian and Demsetz view the keener incentives offered by the market as a reason why firms are subject to more shirking than are markets! This brings us to the awkward position of stating that firm-like organization is preferred when the advantages of managing opportunism internally outweigh the advantages of managing them through markets, that is, firm organization is preferred when it is superior.

This awkwardness is alleviated somewhat by the fact that Alchian and Demsetz stress team production without special reference to vertical relationships; their emphasis is on the problem of free-riding when production is joint, even when this "jointedness" occurs within a single "horizontal" activity level. The literature on opportunism stresses vertical relationships, and the emphasis is on reneging or guile. It may well be that firm-like organization raises the cost of dealing with free-riding while lowering the cost of dealing with guile. Awkwardness might also be alleviated by asset specificity considerations, for asset specificity can be used to index those situations in which firm-like organization has more of an advantage (but, as Coase points out in these lectures, possibly not enough of an advantage). As of now, this is a frail reed upon which to build a theory of the firm. It is silent in regard to the survivability of firm-like organization in the absence of asset specificity, and it is directed primarily at explaining the vertical depth of firms rather than the existence of firms or other aspects of their internal organization. Moreover (as Coase also points out in the present lectures), the opportunism that is associated with asset specificity may be easier to resolve through contract stipulation.

Perhaps more important, asset specificity may reduce the non-opportunistic costs of maintaining vertically separated organizations. There is less need to manage (through vertical integration) the coordination of assets when they are "dedicated" to specific uses, as they are likely to be under conditions of asset specificity. In such a case, if the legal system is a sufficiently good enforcer of contracts, asset specificity may give rise to vertical disintegration.

The major use to which asset specificity has been put is to make the predictive statement that vertical integration is more likely when assets are specific, vertical integration being presumed to circumvent the opportunistic problems caused by asset specificity. Riordan and Williamson adopt this position in their commendable attempt to make predictive statements about vertical integration. Their claim is that when conditions are such as to require asset specificity to achieve low-cost production, vertical integration is more likely.

But there is more to asset specificity than what is contemplated in their paper (and in the important paper by Klein, Crawford, and Alchian). Owners and management make commitments to each other in order to solicit many years of devoted service; human capital specificity arises as a result of long tenure (and this specificity may be exacerbated by the use of physical assets that are highly specific). Conditions change, requiring these commitments to be broken if the firm is to survive. Unlike the claim made by the literature on opportunism, owners or top management do not rush out to break these commitments. They seek to keep them, both for reasons of personal honor and for reasons of continuing to solicit devoted duty from other employees. This is one reason mergers or takeovers occur. A new broom sweeps clean, and these commitments give way to the exigencies of economic conditions.[7] Such is the claim of much of the writings about takeovers. Here we find mergers (initially) taking place to facilitate opportunism toward those who have invested in human capital. Behavior that is opportunistic toward employees is facilitated through mergers, possibly vertical, by bringing in new owners and management that are personally free of these past commitments.

There is much more to the problem of economic organization than is plausibly subsumed under transaction and monitoring cost. Perhaps the transaction and monitoring approaches to the theory of the firm have confined our search too much. Firms would exist in a world in which transaction and monitoring costs are zero, although their organization might be considered different. In the space that remains, I consider an alternative approach, one based on aspects of information cost considerations that are different than those captured by transaction and monitoring costs. No well-developed model is offered. My intent is only to illustrate one way in which we have ignored considerations that seem important to a theory of the firm. It is desirable first to give some notion of what it is that we wish to explain with a theory of the firm.

4. FIRM-LIKE ORGANIZATION

The firm properly viewed is a "nexus" of contracts. Our interest might center on explaining (1) the persistence of certain types of contracts that are found in this nexus, (2) the variation observed in other types of contracts that are "more or less" included in this nexus, and (3) the (horizontal and vertical) scope of activities covered by these contracts. No doubt this list can be extended greatly. For example, we might want to understand the relationship between the existence of firm-like contracts and problems of unemployment and politics. Past and current interest in the existence, the internal organization, and the vertical and horizontal scope of "the firm" fit comfortably into the three areas of inquiry listed above, and it is in these that I wish to show that information cost has relevance that extends beyond its significance in transaction cost and moral hazard problems.

The defining content of the nexus of contracts referred to above remains rather vague in literature on the theory of the firm.[8] We may as well recognize that we have no clear notion of firm-like contractual arrangements, especially since we now recognize the difficulty of distinguishing between coordination achieved "across markets" and coordination achieved "within firms." It might be useful to adopt legal notions of what a firm is and what it is not, for there do arise cases in which this determination has been called forth because of the important impact it has on which body of law determines the liabilities of the parties involved. I prefer instead to identify three aspects of the nexus of contracts that plausibly influence firm-like coordination. (At least two of them receive mention in case law.) These aspects of firm-like contractual arrangements brush aside the question of absolutes — "When is a nexus of contracts *a firm*?" — and substitute instead a question of relatives — "When is a nexus of contracts *more firm-like*?"

A common feature of corporate charters is a statement about the business of the firm. While this may change over time, one aspect that persists is that the firm produces goods that are to be sold. This implies an agreement to *specialize*, by which I mean to produce mainly for persons who are not members of the firm's team. The complement to this is self-sufficiency or production by and *for* the same persons, which, in the limit, is one person doing for himself without the cooperation of others. Specialization, which can differ in degree between firm-like institutions, is adopted as a characteristic of firm-like contracts in order to maintain compatibility with the theory of price. The firm in the theory of price does not consume what it produces, it sells to others.[9]

The second aspect of the nexus of contracts is the expected length of time of association between the same input owners. Do the contractual agreements entered into contemplate mainly transitory, short-term association, which in the extreme would be characterized by spot market exchanges, or do these agreements contemplate a high probability of continuing association between the same parties? The firm viewed as team production exhibits significant reassociation of the same input owners. The third facet is the degree of conscious direction that is used to guide the uses to which resources are to be put; this is minimal in spot market transactions, but more important in a context in which continuity of association is relied upon. The direction of some by others catches the spirit of managed coordination.

Our interest centers mainly on the cooperative efforts of more than one person, but the one-person firm is not ruled out by these characteristics. The financial advisor, working alone, offers specialized services. Continuity of association and directability of behavior would seem more difficult to imagine in the case of a one-person firm. Still, a person must deal with himself in a relationship that is continuous over a lifetime, and conflicts do arise between the capabilities and tastes of a person today, or in one set of circumstances, and the "same" person tomorrow, or in a different set of circumstances. Because of these conflicts, a person sometimes finds it desirable to restrict his activities by entering into binding precommitments that control his future behavior (Thaler and Shefrin). Deadlines are often accepted as a self-enforcing device and costs are imposed on future errant (from today's perspective) behavior (as when Christmas savings clubs are joined). The agency problem resides within each of us as well as in interactions between us.

Specialization, continuity of association, and reliance on direction are characteristics of firm-like coordination. They substitute for self-sufficiency and spot markets. These are frequently found characteristics of firm-like organization because they are productive in many circumstances. This productivity derives in part from transaction and monitoring cost considerations, but it also depends on other conditions. Particularly important are the conditions that underlie the acquisition and use of knowledge.

5. KNOWLEDGE AND THE ORGANIZATION OF SPECIALIZATION

Smith has enshrined forever the idea that specialization is productive, but Smith's focus is on the changes wrought in the individual worker. The problem of how the activities of cooperating specialists are organized so as to mesh better is largely ignored. He ascribes the productivity gains achieved through specialization to three aspects of the division of labor—improvement in dexterity realized by each workman, time saved by avoiding switching from one task to another, and ease with which workmen conceive of innovating improvements when they are steadily occupied in a single task. He writes as if the examples of specialization that he discusses take place within different departments of a firm, but they could also take place across different firms. Indeed, this is the interpretation adopted by Stigler (1951) in his discussion of the impact of market size on vertical integration. It is safe to ignore the organization problem only if the gains achievable through specialization are independent of the way in which specialization is achieved. This seems implausible, and surely would be thought so by Smith who saw in natural liberty an organizing principle vastly superior to central planning. Even if the details of this organization are best left to the invisible hand of natural liberty, its broad outline is important to the theory of the firm.

Information is also a subject upon which much has been written, at least since Stigler's "The Economics of Information" (1961). It is a subject that has obvious connections to moral hazards and transactions, but here I want to emphasize other, neglected connections to the theory of the firm. Economic organization, including the firm, must reflect the fact that knowledge is costly to produce, maintain, and use. In all these respects there are economies to be achieved through specialization. Although the true conglomerate firm is a puzzle, we generally identify industries, and firms in these industries, as repositories of specialized knowledge and of the specialized inputs required to put this knowledge to work. Steel firms specialize in different stocks of knowledge and equipment than do firms in investment banking or industrial chemicals, and even firms in the same industry differ somewhat in the knowledge and equipment upon which they rely.

Knowledge does not directly convert to utility or living standards. If each of us specialize in a single branch of knowledge but attempt to use this knowledge without relying on others, the standard of living achievable would be less than if everyone had become a jack-of-all-trades. Although knowledge can be learned more effectively in specialized fashion, its use to achieve high living standards requires that a specialist somehow use the knowledge of other specialists. This cannot be done only by *learning* what others know, for that would undermine gains from specialized learning. It cannot be done only by *purchasing* information in the form of facts, for in many cases the theory that links facts must be mastered if facts are to be put to work.

This difference between the economics of acquiring and using knowledge has profound implications for social organization. "Common knowledge," particularly of language and arithmetic, is useful because its possession allows *greater* specialization. There must be a low-cost method of communicating between specialists and the large number of persons who either are non-specialists or who are specialists in other fields. Since this communication cannot consist of extensive education in this knowledge without losing the gains from specialized learning, and since the bare facts contained in this knowledge are often uninterpretable, much communication must consist in the giving of *directions*. These directions may pertain to product use or to work activity. The large cost borne to educate masses of persons in language and calculating skills is worth bearing because it facilitates the giving and taking of directions.

Firms and industries must form a pattern of economic organization that takes account of the need for acquiring knowledge in a more specialized fashion than the manner in which it will be used. Those who are to produce on the basis of this knowledge, but not be possessed of it themselves, must have their activities *directed* by those who possess (more of) the knowledge. Direction substitutes for education (that is, for the transfer of the knowledge itself). Direction may be purchased through short- or long-run commitments, depending partly on the cost of transacting. In either case, direction is involved, and direction is an important dimension of managed coordination. A second way to put information to work without sacrificing specialization in knowledge is to produce and sell goods that require less information to use than is required to produce them: *direction*, in the form of instructions, is involved but, unlike the direction of employees, who are expected to respond in details of timing and execution of their assigned tasks, the users of purchased goods have greater discretion about the timing and application of the instructions that accompany purchased goods. The larger the number of different bodies of knowledge that are required to produce a good, or the more specialized the knowledge that is required, the greater the reliance that must be placed on the direction of some by others. The division of this direction between the direction of employees and the direction of buyers of the good is relevant to the issue of vertical integration. The vertical depth of the firm may be considered from the perspective of the need for conserving on information costs. Other costs matter also, but I wish to focus attention on the consequences of costly knowledge, and I wish to do so without reference to the information costs inherent in transaction and moral hazard problems.

Because it is uneconomical to educate persons in one industry in the detailed knowledge used in another, recourse is had to developing or encapsulating this knowledge into products or services that can be transferred between firms cheaply because the instructions needed to use them do not require in-depth knowledge about how they are produced (and because of transport considerations). The economical use of industrial chemicals by steel firms does not generally require knowledge of how these chemicals are produced; similarly, the use of steel by industrial chemical firms does not require transfer of knowledge of how the steel is produced. A production process reaches the stage of yielding a saleable product when downstream users can work with, or can consume, the "product" without themselves being knowledgeable about its production. Short of this point, it would be necessary to educate downstream users more fully, and this would sacrifice the gains from specialized learning.

However, "products" could continue to be processed into downstream derivatives that are even easier to use. Steel could be set into its structural places by producers rather than by construction companies; this would reduce the need for construction companies to learn the properties of steel that are relevant to riveting and integrating the structure. Steel could be driven for its buyers when they use it in the form of an automobile. The process of further product refinement is halted when the next version of the product will be put to many multiple uses downstream that rely on different bodies of knowledge. A single firm if it was vertically integrated would have difficulty acquiring and maintaining the stocks of knowledge necessary to control cost and quality and to make good managerial decisions when downstream uses are multiple in this sense.

The many uses that are made of steel generally require knowledge that is substantially different from that which is required to produce steel. It is therefore costly to house production of steel in the same firm that is to produce many of these downstream products. Instead, steel is sold. Title passes to others who are masters of the knowledge required to use steel to produce derivative products and services.

Roughly speaking (since other things also matter), the vertical boundaries of a firm are determined by the economics of conservation of expenditures on knowledge. A single firm works a product into new, simpler-to-use (on the basis of directions) products until the diversity of uses further downstream is so great as to require this firm, if it is to continue developing product lines, to bear greater costs of information acquisition and maintenance than are avoided by potential users when there is additional simplification of each product line. Title to "the" product is likely to change hands when this point in the development of product lines is reached, but even if title does not change, further work on derivative products is likely to become the task of other firms. The boundary defining degree of vertical integration will have been established.

It will normally be the case that the boundary suitable for changing title is not coterminous with the point at which one person can economically possess the knowledge required to bring the process to this boundary. Still, the firm that is owned, managed, and operated by a single person is more common than might be supposed. It exists when a person's capacity to absorb knowledge, and to become expert in its use, is great enough for him to learn and use those skills required to bring a product to the boundary at which title is likely to change. The town baker may find it expedient to master knowledge of kitchen chemistry, recipes, and cash accounting himself, and to purchase only products from others. In the more important case, however, the capacity of an individual to acquire and use knowledge is too limited to allow this boundary to be reached without requiring the services of several people each of whom is occupied in a different vertical stage of production.

Economies of scale with respect to number of persons optimally linked to the use of other inputs at any given horizontal level of economic activity may also call for many more than just one person at each stage of production. Information cost may play a role here also. The giving of directions (in substitution for educating) to others may be subject to scale economies of a limited sort. The utilization of the services of a "direction giver" may demand the presence of several "direction receivers" if these services are to be used efficiently.

This brings us to the question of how these services are secured, and to the issue of continuity of association. In many cases it is not practical to purchase the knowledge itself unless someone is to become expert in it; hence, in one way or another a growing reliance on additional knowledge requires securing the services of additional persons. Such services can be secured through short-term transitory purchases or through long-term, less frequently repeated purchases. Transaction cost will influence this decision, but it is not the only important consideration. The decision also turns on the productivity *benefits* derivable from different arrangements. Two firms facing the same labor transaction costs may choose different employment arrangements because the benefits they derive from these arrangements differ. Particularly important in determining these benefits are knowledge-based considerations. Continuing association of the same persons makes it easier for firm-specific and person-specific information to be accumulated (see the large literature on specificity of human capital). Knowledge about the objectives and organization of the firm is learned "cheaply" through continuing association, and so is knowledge about the capabilities and limitations of the persons involved in this association. Continuing association, however, implies commitment, and commitment has the disadvantage of inflexibility. The benefits to be derived from continuing association must be set against the cost of inflexibility in determining the best manner in which to acquire the talents and services of many persons.

Short-term arrangements become more favorable when firms are more likely to change what they are doing in the important respects of objectives, locations, tasks, and style. Long-term arrangements are more suitable when the conditions under which a firm operates are stable. The considerable changes in quantities and types of labor services required by firms who have been forced to shift from a relatively stable regulated environment to a more volatile unregulated environment reflects these considerations, and my guess is that deregulated firms choose an average continuity of association with the typical employee that is shorter than they choose in a regulated environment.

The complete absence of variability in the tasks that are likely to be required by a firm is an incentive to substitute machinery for personnel. Machinery, being very durable, can be thought of as used on a continuing basis by the firm. As task variability increases, the inflexibility of machines exacts a toll. Labor services increase in relative productivity. Great variability in the likely uses to which an employee is to be put creates an even stronger need for flexibility, and long-term employment tends to give way to short-term. Thus, while long-term employment relies on the direction of employees in a changing pattern of tasks, great variability in such tasks makes any one employee less suitable than a series of employees each better suited to the immediate requirements of the job. The resulting variation in continuity of association is affected by transaction cost, but it is also affected (more importantly, I believe) by how the relative productivities of tenure change when the stability of the knowledge requirements of an employee changes.

Theories of transaction cost and agency have greatly enriched our understanding of the nature of firm-like organization. Coase's insight into the importance of the cost of using markets helped to stimulate much of the work that has been done on this topic during the last two decades. My concern is that our thinking may be too constrained by our past successes. Some important problems are amenable to solution by application of the logic of both transaction cost theory and agency theory, but other problems, equally important, are not. Coase's work is best honored by using it as the foundation upon which to build a still richer set of tools. One step in this construction has already been added—the theory of agency relationships. In the present effort to encourage the taking of additional steps, I have found it necessary to outline some of the weaknesses in what has already been accomplished, while suggesting a new direction of inquiry. This would not be needed except for the fact that the work that Coase has done, and that which he has prompted others to do, remains so compelling.

NOTES

I wish to thank Rebecca Demsetz, Kevin James, Ben Klein, George Stigler, Mike Waldman, and Rupert Windisch for useful comments and questions.

1. Free information about production and prices may be contrasted with information about consumption. Knowledge about production and prices is assumed to be *universally* knowable at zero cost. With no one privy to this information, there is no role for a specialized input called management. Knowledge about personal tastes is freely knowable only *to the person* whose tastes they are; hence, individuals as consumers must manage their own affairs, including the hiring of experts, but this requirement for personalized decisions is also satisfied costlessly.

It is this asymmetric, theoretical treatment of knowledge—universally knowable in the case of production, only personally knowable in the case of consumption—that makes socialism appear appealing. The state is viewed by intellectuals as capable when it comes to production, where it is presumed to possess knowledge as good as anyone else's, but incapable when it comes to psychological tradeoffs between consumption goods and between work and leisure. The policy that flows quite naturally from such assumed asymmetry in knowledge is nationalization of industry combined with privatization of consumption and work.

2. If free and full information about technical relationships and prices make it difficult to cap the size of firms in the model of perfect decentralization, they also make it difficult to develop a theory of market concentration. Short of making information costly, the only way out of these dilemmas is to conjure other sources of diseconomies of scale. Conjuring is necessary, because economic theory makes no pretension at knowing these sources or when they will be more and less operative.

3. This analysis of the make-or-buy decision is inframarginal in nature. If the problem of make-or-buy is viewed in the context of completely divisible adjustments, it must be that on the margin all firms are indifferent between making inputs or buying them. The fact that some firms make considerable quantities of their inputs, even while they purchase the same inputs from others, simply reveals that inframarginal comparisons show that over some range of output the sum of these costs is lower if inputs are produced in-house.

4. Williamson may be cited again. In *The Economic Institutions of Capitalism*, he does discuss in three pages (92–94) the role of scale economies in raising the cost of enlarging the scope of activities included within a single firm, and he discusses different ways of organizing work later in the book. It would be wrong to claim that he has completely ignored production cost. Yet, his discussion of these does not emphasize the *differences* that may exist between firms within the same industry. His discussion of scale economies is confined to the problem of where on a given production function, available to all firms, the firm functions (similarly with regard to choice of method of organizing work). That the history of a firm may impose constraints on its knowledge about and its ability to alter the way it functions plays no key role in his discussions. Indeed, preceding his discussion of scale economies, in another short section (86–90), he rejects the importance of technological conditions to economic organization. With respect to asset specificity (which he fails to recognize as at least partly technical), it is not with technology that he is concerned but with the (asserted) fact that asset specificity raises the cost of governance through market arrangements. Even "bounded rationality" is not used to emphasize the *differences in the content of the information* that may be possessed by the personnel and traditions of different firms. It is used to limit the span of control that may be exercised by one person over others, and, thereby, to create a monitoring problem.

5. The question of how transaction cost is to be defined is raised in my 1964 paper, "The Exchange and Enforcement of Property Rights." The questions raised are of two sorts. Should the cost of enforcing agreements be a transaction cost? Should the cost of avoiding the "under revelation" of demand (as when collective goods are purchased) be a transaction cost? My preference is for a more restricted definition, dealing with the cost of negotiating. Otherwise, we come seriously close to a definition of transaction cost that amounts to "the cost of solving a problem."

6. Recognition of the relevance of moral hazard for the theory of the firm both precedes and follows Coase's seminal work on transaction cost. Many writers using the moral hazard theme take the discussion of shirking in Alchian and Demsetz as a starting reference, but Knight, in his classic *Risk, Uncertainty, and Profit*, anticipates much of what they say. Knight clearly understands the shirking problem, which he calls moral hazard; he also recognizes its relationship to the organization of the firm. The failure to appreciate his contribution fully is mainly due to Knight himself, and this for two reasons. First, his interest really is not in the firm, but in the enterprise *system*, so he does not bring his ideas about the inner workings of the firm to center stage or to full maturity. Second, his theoretical perspective is overwhelmed

by his belief in the importance of allocating risk (of compensation loss) efficiently, and this leads him to make the existence of risk his dominant and pervasive explanation for the existence and organization of firms. He views the separation of claims on the firm's revenues into a stable component, the wage that is received by employees, and a less stable component, the profit that is received by owner/entrepreneurs, as reflecting different degrees of aversion to and competence in handling risk. It is this theme that attracts the criticism of Alchian and Demsetz, Coase, and other writers too, and that diverts them from Knight's discussion of the relationship between economic organization and moral hazard. Just as there can be little doubt that transaction cost is relevant to the existence of the firm, and to the existence of moral hazard problems, so there cannot be much doubt that moral hazard problems influence the internal organization of the firm.

7. This role of mergers was brought to my attention by an unpublished econometric exercise of my research assistant, John Simpson.

8. Alchian and Demsetz define the firm implicit in classical economics by the bundle of rights that determines the permissible actions of the owner-monitor. He has the right (1) to be a residual claimant; (2) to observe input behavior; (3) to be the central party common to all contracts with input owners; (4) to alter the membership of the team; and (5) to sell these rights.

9. The large number of activities carried on in specialized fashion is too broad to meet the needs of an inquiry seeking to explain firms as these are commonly identified. Every person who acts as a specialist, and every combination of such persons who act as a team of specialists, can be considered a firm, and in many respects they are different firms. The calculus of choice that motivates a person who provides engineering service to GM is not much different if he functions as an "independent" consultant or as an "employee." Nonetheless, a particular combination of the above dimensions may define a firm that is of special interest and importance. This combination is likely to be a *multiperson* team involving a *central contracting agent* operated mainly for *profit*, whose members associate together on a *continuing* basis and have their actions coordinated in large part by *direction*.

REFERENCES

Alchian, Armen A., and H. Demsetz. 1972. "Production, Information Costs, and Economic Organization," 62 *American Economic Review* 777-95.

Berle, A. A., and G. C. Means. 1932. *The Modern Corporation and Private Property*. New York: Macmillan.

Coase, R. H. 1937. "The Nature of the Firm," 4 *Economica* n.s. 386-405.

Demsetz, H. 1964. "The Exchange and Enforcement of Property Rights," 7 *Journal of Law and Economics* 11-26.

———. 1982. *Economic, Legal and Political Dimensions of Competition*. Amsterdam: North-Holland.

———, and K. Lehn. 1985. "The Structure of Corporate Ownership: Causes and Consequences," 93 *Journal of Political Economy* 1155-77.

Jensen, M. C., and W. H. Meckling. 1976. "Theory of the Firm: Management Behavior, Agency Costs and Ownership Structure," 3 *Journal of Financial Economics* 305-60.

Klein, B., R. G. Crawford, and A. A. Alchian. 1978. "Vertical Integration, Appropriable Rents and the Competitive Contracting Process," 21 *Journal of Law and Economics* 297-336.

Knight, Frank H. 1921. *Risk, Uncertainty, and Profit*. New York: Hart, Schaffner, and Marx; repr. (1965) New York: Harper and Row.

Riordan, M. H., and O. E. Williamson. 1985. "Asset Specificity and Economic Organization," 3 *International Journal of Industrial Organization* 365-78.

Stigler, G. J. 1951. "The Division of Labor Is Limited by the Extent of the Market," 59 *Journal of Political Economy* 185-93.

_____. 1961. "The Economics of Information," 69 *Journal of Political Economy* 213-25.

Thaler, R. H., and H. M. Shefrin. 1981. "An Economic Theory of Self-Control," 89 *Journal of Political Economy* 392-405.

Williamson, Oliver E. 1985. *The Economic Institutions of Capitalism*. New York: Free Press; New York: Macmillan.

11

On Coase, Competence, and the Corporation

SIDNEY G. WINTER

Ronald Coase observed in his first lecture that his contribution to the theory of the firm did not appear to him to be in any sense foreordained, but rather was the result of a conjunction of circumstances in his life that resulted in his exposure to a particular set of influences and facts.[1] These influences and facts he fashioned into an absorbing intellectual puzzle that he then undertook to solve.

I will argue that the broader history of the theory of the firm also reveals the major shaping role of conjunctions of circumstances that are accidental at least in the sense that they do not reflect the internal logic of the subject matter. The legacy of these accidents along the historical track is visible in the present state of the subject. Without demeaning the contributions that any of us have made, I think we must acknowledge that the present state is one of incoherence. If we ask, "What does economics have to say about the role of the business firm in a market economy?" the response will be silence followed by an excited babble of significantly conflicting answers—an interesting babble, but a babble nonetheless.

To develop this thesis, I will first review in the following section the orthodox statement of the theory of the firm and summarize four major critiques of that orthodoxy. In section 2, I attempt to discover order in the present theoretical chaos by arraying and contrasting four contemporary paradigms in the theory of the firm—of which one is the transaction cost paradigm founded by Ronald Coase. Section 3 takes note of some of the conflicts and complementarities between the transaction cost paradigm and the evolutionary approach to economic theory. The principal issue addressed is whether the transaction cost approach provides an adequate basis for understanding the collections of capabilities that particular large firms display—this is the issue of "competence and the corporation" referenced in my title.

1. TEXTBOOK ORTHODOXY: FOUR CRITIQUES

In our book, Nelson and I treat with some care the question of whether it is useful to speak of an "orthodox" viewpoint in economic theory, and if (as we claim) it is, what that orthodoxy amounts to (1982:6–11). I will omit discussion of the first question and give only the short-form answer to the second: "Orthodox economic theory is the theoretical view that dominates the leading textbooks of intermediate microeconomics, together with the extensions and elaborations of that basic viewpoint found in more advanced work." In the case of the theory of the firm, the orthodox view is set out in the textbook chapters variously titled "Theory of the Firm," "Production and Cost," "Competitive Supply," "Monopoly," and so forth.

The basic elements of that orthodox view are as follows. Firms are characterized by the technological transformations of which they are capable—formally, by production sets or production functions. Like consumers, firms are unitary actors and are economically rational; more specifically, they maximize profit or present value. They deal in markets for homogeneous commodities; in almost all cases these appear to be contemporaneous spot markets for inputs and outputs. Contractual arrangements and other institutional supports for the functioning of the business firm are, one infers, assumed to be sufficiently close to being flawless and costless so as to justify the virtually total absence of discussion of these topics. (Look for "contract" in the index; you will probably find "contract curve.") The discussion focuses on how firms, guided by market forces, make the production decisions that form a part of the answer to the overall social resource allocation problem. It is about inputs and outputs and how they relate to the given technology, to each other, and to market forces.

This constellation of assumptions and concerns is also focal for the treatment of the firm in the advanced texts. And in general equilibrium theory, its outline stands out even more starkly than in intermediate price theory.[2] Standard treatments of the modern theory present firms as production sets with profit motives attached. The profit motive may be rationalized as reflecting the stockholders' (unanimous) interests under the prevailing assumptions of complete markets, atomistic competition, and perfect contracts. No such rationalization is provided for the firms per se. Like consumers, they are logical primitives of the theoretical system.[3]

This same general view of the business firm and the contexts in which it functions is pervasive in contemporary economic theory. Particular contributions may explore the consequences of modifying one assumption or another, but basic elements of the structure remain intact. Research in theoretical industrial organization economics has been transformed by the application of more powerful mathematical techniques in the past quarter century, and recently by careful attention to information-theoretic and game-theoretic details of the interactions among firms, or between firms and consumers. But in almost all of this work, firms are what they are in the intermediate microeconomics texts.

Roam on through public finance and labor economics; examine almost any paper in applied econometrics that involves firm behavior, and you will find much the same situation. In short, on this question as on most others, the intermediate texts provide a bare-bones but generally accurate account of what the economics discipline is up to. What they present as the theory of the firm is the orthodox theory of the firm—or more precisely, it is what the orthodox theory of the firm *has been*. I call it "textbook orthodoxy" to distinguish it from the recent work of otherwise orthodox theorists who have concerned themselves with questions relating to the nature of the firm. Textbook orthodoxy today defines the theory of the firm for essentially all economists except those who are working on the theory of the firm.

1.1. First Critique: Conflict with Methodological Individualism

Textbook orthodoxy on the theory of the firm has one characteristic that seems quite bizarre when assessed against the broad background of Western economic thought: it involves a blatant affront to the principle of methodological individualism. This principle disallows, or at least warns against, the practice of grounding theories on assumptions about the behavior of social groups, organizations, or institutions. A careful and restrained explication of the principle is the following:

> Although in modern economics, collections of individuals are sometimes treated as "entities" for analytical purposes (examples of "the household," "the firm," and even occasionally "the state" spring to mind) the *ultimate* unit of analysis is always the individual; more aggregative analysis must be regarded as only provisionally legitimate. In other words, the economist is always sensitive to the possibility that the holistic treatment of groups of individuals may mislead greatly, or involve overlooking dimensions of reality that are extremely important (Brennan and Tullock: 225).

It is interesting to note that, in fact, the textbooks typically prefer the affront to reality involved in the abstraction of the isolated "consumer" over the complexities and the affront to individualism involved in discussing the demand behavior of "the household." In the case of the firm, however, the opposite choice is made and often with little or no apology.[4] Economists can be quite caustic when presented with an argument that speaks of "the public interest." They know (or think they know) that a "public" is not the sort of thing that has an "interest," except perhaps for the interest in a Pareto efficient outcome. They are similarly quick to correct what they consider obvious error when students intuitively recognize an "industry interest" and hence find it difficult to accept the notion that competitive firms routinely engage in mutually disadvantageous behavior, driving price to marginal cost. This dedication to methodological individualism—and, relatedly, to the study of non-cooperative equilibria—is abruptly suspended when the workings of the firm itself are discussed. There, fully cooperative relations among the diverse economic interests organized in the firm are routinely, though implicitly, assumed to be easily achieved through voluntary exchange.

This aberration is a nice example of how an adaptive or evolutionary process can yield a result that is quite puzzling until one examines the path along which it emerged. In classical economics, individualism reigned supreme in the theory of the firm as it did elsewhere. The dominant view of the firm, reflecting the historical context, was that of the small enterprise organized as a sole proprietorship – or, if not that, at least in a form in which "the firm" is no more problematic in its relation to individualism than is "the household." As much care was taken in uncovering the different economic roles that might be combined in "the entrepreneur" as in discussing the problems that arise if the roles are divided among many individuals.[5] Indeed, as regards the "separation of ownership and control," it seems that there was so much skepticism regarding the viability of such arrangements as to make detailed discussion of them unnecessary. Thus, for example, J. S. Mill:

> Management, however, by hired servants, who have no interest in the result but that of preserving their salaries, is proverbially inefficient, unless they act under the inspecting eye, if not the controlling hand, of the person chiefly interested: and prudence almost always recommends giving to a manager not thus controlled a remuneration partly dependent on the profits; which virtually reduces the case to that of a sleeping partner (J. S. Mill: 390).

Note that it is the owner who becomes the "sleeping partner," and the enterprise itself is thus associated directly with the individualistic interests of the hired management.[6]

No major technical difficulty stands in the way of developing the theory of the firm explicitly as a theory about individual entrepreneurs. There are a few unfamiliar issues to be dealt with – such as how the idea of "profit maximization" is to be adapted to allow for the income-leisure tradeoff of a utility-maximizing consumer whose work is running his business.[7] Minor modifications to the familiar structure of general equilibrium theory would be required. Production sets would enter the theory associated with consumers; presumably there would be an axiom denying the possibility of output without an input of some of the consumer's own time – that is, without a positive level of "entrepreneurial activity" by that consumer. Among other advantages, this approach would rationalize the upward sloping portion of the U-shaped long run average cost curve of Marshallian theory; in fact, with a slight strengthening of the axiom just stated, one could derive the proposition that average costs must ultimately increase. The question of which consumers were also entrepreneurs would simply be among the many questions subsumed in the concept of "an allocation."[8]

This development of the theory of the firm would be consonant with methodological individualism – not to speak of the nonmethodological aspects of economic theory's association with individualism. Why is this not the standard development of the subject? I will propose an answer to this question in introducing the fourth critique.

1.2. Second Critique: Failure to Explain Economic Organization

It is hardly necessary to observe here that Ronald Coase (1937) provided a profound critique of textbook orthodoxy well before that orthodoxy was fully developed. Orthodox theory recognizes two aspects of the problem of coordinating economic activity, the interfirm aspect and the intrafirm aspect. Markets are shown to be the answer to the interfirm aspect. What the answer to the intrafirm aspect may be is not explicitly addressed, but presumably it is the contractually based authority of the "entrepreneur." However, since both the functioning markets and the firms-qua-production sets are given data of the theory, there is no opportunity for an analysis of the division of labor between these two coordination modes. Hence, as Coase observed, there is no answer to the question of why markets do not do the coordinating that firms do, and no answer to the obverse question of why one big firm would not work as well as a market economy. In short, textbook orthodoxy provides no basis for explaining the organization of economic activity. This is more than a mere embarrassment concerning the logical structure of the theory, since the organization of activity is in continuing flux. Markets appear and disappear; firms expand in scope and then turn back toward specialization; quasi-firms and quasi-markets proliferate. Why and according to what principles do these things happen?

1.3. Third Critique: Lack of "Realism"

Discussion of the merits of the orthodox theory of the firm has long been a feature of the methodological controversy over "realism of assumptions." From the tangle of issues involved in that controversy, I pull out the following thread of related questions: Is observation of the internal workings of business firms (1) a legitimate area of economic inquiry? (2) a potential source of fruitful hypotheses about firm behavior? (3) a potential source of data with which to test competing hypotheses about firm behavior? Defenders of orthodoxy have been known to claim, among other things, that the correct answers to these questions are no, no, and no. Those who have complained of the lack of "realism" in orthodox theory have argued, among other things, that the correct answers are yes, yes, and yes.[9]

Coase's lectures in this volume clearly place him in the latter camp. In the period of his 1931–1932 visit to the United States, during which he gradually achieved a clear formulation of the question addressed in his article, he spent most of his time "visiting businesses and industrial plants." The contrasting examples of the acquisition of Fisher Body by General Motors and the successful long-term contractual relationship of GM with A. O. Smith and Co. were particularly important to him. His discussions with businessmen led him first to recognition of the hazards of opportunism involved in long-term contracting, and subsequently to the realization that these problems could sometimes be controlled by suitable contract provisions (for example, the customer's ownership of transaction-specific assets employed by the supplier), and are mitigated by the incentives to continue a mutually advantageous relationship. These latter considerations led him to reject then (and apparently lead him to reject now) the proposition that opportunism hazards in long-term contracting where asset specificity is involved are a quantitatively important motive for vertical integration. Whatever the final verdict on that particular issue, Coase's methodological stand on the relevance of evidence about actual business behavior is clear.[10]

It is hardly a surprise that Coase takes this stand in relation to the third critique, given his association with the second. If the boundaries of the firm—or, more broadly, the roles of different modes of governance of transactions—are to be endogenously determined in economic theory, then it is hard to understand how the inner workings of firms could possibly be declared "off limits" to the discipline. But, collectively and individually, economists seem to be of two or more minds on this issue. On the one hand, there is today little vigorous support for the "off limits" view as put forward by, in particular, Fritz Machlup.[11] On the other hand, I doubt that a dissertation prospectus outlining the sort of research program Coase conducted in 1931–1932 would pass muster in most economics departments today. Indeed, even a much more structured plan of inquiry into actual business practice would be likely to confront great skepticism regarding the value of such research. And certainly the reason is not that we have accumulated so many good observations about how firms work that we do not need any more. Quite the opposite is the case (see Simon).

1.4. Fourth Critique: Simplistic Treatment of Its Focal Concern

The strong point of textbook orthodoxy is its concern with the role of firms as repositories of productive knowledge.[12] This, I propose, is the significant benefit that has motivated acceptance of the "opportunity cost" of methodological individualism foregone—and it is this tradeoff that makes the concept "everyone is a potential entrepreneur" unappealing as an approach to the theory of the firm. The clash of these two considerations was nicely framed by J. de V. Graaf in a (once) well-known exposition of welfare economics:

> When we try to construct a transformation function for society as a whole from those facing the individual firms comprising it, a fundamental difficulty confronts us. There is, from a welfare point of view, nothing special about the firms actually existing in an economy at a given moment of time. The firm is in no sense a "natural unit." Only the individual members of the economy can lay claim to that distinction. All are potential entrepreneurs. It seems, therefore, that the natural thing to do is to build up from the transformation functions of the men, rather than the firms, constituting an economy.
>
> If we are interested in eventual empirical determination, this is extremely inconvenient. But it has conceptual advantages. The ultimate repositories of technological knowledge in any society are the men comprising it, and it is just this knowledge which is effectively summarized in the form of a transformation function. In itself a firm possesses no knowledge. That which is available to it belongs to the men associated with it. Its production function is really built up in exactly the same way, and from the same basic ingredients, as society's (1957:16).

What Graff calls the "conceptual advantages" of the approach he describes I would call the philosophical advantages—specifically, the straightforward conformity with methodological individualism. Where he says that it is an "extremely inconvenient" approach empirically I would say that it is false. At least, it is false that "the ultimate repositories of technological knowledge in any society are the men comprising it" and that "in itself a firm possesses no knowledge," although it is true enough that individuals are *among* the ultimate repositories of technological knowledge.

Examine the top of the Fortune 500; you will typically find companies that have existed for large percentages of the time since the invention of the ancestors of their principal product lines, or which antedate those inventions and became active in the ancestral product lines at an early stage. Thus, for example, IBM antedates the first electronic computer (ENIAC, 1945) and introduced the IBM 650, the "Model T of computers," in 1954. By this very conservative determination of IBM's date of entry to this very modern line of business, IBM has been involved for 78.5 percent of the elapsed time since the product was invented.[13] Other examples, such as General Motors, Ford, AT&T, Boeing, and the oil companies are much more extreme in this regard, and the time spans involved are much larger compared to human lifetimes. It seems undeniable that these large corporations are, *as organizations*, among society's most significant repositories of the productive knowledge that they exercise, and not merely an economic contrivance of the individuals currently associated with them. Thus, "the textbooks are closer (than Graaf) to being right — it is the firms, not the people who work for the firms, that know how to make gasoline, automobiles, and computers" (Winter, 1982:76).

Although founded on the defensible claim that the central characteristic of the business firm is its role as a repository of productive knowledge, textbook orthodoxy falls far short in its account of that role. It suffers in this regard from defects analogous to those that make it inadequate as an approach to economic organization. By taking production sets or functions as given, it fails to provide a framework for explaining why society's capabilities should be packaged at a particular time in one particular way and not some other way. By treating the storage of productive knowledge as costless — the analogue in this context of the assumption of costless and perfect contracts — it forecloses to economic analysis the performance of the very role that it claims is central.

Most important, textbook orthodoxy fails to provide a basis for understanding the incentives and processes in business firms that produce technological and organizational change. This failure is closely related to its inadequacy in accounting for the boundaries of the firm — or, more broadly, for the diverse array of means by which rent-streams are protected and transactions organized in relation to productive knowledge of diverse types (Teece, 1982, 1987). It is also closely related to orthodoxy's utter neglect of the problem of how firms actually perform the task of storing the knowledge that underlies productive competence; to acknowledge that maintaining competence may not be a straightforward matter is to see that static competence may be an exceptional case arising only when the forces making for advance happen to balance those making for regression.

There are other major problems with the orthodox framework as a starting point for understanding economic change — but since Richard Nelson and I have written at considerable length about these issues, I will forgo further discussion here. (See Nelson and Winter, 1982 [esp. ch. 3]; Nelson, 1980; Winter, 1982).

2. CONTEMPORARY PARADIGMS IN THE THEORY OF THE FIRM

As I have suggested, textbook orthodoxy provides the theory of the firm mainly for economists who are not much interested in the theory of the firm per se. Those who are interested are generally seeking to remedy the deficiencies noted in one or more of the four critiques set forth above. The critiques thus provide one sort of taxonomic structure for contemporary research on the theory of the firm — one can ask which critique(s) the researcher appears to take seriously. In this section I propose a different taxonomic structure, identifying and relating four research "paradigms."

Textbook orthodoxy on the theory of the firm has been adequately characterized above. "*Working paper orthodoxy*" is the term I will use to refer to recent research (much of which has been published, of course — but "article orthodoxy" does not carry the needed connotation of recency) by theorists who work in an optimization framework and are concerned primarily with the structure of relationships among the actors involved in the firm. The substantive issues addressed include those of incentives, information, and control as between owners and managers or between managers and workers. Much of this research is in the principal-agent framework; noncooperative equilibria and outcomes that are "second-best" optimal because of the imperfect enforceability of contracts are its hallmarks. But I also include under this rubric other studies of optimal organization, including team theory.

Transaction cost economics is the paradigm founded by Ronald Coase in the article honored at this conference and extensively developed by a number of participants here, and in particular by my colleague and coorganizer, Oliver Williamson. As Coase succinctly puts it at the end of his first lecture, this approach "succeeded in linking up organization with cost." More specifically, it recognizes that there are different ways of organizing transactions (or different "modes of governance" for transactions), that these differ in costs, and that the costs are likely to differ in systematic ways depending on observable characteristics of the transactions in question. Much progress has been made in strengthening the operational content of models in this paradigm, that is, in rebutting the charge that transaction costs can explain anything. An interesting methodological point is that this progress has been achieved not by the development of techniques for measuring transaction costs directly but by the development of operationalizing hypotheses to suggest where transactional difficulties are likely to be severe. As compared with working paper orthodoxy, the scope of transaction cost economics tends to be broader, and the alternative modes of organization it is concerned with tend to be modeled closely on those observed in the world rather than hypothetical ones suggested by a formal structure.

Evolutionary economics relates to Armen Alchian's classic paper, "Uncertainty, Evolution, and Economic Theory," in much the same way that transaction cost economics relates to Coase and "The Nature of the Firm." It emphasizes the inevitability of mistaken decisions in an uncertain world, and the active, observable role of the economic environment in defining "mistakes" and suppressing the mistakes it defines. Relatedly, the sort of explanation it offers for states of affairs is evolutionary explanation — some antecedent condition existed, and the state of affairs now observed reflects the cumulative effect of the laws of change operating on that antecedent condition. In other words, the focus of explanatory effort is on dynamics. Like transaction cost economics, evolutionary economics tends to direct attention to observed economic behavior rather than hypothetical sets of alternatives. Like evolutionary biology, it is much concerned with how patterns are reproduced through time in the face of continuing turnover in the population of individuals displaying the pattern. Finally, it regards understanding of the ongoing, interrelated processes of change in technology and organization as the central intellectual problem to be confronted by a theory of the firm.

Figure 11.1 is a bold attempt at placing these four paradigms in understandable relation to one another. At the risk (no, at the *cost*) of oversimplification, it proposes contrasts along two dimensions — dimensions whose nature has been only partly foreshadowed in the discussion thus far.

The columns of the two-by-two array are distinguished according to the emphasis placed on *production* versus *exchange*. It will be objected immediately that any theory of the firm has to deal with both: textbook orthodoxy, for example, starts with a production set but immediately turns that concept to the analysis of behavior in the markets for inputs and outputs. This is quite true, and analogous remarks apply in the other three cases. On the other hand, one certainly would gather from the textbooks that the choice of input proportions is quite interesting, while the choice of contract terms is not. There is not, in other words, an evinced concern with the *structuring of deals*, and it is in that sense that exchange is not a focal concern of textbook orthodoxy.

In evolutionary economics, the specifics of the ways firms relate to owners, customers, and input suppliers are subsumed under the heading of organizational routines. These relationships are aspects of the productive performance as a whole, and what matters is whether the performance as a whole is profitable at any

		Focal concern	
		Production	*Exchange*
	Unbounded	Textbook orthodoxy	Working paper orthodoxy
Rationality viewed as			
	Bounded	Evolutionary economics	Transaction cost economics

Figure 11.1 Four Contemporary Paradigms in the Theory of the Firm

particular time and likely to improve over time. Thus, in the same sense as in the case of textbook orthodoxy, exchange is not a focal concern of evolutionary economics.

The fact that working paper orthodoxy and transaction cost economics place deal-structuring at center stage, and cast the economics of production and cost in a supporting role, requires little argument.

What may be more controversial is my claim that transaction cost economics is fundamentally associated with the view that economic rationality is bounded. I am pleased to be able to invoke the authority of my esteemed colleague Oliver Williamson in support of this position.

> Bounded rationality is the cognitive assumption on which transaction cost economics relies (1985:45).

> Confronted with the realities of bounded rationality, the costs of planning, adapting and monitoring transactions need expressly to be considered. Which governance structures are more efficacious for which types of transactions? *Ceteris paribus*, modes that make large demands on cognitive competence are relatively disfavored (1985:46).

Ronald Coase, on the other hand, makes it clear that among the fundamental propositions he learned from Arnold Plant was that firms maximize profits—in fact, that the notion of a shortfall from such profit maximization was "bilge." Other major contributors to the transaction cost paradigm no doubt share this view.

Although there are important theoretical issues at stake here, I suspect that there is less to this Coase-Williamson conflict than meets the eye. Coase would probably reject the following reformulation of his pro-profit maximization position: "The costs of planning, adapting and monitoring transactions are always negligible and should be ignored." In fact, he might reject as absurd the suggestion that the idea of profit maximization could be rendered in this way. He would be justified in this reaction to the extent that, for him, "profit maximization" means something little different from what I would call "profit seeking." When the implications of the idea of profit maximization are explored primarily with ordinary language, the distinction between "seeking" and "maximizing" is frequently elided—and often, as in Coase's work, to fruitful effect. When, however, theoretical argument about profit maximization is expressed in terms of the mathematics of optimization, the costs associated with the cognitive operations of the optimization itself inevitably disappear from the analysis. The costs lost from view in this way may include those of planning, adapting, and monitoring transactions. Even if some attempt is made to treat these costs explicitly, it remains true that they are not realistically very different from the information processing costs of optimization per se. Then the question arises, if the information processing used in optimization is available for free, why isn't all of it free? Isn't it the value of the marginal unit that sets the shadow price?

Williamson, following Herbert Simon, stresses the point that recognition of economic behavior as *intendedly* rational suffices to provide an "economizing orientation" for the analysis of economic institutions (1985:45). Similarly, in evolutionary models, firms are typically represented as profit-*seeking* organizations. Sometimes, of course, these assumptions may be conveniently expressed in an optimization framework; few if any advocates of transaction cost or evolutionary economics have sworn to abstain entirely from optimization calculations. The significant issue is whether it is worth great effort to adhere to a theoretical aesthetic of strict formal optimization, given the inescapable fact that there is nothing "strict" about the treatment of information processing costs in that sort of analysis. For example, to assume that there is some degree of myopia in the profit-seeking process of a firm may be a more balanced way of representing behavioral response to all of the relevant scarcities (including cognitive limitations) than is strict optimization.

It is not actually up to me to establish the qualifications for membership in the transaction cost club, so I will not pursue this issue further. I do want to make it clear that Ronald Coase remains eligible according to my characterization of the club, his remarks about profit maximization notwithstanding. His dedication to English prose as a mode of theoretical expression largely immunizes him from the dangers of that idea.

If figure 11.1 is accepted as reasonably descriptive of important differences among the four schools of thought, some interesting patterns of row and columnwise alliance and conflict are implied. In particular, note that evolutionary economics stands with textbook orthodoxy, and in opposition to transaction cost economics, in having production as its focal concern. This observation provides the theme for the following section.

3. EVOLUTIONARY VS. TRANSACTION COST PERSPECTIVES ON THE FIRM

Fundamentally, business firms are organizations that know how to do things. Profitability is the imperfect signal that market economies employ to tell firms how useful their activities are to society, and whether more or less of the same is wanted. The scope of a firm's productive knowledge may be broad or narrow; even if it is narrow it may be reflected in the firm's output markets by a long list of quite different products. As Teece has observed, "a firm's capability lies upstream from the end product — it lies in a generalizable capability which might find a variety of final product applications" (1982:45). Even very large and highly diversified firms, however, are typically active in a very small fraction of the total number of output markets in the economy. It is not difficult to identify and distinguish the areas of competence of most of the largest corporations.

The foregoing is a basic, though partial, account of how business firms appear to the eye of an evolutionary theorist. As far as it goes, it is not blatantly in conflict with textbook orthodoxy — although it is somewhat closer in spirit to activity analysis than to the single-product production function treatment that is most common in the intermediate texts. Firms are repositories of productive knowledge. In fact, though this is not much emphasized in the textbooks, a particular firm at a particular time is a repository for a quite specific range of productive knowledge, a range that often involves idiosyncratic features that distinguish it even from superficially similar firms in the same line(s) of business.

As was noted in section 1, although textbook orthodoxy has the virtue of focusing on the important role of the firm as a repository of knowledge, it is open to serious objections both in its treatment of that role and in other respects. In our book, Nelson and I put forward an alternative view that responds in a significant way to each of the four critiques of orthodoxy—but still regards firms as, fundamentally, organizations that know how to do things. For example, to address the conflict with methodological individualism it is necessary to unpack the metaphorical statement that "organizations know how to do things" into an account of the processes by which productive knowledge is preserved in an organization while individual human members come and go. Whether our account would be fully satisfying to a hard-core methodological individualist is unclear; we believe that it at least gives the concept of organizational knowledge something more than the provisional legitimacy to which Brennan and Tullock refer—and which is clearly all that textbook orthodoxy can claim.

What is of greatest interest in the present context is the nature of our response to the second critique, and the relationship of that response to the transaction cost analysis of the same issues. In the evolutionary view the question of how the boundaries of a firm are determined is akin to the question of how the boundaries of a tropical rain forest—or a population of house mice—are determined. The thing "knows" (metaphorically speaking) how to reproduce itself. It *must* reproduce itself through time to continue to exist, and the processes that are involved in reproduction through time are the basis of growth in spatial or other dimensions. Give it the appropriate environment and it will grow. Encroach upon it by some method; it will tend to grow back. The rain forest metaphor is particularly appropriate because the "competencies" of the forest are diverse; it can exploit many differentiated environments in differentiated ways—but as a whole it is a collection of competencies quite different from those exhibited by a deciduous forest of the temperate zone.

Putting aside the metaphor:

The point emphasized by evolutionary theory is that a firm with an established routine possesses resources on which it can draw very helpfully in the difficult task of attempting to apply that routine on a larger scale. . . . The replication assumption in evolutionary models is intended to reflect the advantages that favor the going concern attempting to do more of the same, as contrasted with the difficulties that it would encounter in doing something else or that others would encounter in trying to copy its success" (Nelson and Winter: 119).

Of course, when a firm grows by vertical integration, it is not just a question of "more of the same." But it is more of something closely related, something about which the firm already has some degree of relevant knowledge. The evolutionary view suggests that this "degree" is probably an important determinant of where integration takes place and where it does not.

What is the relationship between this evolutionary view and the transaction cost approach to the same issues? This is quite a complicated question, with many levels and facets. At a very basic level, it is not clear whether transaction cost economics aspires to a historico-evolutionary mode of explanation or, instead, to something more like the timeless, abstract deduction from presumed "data" that characterizes general equilibrium theory. The frequent use of historical evidence in the transaction cost paradigm is consistent with the former, and not the latter, interpretation of its explanatory program.[14] On this interpretation, transaction cost economics is fully compatible with evolutionary thinking. Transaction costs shape economic organization over time because organizational innovations occur that permit previously experienced transactional difficulties to be circumvented. Firms that make such innovations prosper and grow at the expense of their rivals, except perhaps those that are quick to imitate the innovation. This is the evolutionary view of how "cost minimization" — whether of transaction costs or production costs — really works. Something is tried, some problems are encountered: something else is tried and may be found to work better.

However, if this is the style of explanation, the axiom that "the transaction is the basic unit of analysis" seems troublesome. Firms perform their function as repositories of knowledge largely by virtue of the extension in time of the association of inputs, especially human service inputs, with the firm. At any particular time, the costs and benefits of adjustments in governance modes for particular classes of transactions are substantially influenced by the network of transacting patterns already in place. Thus, the process of change in a firm's way of doing things most typically involves incremental adjustment in a complex, interdependent system. Such a process may well produce progress, but it does not produce an "answer" to any well-specified question or list of questions about how activity should be organized.

Relatedly, it is the interdependent system as a whole that is subject to the most significant informational feedback the market provides to the firm — its overall profitability. Of course, individual organizational problems, like individual technical problems, can be the object of "intendedly rational" problem-solving efforts by firm participants. Experience, learning, and adaptation can bring about improvement, or even an approximate local optimization, with respect to performance of a particular production task or the determination of the firm's boundaries at the micro level of a make-or-buy decision. But since it is the performance of the system as a whole to which the most important feedback relates, it is quite possible that a very good solution to one part of the system problem can carry, at least for a time, the cost burdens of a number of blunders in other areas. In that case, the profit incentives and evolutionary mechanisms favoring the replication of overall success can lead to the replication of the blunders along with the competitive advantages of the total system.

Given complex interdependence of sub-problems, given the size of the problem space generated by the need to specify one of M_i alternative solutions to each of N

sub-problems (with M_i's and N typically large), and given the economies of replicating routines of known effectiveness to achieve timely expansion of profitable activity, it seems unreasonable to expect in general that observed sub-problem solutions can be shown to be subtly responsive to contemporary features of their individual contexts. Rather, one should expect that many of the micro level "solutions" observable today may be understandable as "satisficing" choices, as adaptive responses to conditions that prevailed in the past, or as the consequences (for some reason durable) of past chance events.

Related observations apply to the question of the boundaries of the firm at the macro level, the overall size of the firm. In the evolutionary view—perhaps in contrast to the transaction cost view[15]—the size of a large firm at a particular time is not to be understood as the solution to some organizational problem. General Motors does not sit atop the Fortune 500 (at over $100 billion in 1986 sales) because some set of contemporary cost minimization imperatives (technological or organizational) require a certain chunk of the U.S. economy to be organized in this way. Its position at the top reflects the cumulative effect of a long string of happenings stretching back into the past, *among which* were the achievement of relatively good solutions to various technological and organizational problems,[16] the success of its ancestral companies in establishing strong positions in a young market that turned out to be a big one, and of course the creation by merger of the company itself. In short, a position atop the league standings is not a "great play." It may express the cumulative effect of many great plays; it does not exclude the possibility that there were also several not-so-great plays.

With respect to narrower issues, it seems that evolutionary economics and transaction cost economics typically offer refinements to the categories of the other approach. For example, the transaction cost approach urges attention to the organization of transactions across the boundaries of the firm as part of the problem that organizational "routines" must solve. This in turn suggests the need to characterize different transacting environments in ways that provide a basis for analyzing what sorts of transacting routines will prove viable in different environments. Transaction cost economics obviously offers a great deal of useful guidance to this effort.

Evolutionary economics suggests that the concept of human asset specificity is central to understanding the functioning of the firm as a repository of knowledge. For understanding to progress, however, the idea of "specificity" must be refined and linked to the broader context in which quasi-rents to various sorts of productive knowledge are determined. Thus, for example, the "hazards of opportunism" faced by an innovating firm include the possibility that several key employees will simultaneously quit and found a rival firm. Considered one by one, these employees may be strongly bound by human asset specificity to transacting with the original innovator. Considered as a coalition, however, the group's freedom of action may be much greater than the one-by-one analysis would suggest. The "specificity" of the investments involved is not really to the transaction pattern per se (that is, to transacting with the original innovator), but rather to the context that the innovator provided. If enough of the context can be moved simultaneously, the innovator may be left behind.

In sum, there are conflicts and complementarities between the transaction cost and evolutionary paradigms. Both provide opportunities for fruitful inquiry to advance understanding of the nature of the firm.

4. CONCLUDING COMMENT

In the past half-century, it has been clearly demonstrated that the economy is much better at changing itself than economists are at changing their minds. These divergent growth trends are grounds for dismay. But, after wasting at least a third of a century by not taking "The Nature of the Firm" seriously, the discipline now shows signs of a notable acceleration of progress. Perhaps the gap between our understanding and an increasingly complex reality is at last beginning to close.

NOTES

Financial support from the Sloan Foundation is gratefully acknowledged.

1. Instances of multiple independent discoveries of the same invention or scientific principle are frequently cited in support of the view that advances are "foreordained" in the sense that their elements are introduced to the intellectual environment by previous advances, and once they are there any number of investigators may perform the crucial juxtaposition of these elements to produce the advance in question (Merton). By this standard, Coase has a strong claim to having made an advance that was far from foreordained when he made it. Not only was there no codiscoverer, but decades passed before the discipline was ready to make use of the contribution. And one thing that happened during those decades was that Coase wrote another classic article — "The Problem of Social Cost" — that employed some of the same basic ideas in the context of a different problem.

2. An even more dramatic decline in institutional content and plausibility occurs between the elementary and intermediate levels. As Martin Shubik once observed, "The more elementary the textbook is, the more likely there will be information on different organizational forms. However, as soon as our study becomes 'advanced,' we do not bother to differentiate between General Motors and the local candy store" (413).

3. See Debreu, and Arrow and Hahn.

4. Walter Nicholson's distinguished text provides an example of a relatively high level of attention to these problems (ch. 10).

5. See J. S. Mill (1848: v. 1, book II, ch. XV).

6. Similarly, Adam Smith's comments on joint stock companies reflect a negative assessment of arrangements that empower directors who have little or none of their own capital at stake: "Like the stewards of a rich man, they are apt to consider attention to small matters as not for their master's honour, and very easily give themselves a dispensation from having it. Negligence and profusion, therefore, must always prevail, more or less, in the management of the affairs of such a company" (1776:700).

7. It is interesting to note that this problem is the subject of an article by Scitovsky that follows "The Nature of the Firm" in the AEA *Readings in Price Theory*.

8. Special-purpose general equilibrium models that address the question of who becomes an entrepreneur include those of Lucas, and Kihlstrom and Laffont. In the former case, entrepreneurial status goes with high managerial ability, which in turn corresponds to a

Hicks-neutral productivity factor modifying the given technology. In the latter case, everyone has equal access to the same technology and entrepreneurs are distinguished by their low risk aversion.

9. They sometimes proceed to engage in the testing activity endorsed by the third yes and then frequently come to the conclusion that the orthodox theory of the firm stands refuted. This empirical conclusion is obviously quite distinct from, and not entailed by, the yes-yes-yes methodological view. See Blaug (ch. 4 and 7) for an overview of the methodological controversy.

10. In lecture 2, Coase addresses the irrelevance-of-assumptions thesis directly and indicates his disagreement with it.

11. When I gave this issue serious attention in a recent paper (1986), noting in particular the opposition between Coase (1937) and Machlup, my discussant politely intimated that I was flogging a dead horse.

12. I use the term "productive knowledge" rather than, for example, "technology" because I view technology and organization as inseparable constituents of the ability to do things.

13. Actually, IBM developed a one-of-a-kind computer, the Selective Sequence Electronic Calculator (SSEC), over the period 1944–1947. Thomas J. Watson, Sr., felt that the one SSEC machine "could solve all the important scientific problems in the world involving scientific calculations." IBM sold specialized computers to the armed services and produced and leased a limited number of the "Defense Calculator" machine, later renamed the IBM 701, before producing the IBM 650. Thus, it could well be argued that IBM was in the industry from the start, though not as vigorously as some of its early rivals, particularly Remington Rand (Katz and Phillips: 169, 171, 177–78).

14. For a penetrating discussion of this and other methodological issues relating to the transaction cost paradigm, see Dow.

15. I will not take up the considerable challenge of describing where Coase, Williamson, and other transaction cost theories stand on the question of the determination of firm size. It is interesting to note that Williamson (1975: ch. 11) is quite consistent with the evolutionary view.

16. Of course, among the various problem solutions on the string are some that have provided recurring themes in transaction cost economics — for example, the invention of the M-form and the acquisition of Fisher Body. It may well be the case that *but* for these solutions and others, GM would not be atop the Fortune 500.

REFERENCES

Alchian, A. 1950. "Uncertainty, Evolution and Economic Theory," 58 *Journal of Political Economy* 211–21.

Arrow, K. J., and F. H. Hahn. 1971. *General Competitive Analysis*. San Francisco: Holden-Day.

Blaug, M. 1980. *The Methodology of Economics, or How Economists Explain*. Cambridge: Cambridge University Press.

Brennan, G., and G. Tullock. 1982. "An Economic Theory of Military Tactics: Methodological Individualism at War," 3 *Journal of Economic Behavior and Organization* 225–42.

Coase, R. H. 1937. "The Nature of the Firm," 4 *Economica* n.s. 386–405.

_____. 1960. "The Problem of Social Cost," 3 *Journal of Law and Economics* 1–44.

Debreu, G. 1959. *Theory of Value*. New York: John Wiley & Sons.

Dow, G. K. 1987. "The Function of Authority in Transaction Cost Economics," 8 *Journal of Economic Behavior and Organization* 13–38.

Graaf, J. de V. 1957. *Theoretical Welfare Economics*. Cambridge: Cambridge University Press.

Katz, B. G., and A. Phillips. 1982. "The Computer Industry." In R. R. Nelson, ed., *Government and Technical Progress: A Cross-Industry Analysis*. New York: Pergamon Press.

Kihlstrom, R. E., and J.-J. Laffont. 1959. "A General Equilibrium Entrepreneurial Theory of Firm Formation Based on Risk Aversion," 87 *Journal of Political Economy* 719–48.

Lucas, R. E., Jr. 1978. "On the Size Distribution of Business Firms," 9 *Bell Journal of Economics* 508–23.

Machlup, F. 1974. "Situational Determinism in Economics," 25 *British Journal for the Philosophy of Science* 271–84.

Merton, R. K. 1961. "Singletons and Multiples in Science." In N. W. Storer, ed., *The Sociology of Science: Theoretical and Empirical Investigations*. Chicago: University of Chicago Press.

Mill, J. S. [1848] 1899. *Principles of Political Economy*, v. 1. New York: The Colonial Press.

Nelson, R. R. 1980. "Production Sets, Technological Knowledge and R and D: Fragile and Overworked Constructs for Analysis of Productivity Growth?," 70 *American Economic Review* 62–67.

———, and S. G. Winter. 1982. *An Evolutionary Theory of Economic Change*. Cambridge: Belknap Press of Harvard University Press.

Nicholson, W. 1972. *Microeconomic Theory: Basic Principles and Extensions*. Hinsdale, Ill.: Dryden Press.

Scitovsky, T. 1943. "A Note on Profit Maximization and Its Implications." Repr. (1952) in G. Stigler and K. Boulding, eds., *AEA Readings in Price Theory*. Homewood, Ill.: R. D. Irwin.

Shubik, M. 1970. "A Curmudgeon's Guide to Microeconomics," 8 *Journal of Economic Literature* 405–34.

Simon, H. A. 1984. "On the Behavioral and Rational Foundations of Economic Dynamics," 5 *Journal of Economic Behavior and Organization* 35–55.

Smith, A. [1776] 1937. *An Inquiry into the Nature and Causes of the Wealth of Nations*. New York: The Modern Library.

Teece, D. J. 1982. "Towards an Economic Theory of the Multiproduct Firm," 3 *Journal of Economic Behavior and Organization* 39–63.

———. 1986. "Profiting from Technological Innovation: Implications for Integration, Collaboration, Licensing and Public Policy," 15 *Research Policy* 285–305.

Williamson, O. E. 1975. *Markets and Hierarchies*. New York: Free Press.

———. 1985. *The Economic Institutions of Capitalism*. New York: Free Press.

Winter, S. G. 1982. "An Essay on the Theory of Production." In S. H. Hymans, ed., *Economics and the World around It*. Ann Arbor: University of Michigan Press.

———. 1986. "The Research Program of the Behavioral Theory of the Firm: Orthodox Critique and Evolutionary Perspective." In B. Gilad and S. Kaish, eds., *Handbook of Behavioral Economics*, v. A (Behavioral Microeconomics), Greenwich, Conn.: JAI Press.

12

A Legal Basis for the Firm

SCOTT E. MASTEN

Fifty years after the publication of Ronald Coase's seminal deliberations on the subject, economists have yet to reach a consensus on the nature of the firm. While many continue to regard the firm as a distinct institution, usually ascribing to it some superior control, information, or adaptive properties, others reject the notion that any unique governance advantages accrue to integration, noting that neither human nature nor technology or information are altered by the purely nominal act of "internalization." For the latter, the word *firm* is merely descriptive, a collective noun denoting a particular cluster of otherwise ordinary contractual relationships.

The purpose of this article is not to offer another theory of vertical integration but rather to explore in more depth the logically antecedent question of whether it even makes sense to talk about the firm as a distinct organizational form. Specifically, is there a basis for associating special properties with internal organization, or is the designation *firm* really just descriptive of a set of commonly observed but otherwise unexceptional contractual relationships?

After briefly reviewing key elements of the controversy, I argue that the answer to this question lies in an examination of the broader legal and political institutions that regulate economic activity. The body of the paper is then devoted to exploring the status of the employment relationship in the legal system and a comparison of corresponding doctrines in commercial contract law to see whether legal rules establish an institutional basis for the advantages and limitations most commonly associated with internal organization.

1. THE NATURE OF THE DEBATE

The ambiguity regarding the nature of the firm in the economics literature can be traced back to Ronald Coase's original contribution. The language Coase adopts often suggests a conception of the firm as a distinct alternative to market exchange (chapter 2: 19):

Outside the firm, price movements direct production, which is co-ordinated through a series of exchange transactions on the market. Within a firm, these market transactions are eliminated and in place of the complicated market structure with exchange transactions is substituted the entrepreneur-co-ordinator, who directs production. It is clear that these are *alternative methods* of co-ordinating production (emphasis added).

But this apparently discrete view of the firm is subsequently qualified: "Of course, it is not possible to draw a hard and fast line which determines whether there is a firm or not. There may be more or less direction" (337, n. 21). Rather, the firm is characterized by the existence of a central contracting agent and a contract "whereby the factor, for certain remuneration (which may be fixed or fluctuating), agrees to obey the directions of the entrepreneur *within certain limits*" (336–37, emphasis in original). Hence, for Coase, the distinction between the firm and the market appears to be more a matter of degree than kind, the existence of the firm depending on the *amount* of discretion accorded the manager in the contract.[1]

While the conception of the firm offered by Coase is essentially descriptive, a number of more recent treatments of the vertical integration decision have clearly taken a more constructive view, crediting the firm with superior access to information and greater managerial control and flexibility.[2] But the source of those advantages has remained obscure. Where does the authority of management to direct production or settle disputes come from, and why are employees less able to hide or distort information than independent contractors? Armen Alchian and Harold Demsetz offered a major indictment of authority-based theories of the firm in their 1972 article (777):

It is common to see the firm characterized by the power to settle disputes by fiat, by authority, or by disciplinary action superior to that available in the conventional market. This is delusion. The firm does not own all its inputs. It has no power of fiat, no authority, no disciplinary action any different in the slightest degree from ordinary market contracting between any two people. I can "punish" you only by withholding future business or by seeking redress in the courts for any failure to honor our exchange agreement. That is exactly all that any employer can do. He can fire or sue, just as I can fire my grocer by stopping purchases from him or sue him for delivering faulty products.

The possibility that integration relieves information asymmetries has also been explicitly rejected: "Common ownership creates neither new information nor expertise. Nor does it create new auditing opportunities. Nonintegrated companies permit arbitrators to audit their operations when there is a dispute between them" (Evans and Grossman: 119–20). Such criticisms have led many economists to deny the existence of administrative solutions to contractual failures, asserting that the same transactional frictions confront employers as independent contractors. The firm, at least in governance respects, thus becomes no more than a coalition or "nexus" of contractual relationships, and the choice faced by transactors is only among the details to include in the contract. As Steven Cheung puts it, "It is *not* quite correct to say that a 'firm' supersedes 'the market.' Rather, one type of contract supersedes another type" (10). "Thus it is futile," he continues, "to press the issue of what is or is not a firm. . . . The important questions are why contracts take the forms observed and what are the economic implications of different contractual and pricing arrangements" (18; cf. Jensen and Meckling: 310–11, and Alchian and Demsetz: 778).

2. AN INSTITUTIONAL BASIS FOR THE FIRM

The issues that concern me are these: Are all economic relationships only contractual and therefore subject to the same economic calculus, or do institutional designations sometimes carry with them certain rights, responsibilities, or authority? And if institutions do exhibit special properties, what is the source of those distinctions?

The dissonance surrounding this issue derives, at least in part, from the many uses of the terms *contract* and *institution*. Both economists and lawyers often use the term *contract* in a broad sense encompassing both "agreement" and "transaction" in meaning. Accordingly, a promise to deliver steel in sixty days and a purchase from a grocer are often categorized equivalently as contractual. To define the firm as a collection of contracts under this expansive usage is tautological.

There is, however, another more restrictive connotation to the term *contract*, and that is as a formal, legal commitment to which each party gives express approval and to which a particular body of law applies (compare, for example, Klein, 1980:358; and Clark: 60–61). Not all transactions and agreements are contractual in this way. Thus, it is meaningful, in this sense, to distinguish between a simple exchange and a bona fide contract: "cancelling an order" differs from "breaching a contract," to use Stewart Macaulay's dichotomy (61). In this narrower sense the nexus-of-contracts definition of the firm is disputable. Employees with special skills or those represented by a union may have an explicit contract with management, but the typical employment relationship is "at will," that is, "a simple exchange of a day's work for a day's pay" (see, for example, *Journal of Law Reform*, 1983:449–50, n. 5).

The real issue in contemplating the nature of the firm, however, is not whether the relationships among members are contractual but whether the firm represents a distinct institution in the constructive sense of the word. Like *contract, institution* has broad and narrow applications. The broad sense is essentially descriptive; it includes all modes or conventions for transacting as well as the organizations embodying them and is aptly applied to any pattern of behavior or collection of relationships that occurs with enough frequency to merit a label. Markets and credit in their generic senses are examples of economic institutions under this definition.

In its narrower sense, *institution* denotes a more established arrangement, a relationship or organization whose existence or boundaries are defined and administered by an exogenous authority. Membership or participation in such an institution typically confers particular rights or responsibilities and establishes the rules and procedures that govern the conduct of the transactors. Congress is governed by the Constitution, an agency of government by its enabling legislation, and a corporation by its charter and the laws of incorporation. The relationships among members of these bodies are all contractual in the broad sense, but the organizations themselves represent distinct institutions in that term's narrow sense by virtue of the peculiar rules and procedures that regulate admissible behavior within them. It is only by the definition and regulation of allowable behavior by a dominant authority or set of institutions that institutional designations achieve constructive as opposed to merely descriptive meaning.

The question of the nature of the firm can now be reformulated in these terms. Does the law, for example, really treat commercial and employment transactions equivalently? In particular, are any rights, authority, or responsibilities given to employers or employees (or any limitations placed on them) that are not available in analogous form to commercial transactors? Whether internal organization represents a distinct alternative to market exchange depends on whether such differences exist and how they influence the incentive structure within and between firms. Thus, the issue of whether the firm is a distinct institution is ultimately a question of fact: Are there mechanisms or sanctions available in employment transactions that are not similarly available to independent contractors?[3]

2.1. Duties and Obligations

Ironically, economists have either downplayed or rejected outright the role of the law in defining the firm, divorcing the economic concept from the "legal fiction" (see Jensen and Meckling: 310–11; and Rubin: 225).[4] Even a cursory examination of the case law governing the relationship between employers and employees, however, reveals a set of obligations and responsibilities that are indeed unique to employment transactions and which often coincide precisely with the traditional emphasis in economics on the information and authority advantages of internal organization. Upon entering an employment relationship, for example, every employee accepts an implied duty to "yield obedience to all reasonable rules, orders, and instructions of the employer" (53 American Jurisprudence [2nd] §97; Restatement of Agency [2nd], §§2, 220, 385). The importance of authority in employer-employee relationships is given further weight by the criteria that courts use to adjudicate disputes over the nature of a particular transaction. The overriding consideration expressed by the courts in such cases is the control exercised by an employer and, especially, whether the latter is concerned with the manner in which work is performed and not solely with its outcome. In evaluating a transaction, "the first, and seminal, inquiry is whether the alleged employer . . . has the *right* to control . . . the details of the alleged employee's work" (Pitts *v.* Shell Oil Co., 463 F.2nd 331 [1972], emphasis in original; also see Restatement (2nd) of Agency, §2); whereas, "an 'independent' contractor is generally defined as one who in rendering services exercises an independent employment or occupation and represents his employer only as to the results of his work and not as to the means whereby it is to be done" (56 Corpus Juris Secundum (hereafter CJS) 45; Restatement of Agency [2nd], §§2, 14). Hence, the traditional emphasis in economics on the authority of management to direct the efforts of employees is at least nominally supported by the law governing employment transactions.

Comparison of commercial and employment law also provides support for the informational advantage commonly attributed to internal organization in the traditional view of the firm. In commercial transactions, laws regarding the transfer of information are fairly liberal. As a rule, "one party to a business transaction is not liable to the other for harm caused by his failure to disclose to the other facts of which he knows the other is ignorant and which he further knows the other, if he knew them, would regard as material in determining his course of action in the transaction in question" (Restatement [2nd] of Torts, §551; also see Restatement of Contracts [2nd], §303). The most prominent exception to that rule concerns the existence of a fiduciary relationship between the transactors such as that of principal and agent or employer and employee.[5] Where such a relationship exists, the agent is legally obligated to reveal relevant information to the principal (see Restatement of Agency, §381, Restatement of Torts [ibid.] and Kronman). This exception to the general rule of nondisclosure has also become codified in the law of master and servant as the employee's duties to disclose and account, under which a subordinate is obliged "to communicate to [his employer] all facts which he ought to know" (56 CJS 67; see also Clark: 71–72, and Michigan Crown Fender Co. v. Welch, 13 American Law Reports 896 [1920]). Again, the law distinguishes between employment and commercial transactions in a way that apparently supports the superior access to information traditionally assumed to accrue to integration in the economics literature.

The obligations of an employee to an employer, moreover, involve much more than simple compliance to managerial directives and disclosure of information. In addition to obedience, an employer has the right to expect loyalty, respect, and faithfulness from his employees and that each will "conduct himself with such decency and propriety of deportment as not to work injury to the business of his employer" (53 Am. Jur. 2nd; see also Restatement of Agency [2nd], §§380, 387). These duties extend so far as to require the employee to maintain "friendly relations" with the employer (Restatement of Agency [2nd], §380). Criticizing the concept of the firm used by agency theorists, Robert Clark discusses some of the specific implications the requirement of loyalty has for managers.[6] For example, in comparison to the obligations of an independent contractor, the duty of loyalty places larger demands on a manager employed to run a business on behalf of others:

> The independent contractor usually has relatively fixed obligations under his contact. If the contract does not call for a particular performance, he does not have to do it [whereas] with corporate managers, the open-endedness of legally imposed duties is more substantial. . . . Case law on managers' fiduciary duty of care can fairly be read to say that the manager has an affirmative, open-ended duty to maximize the beneficiaries' wealth (73).

The duty of loyalty also restricts the ability of a manager to benefit at the expense of owners. "Essentially," Clark continues, "the fiduciary cannot take any compensation from the beneficiaries or any other advantages from his official position (even when doing so does not seem to deprive the beneficiaries of any value they would otherwise get) except to the extent provided in an above-board actual contract" (73).[7] The law affords independent contractors considerably more leeway in exploiting business opportunities (see below).

Finally, although I have to this point emphasized the employee's duties, employers also assume certain responsibilities upon entering an employment transaction. Along with authority to direct an employee's behavior comes liability under the doctrine of *respondeat superior* for any harms the employee causes to third parties in the course of his employment. "This doctrine," however, "does not apply to the relationship between employer and independent contractor because the employer cannot exercise control over the manner of the contractor's work" (Dykstra and Dykstra: 356). Thus, responsibility for outcomes is assigned to the party ostensibly in control.

Overall, the duties accruing to employment transactions under the law are consistent, at least superficially, with the authority and information properties often associated with internal organization. In fact, the intent of employment law seems to be to make the employee as much as possible an extension of the employer. The duties discussed above, moreover, accrue independently of whether or not they are explicitly contained in a contract (Restatement of Agency [2nd], §§220, 225). The body of law applicable in each case depends on whether the relationship is between independent contractors or employer and employee. In other words, the set of rules that govern the relationship depend on the institution chosen.

2.2. Sanctions and Procedures

Duties of obedience and disclosure, of course, have force only if mechanisms exist to implement them. Statements such as the following, quoted in Batt's *The Law of Master and Servant*, have tended to undermine such distinctions (from Mercy Docks and Harbour Board *v.* Coggins and Griffith [Liverpool] Ltd., [1947] A.C. I):

> "I take no orders from anybody," said the cranedriver.
> "A sturdy answer," said Lord Simmons, "which meant that he was a skilled man and knew his job and would carry it out in his own way. Yet ultimately he would decline to carry it out in [his employers'] way at his own peril, for in their hands lay the only sanction, the power of dismissal" (2).

If the power of management to enforce its directives rests solely on the threat of dismissal, as this passage suggests, then — a nominal duty to obey notwithstanding — the authority of management is no different from that of an independent transactor engaged in ordinary market exchange. Absent an express contract to the contrary, the ability to terminate negotiations and any further dealings is also the "only sanction" normally available to commercial transactors dissatisfied with the terms of trade currently tendered. Obviously, the claim of special authority in employment transactions cannot be based on the threat of termination alone. Otherwise, as Alchian and Demsetz maintained, there can be no material distinction between employment transactions and any other simple exchange in a market setting.

The large volume of case law devoted to defining and differentiating between employment and commercial transactions makes it difficult, however, to dismiss the notion that institutional form matters. If courts cared only about the *details* of a relationship as stipulated in a contract when evaluating performance, then the *type* of relationship the parties had entered would be irrelevant. That transactions are willing to spend resources litigating the designation of a transaction is a strong indication that institutional labels do create legal distinctions having practical implications for the transacting parties. This suggests that it may be appropriate to look beyond the duties nominally accruing to employment transactors to a more fundamental set of questions: Is termination really the only sanction or are there other penalties available to employers and employees and, if so, how do these differ from those available to commercial transactors? Is the ability to write and enforce contracts the same in commercial and employment settings or do the criteria for performance and the penalties for breach differ across institutions? In other words, do the circumstances under which an employer can *fire* or *sue* and the remedies and penalties prescribed by the law differ depending on the mode of organization?

Although a fairly well-established body of common law governs both employment and commercial relations and many of the basic rules of behavior apply to both (see below), a closer look at the case law reveals there are indeed a number of differences in the mechanisms and penalties available to commercial and employment transactors and in their application by the courts. For instance, despite the passage from Batt's *The Law of Master and Servant* quoted above, the threat of dismissal is not the only sanction available to employers. An employee who fails to uphold his duties may actually be held liable for damages if that failure were to cause injury to his employer's business. "In an absence of a waiver of the breach, the employer may recover damages from his employee . . . for involving his employer in loss through his own negligence or wrongful act . . . , or *generally for any failure to perform the duties devolving on him under the employment contract*" (56 CJS 500, emphasis added; Restatement of Agency [2nd] §§399, 400, 401).

Again, whereas the personal conduct and loyalty of participants in commercial exchanges are strictly a matter of business judgment, the law obligates an employee, with few exceptions, to act in his employer's interest. Disloyalty may, of course, be tempered by reputation considerations in both types of transactions, but formal legal sanctions for such behavior are available only to employers. An independent supplier who recruited personnel from a commercial customer might jeopardize future dealings but could not generally be held legally accountable for the customer's loss. Were the raider an employee, however, the enticement of fellow workers to join a competing concern is likely to constitute a breach of the duty of loyalty and entitle the former employer to recover damages (see Frederick Chusid & Co. *v.*

Marshall Leeman & Co., 326 F. Supp. 1043 [1971]). This aspect of the law is also what creates common law remedies for insider trading as well as a number of other practices prohibited to employees but open to outside contractors (see Clark: 74–75). The important point is that the law entitles an employer to recover damages from a disloyal or uncooperative subordinate and thereby differentiates the incentives of employees from those of independent contractors in a discrete fashion, altering the payoff to uncooperative employee behavior in a way that arguably supports the authority commonly attributed to employers in the theory of the firm.

Similar sanctions support the employee's disclosure duty. Specifically, an employee is legally accountable for any pecuniary losses sustained by his employer as a result of failing to disclose relevant facts and is liable for damages and the return of any ill-gotten gains derived from that failure.[8] An independent subcontractor bears no such responsibility and is free, among other things, to exploit profit opportunities that arise in the course of the contract's performance (see, for example, Clark: 73–75). The fact that an employee is less likely to profit successfully from nondisclosure should reduce his incentive to distort or conceal information from his employer.

The objection made by Evans and Grossman that commercial contractors may employ arbitrators to audit a firm and resolve disputes does not undermine this argument. Ultimately, arbitrators must rely on the provision of information by the disputants. An uncooperative actor (especially one that assessed a small probability of success but wished to buy time) could impede arbitration and conceivably force the issue into court. The differential treatment courts bestow on integrated and independent transactors under the laws regarding disclosure will influence both the prospect and timing of successful access to information. The employee's duty to disclose makes it much more likely that an employer would receive a summary judgment in his favor than would an independent contractor in an otherwise similar situation. The prevailing doctrine would place a larger burden on a plaintiff to demonstrate a right to access the internal records of a nonintegrated defendant. Obviously, the delays and other costs such litigation could impose are likely to create a greater barrier to accessing information from an independent contractor than from an integrated division. In this light, the radical change from asymmetric to costless information that traditional theories associate with integration exaggerates but does not contradict the reduction in institutional barriers to information that prevailing legal doctrine affords internal organization.

The procedures for resolving disputes in commercial and employment transactions also differ—and do so in ways that enhance the flexibility of internal organization. As Williamson points out, managerial directives possess a presumptive validity that is reflected in the rules governing conflicts between employers and employees, even in collective bargaining settings:

> Even where the collective agreement lists certain offenses or the parties negotiate plant rules, management may normally supplement the listed offenses or negotiated rules. Rules prescribed by management are subject to arbitrator review, but they carry a presumptive validity and will be upheld so long as

they are reasonably related to achieving efficient operation and maintaining order and are not manifestly unfair or do not unnecessarily burden employees' rights. Management also is entitled to have its orders obeyed and may discipline employees for refusing to obey even improper orders. Arbitrators almost uniformly hold that an employee must obey first and then seek recourse through the grievance procedure, except where obeying would expose him to substantial risks of health and safety (Summers, cited in Williamson, 1985:249).

Disagreements in commercial dealings, by comparison, require "mutual consent before adaptations can be effected" (Williamson, 1985:249). This difference can be important. In the time necessary to negotiate a mutually advantageous adjustment, the opportunity to act may well have passed. The potential liability of an employee for failing to obey or delaying performance of a reasonable directive, on the other hand, is likely to encourage immediate compliance, thereby promoting responsive adaptation to changing circumstances.

The extension of liability for the torts of the employee to the employer under the doctrine of *respondeat superior* also affects incentives in employment transactions. First, it motivates employers to monitor employees' activities more closely. And second, to the extent that an employee may seek legal compensation from an employer for personal liability to third parties for actions undertaken at the direction of the employer, it may reduce the employee's reluctance to follow orders by lessening his need to assess the consequences of those actions. Interestingly, while the monitoring function per se does not define the firm, as Alchian and Demsetz and others have suggested it does, the incentives created by the supporting institutional structure is likely to encourage more intensive monitoring within firms than between them—even holding claims on residual income constant.[9]

Thus, there appears to be differences both in the obligations assumed to accrue to transactors in employment and commercial settings and in the sanctions and procedures that support those obligations. In other words, although both employment and commercial transactors have the right to sue, what they can sue for and their expectations of success differ in relation to the transaction's designation and the common law that applies. Again, the legal distinctions examined so far seem to support the authority and information properties often ascribed to internal organization in the traditional view of the firm.

2.3. Termination and Contracting

Another property often associated with the firm is the greater flexibility to terminate a relationship that the doctrine of employment-at-will affords an employer (see, for example, Rubin). Employment-at-will empowers either party to an employment transaction to terminate the relationship "for good cause, bad cause, or no cause at all" (see, for example, *Stanford Law Review*: 335). The doctrine is more a source of symmetry than contrast between commercial and employment exchanges, however. Commercial transactors engaged in a simple exchange across a market interface also have the right, in the absence of a contract, to discontinue a trading relationship unilaterally. Thus, rather than distinguishing the firm, the doctrine of employment-at-will seems to place employment and commercial dealings (again, absent a formal contract) on an equal footing with regard to termination.

The law also treats employment and commercial *contracts* similarly in many respects. First, employers and employees, like commercial transactors, can generally contract out of the at-will setting by mutual consent (see Epstein). Stipulated damage provisions, for instance, are generally upheld under the same circumstances in both contracts *of service* and contracts *for services* (see *Journal of Law Reform*: 457). The rules governing employment and commercial contracts of unspecified duration are also similar. While employment contracts of unspecified term provide no guarantee of continued performance (*Stanford Law Review*: 345), indefinite-term commercial contracts require only "reasonable notification" for unilateral termination (see UCC §2–309).

Even statutory prohibitions against specific performance in employment contracts offer little distinction in practice. Even though an employee cannot ordinarily be compelled to render services to an employer, specific performance is infrequently applied in commercial settings as well.[10] Rather, the penalties normally imposed for nonperformance of commercial and employment agreements are similar: lost profits versus lost wages less what can be earned "by reasonable effort in other similar employment" (Corbin, §958).

Yet despite these similarities, differences do exist in the treatments courts afford employment and commercial contacts. In particular, the duties discussed above provide an important distinction regarding what constitutes breach of contract in employment and commercial settings. Although only "substantial performance" of the contract is required in either contracts for services or of service, the duties and obligations automatically accruing to every employment transaction provide employers wider latitude to suspend employment contracts: an employment contract may be discharged on the basis of employee indolence, dishonesty, disloyalty, or disrespect, among other offenses. Even where employment is protected under a collective bargaining agreement, fighting, insubordination, the use of profanity or abusive language to supervisors, theft, dishonesty, gambling, and the possession or use of drugs or alcohol have all been found to constitute "just cause" for termination of an employment contract (see Steiber and Murray: 323). But although indolence or disrespect may be bad business in commercial transactions, such behavior would not constitute an actionable cause for discharge of a commercial contract.

The burden of proof in contract disputes also supports the employer's authority. Although an employee may contest a claim of unsatisfactory performance, it is the employee's burden to show that his behavior was in fact satisfactory: "The general rule . . . is that the employee may question the honesty and good faith of his employer's dissatisfaction, and a feigned dissatisfaction is not sufficient justification to avoid continuation of a contract of employment . . . , [but] the burden of proof [rests] upon the employee to show that the claimed dissatisfaction is not in good faith" (Coker *v.* Wesco Materials Corp., 308 S.W. 2nd 884 [1963]). Given the inclusiveness of employees' duties, proving bad faith termination is likely to be difficult in practice.

Such differences in the criteria for discharge of contractual obligations can be interpreted as further contributing to employers' control over the method of production relative to commercial contractors. In comparison to an employee, an independent subcontractor is relatively immune to contract cancellation on the basis of behavior that is largely extraneous to the central purpose of the agreement. The difficulty of proving bad faith termination in employment transactions, moreover, further increases the incentive of employees (relative to independent contractors) to perform satisfactorily and avoid conflicts, especially in cases where the unsatisfactory performance is either marginal in nature or difficult to substantiate in court. In these respects, then, the law serves to make dismissal a more credible threat when made by an employer than by an independent contractor. As a result, an employee under threat of dismissal is more likely to accept managerial redirection—holding reputation considerations constant—than a commercial supplier with common law protections against breach of contract.

Finally, even where an express contract does not exist, there may still be differences in the ability of parties to terminate the relationship. Although an agreement normally carries the force of law only if the parties have expressly bound themselves to performance in writing or by other express means, modern contract law will sometimes infer the existence of a contractual obligation if, for instance, one party has relied on the performance of the other. In particular, if one party is induced to undertake investments in support of a transaction, the value of which would not be recoverable if the other party failed to perform, the courts may treat the transaction as though a formal agreement had in fact been accepted despite insufficient evidence that an explicit bargain had been struck. A distributor who incurred advertising expenditures in reliance on the delivery of brand name merchandise, for example, might be able to recover damages if the manufacturer failed to deliver as promised, even if a formal contract was never stipulated.

Related doctrines under which courts have inferred contractual obligations despite the lack of formal written agreements include promissory estoppel and implied or quasi-contract (see, for example, *Stanford Law Review* and *Journal of Law Reform*). Such remedies have generally been denied in an employment setting, however: "Most courts have been reluctant to find any contractual obligation of just cause discharge in an at-will setting, despite employee reliance on express or implied promises of job security" (*Journal of Law Reform*: 455). Instead, the inference of a contractual obligation has been held to a stricter standard requiring "independent consideration": "To avoid arbitrary discharge, employees must provide their employers with consideration, such as monetary contribution, property transfer, or other financial benefit, arising independently of their jobs. Only after providing such 'independent' consideration have employees been able to enforce employer promises of job security. . . . In any other commercial setting these employer promises would create binding contractual obligations; in the employment setting, however, they have not been viewed as legally binding" (ibid.: 449–50).[11] As a result of this distinction, the threat of termination may be more powerful in employment than in commercial settings. A commercial transactor who has relied on the performance of another would have less fear of termination given the potential of recovering the value of his reliance in a court of law. An employee, on the other hand, who does not have such protection would likely be much more careful to avoid giving an employer reason to reconsider the relationship. Hence, on the margin, the employee again has a greater incentive to accede to the employer's demands than would a commercial contractor.

3. CONCLUSION

Ex ante, contracting is a flexible institution. Transactors can, at least in principle, design each relationship to suit their particular needs. In all but the simplest exchanges, however, the process of exploring and stipulating details of a transaction can become expensive very quickly. In addition, many basic terms and conditions are likely to be common across transactions. To minimize the costly duplication of identical provisions in individual contracts, the law provides a set of standard doctrines and remedies to deal with recurring contractual events. Thus, both court-determined penalties for contract breach and common law application of force majeure criteria can be interpreted as substitutes for the redundant stipulation of common provisions by individual transactors. At the same time, courts recognize the diversity of transactions and give parties wide latitude to augment or modify the terms of the agreement by mutual consent. The existence of a standard set of doctrines to govern contractual exchange and the ability to "'contract out of or away from' the governance structures of the state by devising private orderings" (Williamson, 1983:520) combine to provide a degree of both economy and flexibility in constructing contractual relationships.

There is, however, no reason to believe that the distribution of transactions is unimodal, so that the logic that justifies the existence of an original set of common law doctrines may also warrant the establishment of alternative sets of norms and conventions (namely, institutions) to govern disparate clusters of transactions. Granted, the flexibility afforded transactors in designing contracts admits the possibility of altering rules and remedies to effect any desired structure. Employer-employee relations could be replicated, for instance, through detailed stipulation of the duties and sanctions defined in the law of master and servant in a contract, in which case the contract rather than the case law would become the reference point in the event of a dispute. But accomplishing this would, for all intents and purposes, require reviewing and repeating the entire case law in each contract, obviously forfeiting a substantial economy.[12] Reliance on common law doctrines, in contrast, permits transactors to choose that combination of legal "defaults" or "presets" that most closely approximates the ideal arrangement simply by identifying the class of transactions that the parties intended, to which they may again make incremental adjustments by mutual consent.

The differences in legal defaults, sanctions, and procedures governing commercial and employment transactions provide a constructive, as opposed to merely descriptive, connotation to the notion of the firm. The failure to document adequately such differences made it difficult for traditional theorists to identify a basis for the special managerial authority or access to information usually attributed to integration and led a number of prominent authors to deny the existence of a governance role for internal organization. At most, the firm took on constructive meaning only relative to "those assets (e.g., machines, inventories) that it owns" (Grossman and Hart: 692).

In a formal sense, the distinction between the ownership and governance roles of the firm is a spurious one, however. Ownership itself is a condition sustained by legal rules and remedies. But a change in legal status obviously does not physically transform an asset. What is altered is the relationship of economic actors to those assets, their rights and responsibilities as defined and supported by the legal system. As Harold Demsetz put it, "The problem of defining ownership is precisely that of creating properly scaled legal barriers to entry" (52), that is, of establishing penalties that promote or discourage specific behavior. In this respect, there is no substantive difference between the power of a manager to direct an employee and an owner's ability to restrain the use or removal of an asset. Just as control over individuals is influenced by the rules and penalties prescribed in the law, so is control over physical capital. In either case, an agent's incentives to comply depend on the sanctions the principal can bring to bear. Thus, although particulars may differ—sanctions for disobedience versus those for theft, for instance—ownership, like managerial authority, is ultimately a governance issue.[13]

In this paper, I have addressed the question of what distinguishes organization within the firm from external or market exchange by reviewing the legal literature on employment transactions and comparing it with corresponding doctrines in commercial contract law. Although by no means comprehensive, the investigation reveals that the law does in fact recognize substantial differences in the obligations, sanctions, and procedures governing the two types of exchange, and that these distinctions are likely to alter the incentives of actors across institutional modes in a meaningful way. Moreover, they do so in a manner that appears to support the conventional view of the firm in economics. On one side, the results lend support to the authority, flexibility, and information advantages commonly attributed to internal organization. The effects of the law are such that an employee interested in preserving an employment relationship appears to have stronger incentives to comply with the demands of his employer than would an independent contractor similarly situated. Again, the distinctions and responsibilities uncovered seem to have the intent of making the employee, to as great an extent as possible, an extension of his employer.

At the same time that the laws promote obedience and disclosure by an employee, however, they are also likely to discourage employee initiative and investments in information acquisition and, generally, to require greater monitoring by the employer. An employee's liability for nondisclosure, for instance, not only decreases his incentive to withhold information from his employer but also his incentive to accumulate information in the first place, increasing the need for employee oversight. The employer's liability for the torts of his employees is also likely to encourage greater supervision of subordinates. The strain that this increased attention places on the finite capacities of managers to effectively administer production and exchange represents the principle disadvantage of internalizing successive transactions and ultimately limits the size of the firm.

As Ronald Coase made clear, the decision to integrate depends on the relative merits of the alternatives. My goal in this article has been to identify some of the legal rules that might bear on the outcome of those comparisons. The question of how such rules evolve in the first place, and whether specific rules, such as the doctrine of employment-at-will, promote efficient organization, are beyond the scope of this paper but obviously worthy of attention. Just how important formal legal doctrines are in organizational decisions is also an open question. Changes in legal rules over time and cross-jurisdictional differences in the way courts handle employment disputes should, according to this argument, alter the incentives of transactors to integrate exchange and the form that integration takes, raising the possibility of empirical tests.

NOTES

I would like to thank Keith Crocker, James Krier, Frank Easterbrook, Michael Rosenzweig, George Siedel, Ted Snyder, Valerie Suslow, and Martin Zimmerman for helpful comments on an earlier draft of this essay. The comments of Ronald Coase, Oliver Williamson, and an anonymous referee are also gratefully acknowledged, as is research support from the University of Michigan Graduate School of Business Administration. All of the usual disclaimers apply.

1. Herbert Simon's early treatment of the employer-employee relationship offers a similar view. For Simon, like Coase, the essential feature of the employment contract is the discretion left to the employer to direct some dimension of the employee's behavior (294). Under this definition, however, the employment relationship is analytically indistinguishable from any contract in which one party is empowered to alter some aspect of performance unilaterally. An example would be a fixed price, variable-quantity contract in which the buyer has the "authority" to determine the volume of trade under the agreement and can thus "direct" the production level of the seller. Such arrangements are not at all uncommon in long-term contracts. But although they conform in a technical sense to Simon's definition of an employment transaction, the relationship between the buyer and seller in such contracts would not generally be considered that of employer and employee. At best, the distinction between employee and supplier is again a matter of degree. Only the details and not the type of contract entered separate an employment from a commercial transaction, and neither the label *firm* nor *employee* has any force beyond the provisions explicitly adopted in the contract itself.

2. In *Markets and Hierarchies*, for instance, Oliver Williamson ascribes to the firm superior auditing and conflict resolution properties: internal auditors are believed to have superior access to the information necessary for decisionmaking; and internal dispute resolution mechanisms are perceived as more responsive to changing circumstances than court adjudication, encumbered as it is by strict procedural requirements (1975:29–30). Changes in the information structure of exchange have also formed the basis for more formal models of

the vertical integration decision, such as in Kenneth Arrow's analysis that treats integration as "essentially a way of acquiring predictive information" (176; also see Crocker). Similar advantages are implicit in virtually every model of vertical integration.

3. In what follows, I have attempted to cite the most common rules of law as reported in original cases, legal treatises, and case books. While some exceptions and cross-jurisdictional differences in either the laws of how they are applied exist, the general principles cited are fairly standard in American common law.

In an earlier draft I had also relied on a number of legal encyclopedias for statements of the general rules governing employment transactions. I was advised by legal counsel (see the acknowledgments), however, that legal scholars considered such sources less than authoritative. Although for expository purposes I have sometimes found it convenient to retain the language of these sources, in every case I have supported the quotations with supplementary citations from more authoritative sources.

4. Jensen and Meckling, to whom the phrase "nexus of contractual relationships" is attributable, offer seemingly contradictory statements on the importance of law to organization. On one hand they assert, "It makes little or no sense to try to distinguish those things which are 'inside' the firm (or any other organization) from those things that are 'outside' of it. There is in a very real sense only a multitude of complex relationships (i.e., contracts) between the legal fiction (the firm) and the owners of labor, material and capital inputs and the consumers of output" (311). In a footnote following shortly thereafter, however, they observe, "This view of the firm [as a nexus for contracting relationships] points up the important role which the legal system and the law play in social organizations, especially, the organization of economic activity. . . . [Various] government activities affect both the kinds of contracts executed and the extent to which contracting is relied upon. This in turn determines the usefulness, productivity, profitability and viability of various forms of organization" (311, n. 14).

5. For other exceptions, see Kronman. Note that a servant or employee is always an agent but that not all agents are servants. For the legal definitions of principals and agents, master and servants, and independent contractors, see Restatement of Agency (2nd), §§1 and 2.

6. Clark's position on the concept of the firm adopted by agency theorists is consonant in many respects with the one advanced here. The present paper goes further, I believe, in its analysis of the controversy over the nature of the firm, in examining the sanctions supporting the duties accruing to employees and the role of termination, and in interpreting the economic implications of the legal distinctions between employment and commercial relationships, especially as they apply to the advantages commonly associated with internal organization.

7. The rules that apply to the relationship between an owner and manager also apply to master and servant or employer and employee relationships; see Restatement of Agency (2nd), §25.

8. See Michigan Crown Fender Co. *v.* Welch, ibid. Moreover, "It is not necessary that the employer suffer actual loss before he is entitled to recover ill gained profits from an employee or agent" (Byer *v.* International Paper Co., 314 F. 2nd 831 [1963]).

9. More recently, Armen Alchian has placed some distance between himself and this definition of the firm; see Alchian, 1984.

10. Specific performance may be required if a service involves a special or unique ability. In these cases, however, the contract is considered as being *for services* rather than *of service*, that is, as a commercial rather than employment transaction.

11. Courts have applied a number of public policy exceptions to the "at-will" rule; see Steiber and Murray: 322. In addition, some courts have recently begun to impute just-cause

protections to a wider range of employment relationships, in effect, inferring the existence of contractual guarantees where no explicit written contract exists (on the evolution of these changes, see Finkin). This apparent change in the rules applying to employment transactions has the effect of reducing flexibility of employment relationships relative to simple commercial exchanges. As discussed above, however, the variety of behavior constituting just cause for dismissal of an employee still tends to afford transactors more flexibility to terminate an employment relationship than a commercial *contract*.

12. Clark suggests that exact replication may not, in fact, be possible: "[Basic fiduciary duties] cannot be bargained around (unless, perhaps, one is willing to depart from the manager or stockholder roles or to modify their parameters drastically)" (64). See also n. 10.

13. While Grossman and Hart are generally critical of transaction-cost theories of the firm for reasons similar to those outlined in this paper, their use of legal opinion to define ownership in terms of "residual rights of control over assets" is compatible with the approach adopted here. They also suggest that their theory may be extended to residual rights of control over actions as a basis for analyzing "the relative advantages of contractor-contractee and employer-employee relationships" (717). Among other things, the present paper details the source and nature of those rights in the duties and sanctions defined by the legal system.

REFERENCES

Alchian, Arman A. 1984. "Specificity, Specialization, and Coalitions," 140 *Journal of Institutional and Theoretical Economics/Zeitschrift für die gesamte Staatswissenschaft* 34–39.

———, and Harold Demsetz. 1972. "Production, Information Costs, and Economic Organization," 62 *American Economic Review* 777–95.

Arrow, Kenneth J. 1975. "Vertical Integration and Communication," 6 *Bell Journal of Economics* 173–83.

Batt, E. R. 1967. *the Law of Master and Servant*, ed. G. J. Webber, 5th ed. London: Pitman and Sons.

Cheung, Steven N. S. 1983. "The Contractual Nature of the Firm," 26 *Journal of Law and Economics* 1–21.

Clark, Robert C. 1985. "Agency Costs versus Fiduciary Duties." In J. Pratt and R. Zeckhauser, eds., *Principals and Agents: The Structure of Business*. Boston: Harvard Business School Press, 55–79, 217–19.

Coase, Ronald. 1937. "The Nature of the Firm" [chapter 2 of this volume].

Corbin, A. 1951. *Corbin on Contracts*. St. Paul: West Publishing Co.

Crocker, Keith J. 1983. "Vertical Integration and the Strategic Use of Private Information," 14 *Bell Journal of Economics* 236–48.

Demsetz, Harold. 1982. "Barriers to Entry," 72 *American Economic Review* 47–57.

Dykstra, G. O., and L. G. Dykstra. 1969. *Business Law: Text and Cases* (3rd [Uniform Commercial Code] ed.). New York: Pitman.

Epstein, Richard A. 1984. "In Defense of the Contract at Will," 51 *University of Chicago Law Review* 947–82.

Evans, David, and Sanford Grossman. 1983. "Integration." In D. Evans, ed., *Breaking Up Bell*. New York: North-Holland.

Finkin, Matthew W. 1986. "The Bureaucratization of Work: Employer Policies and Contract Law," *Wisconsin Law Review* 733–53.

Geotz, Charles J., and Robert E. Scott. 1983. "The Mitigation Principle: Toward a General Theory of Contractual Obligation," 69 *Virginia Law Review* 967–1024.

Grossman, Sanford J., and Oliver D. Hart. 1986. "The Costs and Benefits of Ownership: A Theory of Vertical Integration," 94 *Journal of Political Economy* 691–719.

Klein, Benjamin. 1980. "Transaction-Cost Determinants of 'Unfair' Contractual Arrangements," 70 *American Economic Review* 356–62.

Klein, Benjamin, Robert G. Crawford, and Armen A. Alchian. 1978. "Vertical Integration, Appropriable Rents and the Competitive Contracting Process," 21 *Journal of Law and Economics* 297–326.

Kronman, Anthony T. 1978. "Mistake, Disclosure, Information, and the Law of Contracts," 7 *Journal of Legal Studies* 1–34.

Macaulay, Stewart. 1963. "Non-Contractual Relations in Business," 28 *American Sociological Review* 55–70.

Jensen, Michael C., and William H. Meckling. 1976. "Theory of the Firm: Managerial Behavior, Agency Costs and Ownership Structure," 3 *Journal of Financial Economics* 305–60.

Journal of Law Reform. 1983. "Note: Challenging the Employment-At-Will Doctrine through Modern Contract Theory," 16 *Journal of Law Reform* 449.

Rubin, Paul H. 1978. "The Theory of the Firm and the Structure of the Franchise Contract," 21 *Journal of Law and Economics* 223–33.

Simon, Herbert A. 1951. "A Formal Theory of the Employment Relationship," 19 *Econometrica* 293–305.

Stanford Law Review. 1974. "Note: Implied Contract Rights to Job Security," 26 *Stanford Law Review* 335.

Steiber, Jack, and Michael Murray. 1983. "Protection against Unjust Discharge: The Need for a Federal Statute," 16 *Journal of Law Reform* 319–41.

Williamson, Oliver E. 1975. *Markets and Hierarchies.* New York: Free Press.

_____. 1983. "Credible Commitments: Using Hostages to Support Exchange," 83 *American Economic Review* 519–40.

_____. 1985. *The Economic Institutions of Capitalism.* New York: Free Press.

13

Vertical Integration as Organizational Ownership: The Fisher Body–General Motors Relationship Revisited

BENJAMIN KLEIN

I have always considered my work with Armen Alchian and Robert Crawford (1978) on vertical integration to represent an extension of Coase's classic article on "The Nature of the Firm." By focusing on the "hold-up" potential that is created when firm-specific investments are made by transactors, or what we called the appropriation of quasi-rents, I believed we had elucidated one aspect of the Coasian concept of transaction costs associated with market exchange. We hypothesized that an increase in firm-specific investments, by increasing the market transaction costs associated with a hold-up, increased the likelihood of vertical integration. This relationship between firm-specific investments, market transaction costs, and vertical integration was illustrated by examining the contractual difficulties that existed when General Motors purchased automobile bodies from Fisher Body and the corresponding benefits that were created when the parties vertically integrated.

It is clear from Coase's lectures that he considers our analysis not to represent an extension of his earlier work, but rather to be an alternative, incorrect explanation for vertical integration (chapter 5). Coase recognizes that an increase in the quasi-rents yielded by firm-specific investments creates a hold-up potential. However, he argues that there is no reason to believe that this situation is more likely to lead to vertical integration than to a long-term contract. Although long-term contracts are imperfect, opportunistic behavior is usually effectively handled in the marketplace, according to Coase, by a firm's need to take account of the effect of its actions on future business. Coase claims that before writing his classic paper he explicitly considered opportunistic behavior as a motive for vertical integration, in particular as it applied to the General Motors–Fisher Body case, and explicitly rejected it.

Unfortunately, Coase's rejection of the opportunism analysis is based upon too simplified a view of the market contracting process and too narrow a view of the transaction costs associated with that process. A more complete analysis of how vertical integration solved the opportunistic behavior problem in the Fisher Body–General Motors case provides insight into the nature of the transaction costs that are associated with the market contracting process and how vertical integration reduces these costs. The primary transaction costs saved by vertical integration are not the "ink costs" associated with the number of contracts written and executed but, rather, are the costs associated with contractually induced hold-ups. The analysis indicates that hold-up potentials are created not solely from the existence of firm-specific investments, but also from the existence of the rigidly set long-term contract terms that are used in the presence of specific investments. Vertical integration, by shifting ownership of the firm's organizational asset, creates a degree of flexibility and avoids this contractually created hold-up potential, thereby resulting in significant transaction cost savings.

1. LONG-TERM CONTRACTS AS SOLUTIONS TO AND CAUSES OF HOLD-UP PROBLEMS

Coase is correct in believing that in many cases contractual arrangements, rather than vertical integration, can be and are used to solve hold-up problems. For example, consider the case of building a house on a piece of land. It is obvious that you would not build the house on land you had only rented for a short time. After the land lease expired the landowner could hold you up for the quasi-rents on your house investment. However, this does not mean that you need necessarily own the land, that is, vertically integrate, to solve this problem. The hold-up problem potentially could be solved by the use of a long-term rental contract on the land negotiated before the house was constructed. Since land is the type of input where anticipated quality variations are very small or nonexistent, a long-term rental contract is certainly a feasible way to minimize the hold-up potential without vertical integration.

The long-term exclusive dealing contract adopted by Fisher Body and General Motors in 1919 can be explained as an analogous contractual means to avoid a hold-up potential without vertical integration.[1] Since Fisher Body had to make an investment highly specific to General Motors in the stamping machines and dies necessary to produce the automobile bodies demanded by General Motors, a significant hold-up potential was created. After Fisher made the investment, General Motors could have attempted to appropriate the quasi-rents from the investment by threatening to reduce their demand for Fisher-produced bodies, or even to terminate Fisher completely, if price were not adjusted downward. The exclusive dealing clause, which required General Motors over a ten-year period to buy all their closed metal bodies from Fisher Body, limited the ability of General Motors to opportunistically threaten Fisher Body in this manner. The contractual arrangement thereby reduced Fisher Body's reliance on General Motors' reputation and encouraged Fisher Body to make the specific investment.

Although the ten-year exclusive dealing contractual arrangement protected Fisher against a General Motors hold-up, it created a potential for Fisher to hold up General Motors. Fisher could take advantage of the requirement that General Motors could not purchase elsewhere by increasing price or decreasing quality. The contract attempted to protect General Motors against this reverse hold-up potential by specifying a formula by which price would be set over the ten-year period at a competitive level. In addition, in a further attempt to minimize the potential Fisher hold-up of General Motors, the contract also included most-favored nation provisions so that the price could not be greater than what Fisher Body charged other automobile manufacturers for "similar" bodies. Such a "price protection" clause prevents a hold-up because a price increase or decrease to any buyer is guaranteed to be given to all buyers. Hence, established buyers that are "locked-in" by a specific investment or a contractual commitment are protected by the seller's desire to make profitable new sales.

In spite of the existence of a long-term contractual arrangement with explicitly set price and price protection clauses, there is still some probability that a hold-up may occur. This is because not all elements of future performance are specified in the contract. Due to uncertainty and the difficulty of specifying all elements of performance in a contractually enforceable way, contracts will necessarily be incomplete to one degree or another. This creates the possibility for transactors to take advantage of the contract to hold up their transacting partner. For example, the long-term land rental contract in the house construction example may permit the landowner to hold up the house owner by opportunistically controlling the water supply to the house, or by failing to build a wall to prevent erosion of the land under the house, or by closing a road on the land for claimed repairs and thereby threatening to restrict access to the house.

Even though contracts are incomplete, the reputations of the transacting parties limit the economic feasibility of hold-up threats. It is the magnitude of these reputations and the corresponding costs that can be imposed on a transactor that attempts a hold-up that define what can be called the "self-enforcing range" of the contractual relationship. Transacting parties enter contractual arrangements by making specific investments and setting contract terms in such a way so that they are likely to be within this self-enforcing range where a hold-up will not occur. However, there is some probability that market conditions may change (for example, the value of the quasi-rents accruing to one of the parties unexpectedly increases) so that it pays for one transactor to hold up the other in spite of the loss of reputation.[2]

For example, in the General Motors–Fisher Body case demand for the closed metal bodies manufactured by Fisher increased dramatically. When the contract was entered into in 1919 the dominant production process for automobiles consisted of individually constructed, largely wooden, open bodies; closed metal bodies were essentially a novelty. Demand for closed metal bodies grew extremely rapidly and by 1924 accounted for more than 65 percent of General Motors' automobile production.[3] This shift in demand moved the contractual arrangement outside of the self-enforcing range and made it profitable for Fisher to hold up General Motors.

Although Fisher could have taken advantage of many imperfectly specified terms of the contractual arrangement, such as delivery times or quality characteristics, Fisher effectively held up General Motors by adopting a relatively inefficient, highly labor-intensive technology and by refusing to locate the body-producing plants adjacent to General Motors assembly plant.[4] This hold-up mechanism had the advantage, from Fisher's viewpoint, of increasing profitability since the contractually specified price formula set price equal to Fisher's "variable cost" plus 17.6 percent, placing a 17.6 percent profit upcharge on Fisher's labor and transportation costs. The profit upcharge presumably was designed to cover Fisher's anticipated capital costs, which may have been difficult to isolate and measure for General Motors shipments and, therefore, were unreimbursable under the contract formula. The contract may appear to be imperfect, but it was only deficient ex post. If demand had not grown so rapidly, Fisher's reputation (that is, loss of future business with General Motors and possibly other automobile manufacturers) combined with the most favored nation clause may have been an effective constraint on Fisher Body behavior. However, the large increase in demand placed Fisher's short-run hold-up potential of General Motors, even with Fisher being forced to give up new and future sales, outside the self-enforcing range.

The Fisher Body–General Motors case illustrates that while long-term contract terms and transactor reputations may prevent hold-ups and encourage specific investments by tying the hands of the transacting parties, long-term contract terms may also create hold-up problems. Therefore, it is misleading to assert, as Coase does, that "opportunistic behavior is usually effectively checked" in the market by long-term contracts and the existence of transactor reputations. Although the assertion is true, a more complete analysis must recognize that transactor reputations are limited and that contracts may actually create, rather than solve, hold-up problems. It was the long-term, fixed price formula, exclusive dealing contract adopted by the transactors in response to the potential General Motors hold-up of Fisher that created the enormous Fisher hold-up potential of General Motors. The magnitude of this contractually caused hold-up was likely much greater than the quasi-rents on the General Motors–specific investments made by Fisher which the contract was attempting to protect in the first place. Although writing down binding contract terms may economize on limited brand name capital and reduce the probability of being outside the self-enforcing range, the rigidity of long-term contract terms may create a much larger hold-up potential if events actually place the parties outside the self-enforcing range. To avoid this rigidity transactors may intentionally leave their contracts incomplete and thereby give themselves "an out" if market conditions get "out of line."

It is this contractually induced hold-up potential and the costs associated with rigid ex post incorrect contract terms, illustrated so forcefully in the Fisher–General Motors case, that represent the major transaction costs of using the market mechanism to solve the hold-up problem. These transaction costs include the real resources transactors dissipate in the contractual negotiation and renegotiation process in the attempt to create and execute a hold-up. Transactors will search for an informational advantage over their transacting partners and attempt to negotiate ex ante contract terms that create hold-up potentials, that is, that are more likely to imply ex post situations where contract terms are favorably incorrect. Once such a favorably incorrect situation arises, transactors will dissipate real resources during the renegotiation process in the attempt to convince their transacting partner that a hold-up potential does exist. In the Fisher–General Motors case these renegotiation transaction costs consisted of the costs associated with improper plant placement and low capital intensity of production before vertical integration occurred.[5]

These transaction costs associated with the use of a long-term contract represent the theoretical reason why the presence of firm-specific investments are more likely to lead to vertical integration. Specific investments create the necessity for long-term contractual terms which, in turn, imply the rent-dissipating transaction costs associated with the possibility of contractually created hold-ups. In the absence of specific investments, long-term contract terms are unnecessary and spot contracts can be used. Since the costs associated with vertical integration are generally incentive-type costs that are unrelated to the level of specific investments, vertical integration will be more likely the greater the level of specific investments. The greater the level of specific investments and hence the greater the potential costs of using the market (as more explicit and rigid contractual mechanisms must be devised to protect the specific investment), the greater the likelihood that vertical integration will be the solution.

2. PHYSICAL CAPITAL VS. HUMAN CAPITAL

Vertical integration is the form in which the hold-up of General Motors by Fisher Body eventually took place, with General Motors acquiring the Fisher Body stock owned by Fisher at terms that were highly favorable to Fisher. Why did not General Motors merely make a lump sum cash payment to Fisher and renegotiate the contract, fixing ambiguous terms and hoping that another large unanticipated event would not occur in the future to shock the relationship out of the self-enforcing range? One reason is that the change in demand to closed metal bodies made Fisher a much more important specialized input supplier to General Motors, with the Fisher hold-up potential reaching essentially the entire General Motors industry-specific investment. In principle, with an ex post incorrect contract, Fisher could potentially hold up General Motors for their entire automobile manufacturing and distribution organization. This enormous hold-up potential would imply extremely large rent-dissipating transaction costs during the contractual negotiation and renegotiation process as General Motors attempted to protect against and Fisher attempted to take advantage of the hold-up possibilities.

Vertical integration appears to avoid these transaction costs by eliminating the second transactor. This is obvious for cases of physical capital, such as the house construction–land ownership example, where a hold-up, by definition, becomes impossible with vertical integration. It is cases like these that lead to the obvious conclusion that vertical integration will more likely be used when the hold-up potential, that is, the quasi-rents from firm-specific investments, are large. As Joskow (1988) convincingly demonstrates, this insight regarding the economic motivation for ownership of firm-specific physical capital has significant empirical relevance.

However, many real-world examples involve human capital and not merely physical capital as the important firm-specific asset.[6] Since the specific human capital is embodied in individuals who by law cannot be owned and who have the potential to behave opportunistically under any alternative organizational arrangement, vertical integration does not eliminate the other transactor and the hold-up problem. In such cases it is unclear exactly what gains are entailed by vertical integration.

To understand the gains from vertical integration in the context of human capital, the economic question should be phrased not (as we have done in the house construction–land ownership case) as whether to own or rent an asset, but, as Coase essentially phrased it, as whether to make or buy an input. The former question applies only to physical capital while the latter question applies to human capital. When a firm buys an input in the marketplace, it generally does not own the physical capital associated with its production. A firm that produces an input itself also may not own the physical capital associated with its production (for example, the building where the firm has its offices). However, as we shall see, a firm that makes rather than buys an input generally has a particular relationship with the firm-specific human capital.

These issues can be focused by considering the Fisher Body–General Motors case again. If the hold-up problem were based solely on the General Motors–specific physical capital investments made by Fisher Body and had nothing to do with Fisher Body human capital, General Motors could have solved the problem by owning the physical capital. General Motors could have owned their own dies and stamping machines and let Fisher use this capital to make auto bodies for them, avoiding the hold-up problem while taking advantage of whatever cost advantage Fisher possessed in producing bodies.[7]

One problem with this solution is that the extent of the General Motors–specific physical capital investments is likely to be much greater than merely the dies and stamping equipment. There are, for example, complementary physical capital investments that must be made by Fisher in plant, with the associated questions of plant location and the assurance to Fisher of continued General Motors demand for the facility. These questions presumably would have to be handled by contract. To avoid contractual rigidity and the induced hold-up problems associated with ex post incorrect contract terms General Motors could own all the physical capital and merely contract with Fisher to run the operation. While such an arrangement would create marginal distortions regarding the use of the General Motors capital equipment by Fisher, it would appear to solve the hold-up problem if the problem were based solely on specific physical capital investments.

However, much of the specific investment necessary to produce automobile bodies consists of Fisher human capital investments that, by definition, cannot be owned by General Motors. General Motors can finance Fisher's human capital investments but would require some long-term fixed price contractual commitment to prevent Fisher from threatening to terminate the relationship if General Motors did not make a lump sum payment to them equal to the quasi-rents from the human capital investment. Vertical integration, in the sense of making Fisher an employee, rather than an independent contractor, does not eliminate the potential hold-up. As opposed to physical capital, the specialized human capital would presumably still be owned by Fisher even after General Motors' vertical integration. Rather than ownership, a long-term contractual arrangement, with its associated rigidities and potential hold-up problems, must be used by the transactors.[8]

Since, by definition, one cannot own human capital, how did the vertical integration of General Motors with Fisher reduce the hold-up problem? As opposed to the case of physical capital, vertical integration did not eliminate the Fisher brothers. After vertical integration General Motors no longer bought bodies from Fisher Body Corporation. After vertical integration General Motors "made" bodies with the assistance of Fisher. However, did making the Fisher brothers employees compared to being independent contractors change things in any essential way? Although General Motors would now own the plants and presumably be able to tell the Fisher brothers where to locate them, the Fisher brothers became employee managers with the ability to hold up General Motors for their human capital–specific investments by threatening modification on some other dimension.

3. VERTICAL INTEGRATION AS ORGANIZATIONAL OWNERSHIP

Although the use of an employee rather than an independent contractor arrangement may imply important legal differences and hence different constraints on the contracting process, such as the ease of termination by the employer and the required loyalty of the employee, I agree with Coase that the employer-employee contract does not represent the essence of a firm.[9] The transition of the Fisher brothers from independent contractors to employees does not explain what General Motors gained through vertical integration.

Vertical integration not only made the Fisher brothers employees of General Motors, but also converted all the employees of Fisher Body Corporation into employees of General Motors. General Motors moved from "buying" automobile bodies to "making" automobile bodies by obtaining ownership of the Fisher Body organization, including all the labor contracts of the cooperating workers in that organization and all the knowledge of how to make automobiles contained in that organization. It is in this sense of owning a firm's set of interdependent labor contracts and the firm-specific knowledge embodied in the organization's team of employees that an owner of a firm can own the firm's human capital.[10]

Vertical integration may solve a hold-up potential even when it hinges on human capital and, hence, the number of transactors are not reduced by the integration because it involves transferring ownership of a productive team. For example, if we consider the Fisher Body–General Motors case it is unlikely that it was the Fisher brothers themselves who possessed all the relevant firm-specific human capital information. It was much more likely that this information was possessed by the entire group of Fisher employees and was embedded in the Fisher organizational structure. Vertical integration did not merely transfer the Fisher brothers from independent contractor to employee status, but also transferred ownership of the

Fisher organization and the set of interdependent labor contracts to General Motors.

The primary reason a hold-up cannot occur after such a transfer of rights is because collusion is difficult with a large number of entities. If there were only one employee or a few key employees, they could threaten to leave and (subject to legal constraints on trade secret or goodwill theft) take the organization with them. However, with many key individuals involved, the organization will generally be secure. A threat that all the individuals will simultaneously shirk or leave if their wages were not increased to reflect the quasi-rents on the organizational capital generally will not be credible. After vertical integration the Fisher brothers will not be able to hold up General Motors by telling all the employees to leave General Motors and show up on Monday morning at a new address. This is, in general, not economically feasible or, more important, legally possible. It is in this sense of large team organizations that vertical integration can imply ownership of human capital assets in a manner quite similar to ownership of physical capital assets.

Our analysis implies that the General Motors integration with Fisher Body is analytically quite similar to the land–house example. By integrating with Fisher, General Motors acquired the Fisher Body organizational capital. This organization is embedded in the human capital of the employees at Fisher but is in some sense greater than the sum of its parts. The employees come and go but the organization maintains the memory of past trials and the knowledge of how to best do something (that is, how to make automobile bodies). This organizational asset can be thought of as a big machine called the Fisher Corporation. When this machine was owned by the Fisher brothers, it was necessary to write an explicit automobile body supply contract which ex post turned out to create significant hold-up problems. With vertical integration General Motors avoided these contractual difficulties by buying the machine (the Fisher Corporation) and, in the sense of eliminating the need for an automobile body supply contract, eliminating the second transactor (the Fisher brothers).[11]

4. ORGANIZATIONAL OWNERSHIP VS. INPUT COORDINATION

Coase would likely agree that it is useful to consider the firm as an organization. He recognizes that it is the existence of cooperating labor inputs, and not merely a single employee, that represents a firm relationship. "The employer-employee contract approaches the firm relationship but . . . the full firm relationship will not come about unless several such contracts are made with people and for things that cooperate with one another" (chapter 5). However, Coase emphasizes the role of the firm not as an owner of organizational assets, but as a coordinator and controller of cooperating inputs. One must consider the firm, Coase says, as "running a business." And the economic question regarding institutional form involves a "comparison of the costs of coordinating the activities of factors of production within the firm with the costs of bringing about the same result by market transactions or by means of operations undertaken within some other firm" (chapter 5). It is this concept of coordination of a team of inputs that Coase attributes as the essence of a firm.

The concept of a central contracting agent that serves as a hub of a group of interdependent contracts and by coordination eliminates the necessity of contracts between those individuals assumed to be at the end of each of the spokes may appear to provide some insight into the nature of the firm. It is in the sense of coordinating control of a team that the number of market relationships is reduced and substituted for administrative decisions. This concept corresponds to Coase's notion of a reduction in the number of market transactions when vertical integration occurs (1988: lecture 3). However, every transactor in the marketplace purchasing inputs that are assembled into a final product can be considered as a hub of a series of contractual arrangements. The suppliers of the separate inputs need not have any contractual arrangement with one another. Although vertical integration may appear to eliminate the necessity for contractual arrangements between co-operating inputs, it does not.

Unfortunately, in considering whether transactors will adopt a firm or market arrangement, Coase in 1937 and again now has incorrectly identified the costs of using the market mechanism with the narrow transaction costs of discovering prices and executing contracts (chapter 2; chapter 5). However, vertical integration implies small, if any, savings in terms of these shopping and contract execution costs. Ownership of an organization essentially reduces the number of contracts that must be executed by, at most, one. General Motors must still have separate contracts with all the employees of Fisher Body. If the Fisher brothers remain, two new employee contracts must now be written to replace the old independent contractor body supply contract. If the Fisher brothers leave, there will be one less contract.

Rather than a decrease in the number of contracts, what vertical integration alters is the nature of the contractual arrangement. The one contract that is eliminated creates a new relationship between the transacting parties. It is no longer necessary for General Motors to prespecify production conditions (such as body plant locations, capital intensity, delivery times, and so forth) or prices. Although General Motors may actually write many of these conditions down in their internal interdivisional communications and, therefore, not save any "ink costs," these documents no longer have the force of contract law.

The absence of a legal constraint creates increased flexibility and a decreased possibil.y of a contractual hold-up. General Motors and Fisher no longer need to expend real resources in the attempt to determine all of the many events that might occur during the life of the production relationship and write a prespecified response to each event. Most of these events are highly unlikely and, by integrating, General Motors can wait until future conditions emerge before determining what should be done. As discussed above, not only do General Motors and Fisher save the allocatively wasteful transaction costs involved in searching for informational advantages in negotiating prespecified contractual responses, but they also avoid the real resource costs during the renegotiation process once ex post market conditions turn out to be substantially different from the prespecified contract terms. Instead of contractual rigidity and the associated hold-up potential, the relationship becomes flexible to unanticipated market conditions.

While some commentators, including Coase, may identify this increased flexibility associated with vertical integration with the ability to coordinate or "direct" inputs, I do not believe that it is useful to focus on this ability as the central characteristic of a firm. Direction of inputs is neither a necessary nor a sufficient condition for defining a firm. For example, a conglomerate firm may merely own another firm (the organizational asset of another firm) without directing the firm's team of inputs. Alternatively, I may direct my gardener every weekend regarding what I want him to do for me, but I do not own a gardening firm. If the gardener has a group of workers that he uses to carry out my instructions, it is he who owns a gardening firm in the sense of an organization. By my direction I am specifying the particular services I desire. However, I am merely buying the particular services in the marketplace; it is the gardener who is "making" the particular services.

Direction of inputs can be accomplished in the marketplace as long as there are no specific investments made by the transacting parties and, therefore, no need for long-term contracts. Spot contracts in a competitive market can provide, in principle, a mechanism for perfect coordination and direction of cooperating inputs. A miller of flour, for example, may be able to contract in the spot market for supplies of wheat and have complete flexibility to alter quantities and qualities as required by shifts in his demand. The miller may demand in the market (that is, "direct" producers to supply) increased quantities or different qualities of wheat without any fear of a hold-up.

However, most market relationships entail transaction-specific investments and, therefore, the possibility of a hold-up. A magazine publisher, for example, may want to shift production of an issue (say, delay and increase the quantity of a press run to take account of a late-breaking story). Because of transaction-specific investments magazine printing services cannot be purchased in a perfectly competitive spot market. If the publisher purchased printing services from an independent printing firm, the printer may refuse to be "directed" in this manner without some side payment. Because of this hold-up potential, long-term contractual arrangements specifying particular contingencies and payment arrangements will be used. But these contract terms are necessarily imperfect and, as we have seen in the General Motors–Fisher Body case, may lead to the possibility of an even greater hold-up potential.

Transaction-specific investments are pervasive and exist in cases where there are no obvious specific physical capital investments. Even with regard to, say, wheat it may be costly to switch suppliers. It takes time to find new suppliers and to check product qualities and services (delivery times, reliability, and the like). Similarly, wheat suppliers must learn about particular millers' payment practices, delivery requirements, working schedules, and so on. It is because transactors make these specific investments in particular suppliers that real-world demand curves are never perfectly elastic. However, it is important to recognize that if transactor-specific investments were unimportant, spot contracts could be used and transactors would have the full ability to "direct" cooperating inputs in the marketplace. From an analytical point of view, vertical integration is not necessary in order to coordinate or "direct" cooperating inputs in the production process.

5. CONCLUSION

Given the presence of specific investments in an exchange relationship, transactors will have to decide whether to use a long-term contract or vertical integration to solve the hold-up problem. Vertical integration entails the widely recognized possibility of increased costs associated with somewhat reduced incentives and increased bureaucracy. I have discussed here the other side of the equation—the transaction costs associated with long-term contacts. The important element of these transaction costs is not the "ink costs" of writing contract terms emphasized by Coase, but the significant rent-dissipating costs borne during the negotiation and renegotiation contracting process as transactors attempt to create, avoid, and execute the hold-ups implied by necessarily imperfect long-term contractual arrangements.

While vertical integration may imply an increased ability to direct cooperating inputs compared to a long-term contractual arrangement, one must not confuse what an integrated firm may do with the basic economic motivation for the integration. Vertical integration, by shifting ownership of an organizational asset, permits transactors to avoid the transaction costs associated with a hold-up potential in the presence of specific investments. Whether transactors adopt vertical integration as a solution to a particular hold-up potential depends upon the magnitude of these specific investments, combined with the ability to write long-term contracts that flexibly track market conditions without creating an alternative hold-up potential. Since the ability to write and use long-term contracts depends, in part, upon the underlying market uncertainty and on the level of transactor reputations, these factors will also influence the likelihood of vertical integration.

This analysis of the motivation for vertical integration is consistent with the fundamental point recognized by Coase fifty years ago—that a transaction within the firm is something that is inherently different from a transaction in the marketplace. The view of the firm as merely a "nexus of contracts" that has developed in reaction to Coase's fundamental distinction between the firm and the market[12] is incomplete and misleading. I now agree with Coase that there is a useful analytical and not merely legal distinction to make between interfirm and intrafirm transactions. Firms are more than particular groups of explicit and implicit contracts. They consist of valuable team assets and developed mechanisms of handling information and control. By consolidating ownership of these organizational assets in the hands of one firm, vertical integration eliminates the need for one fundamental contract and creates an increased ability to flexibly direct production. As a consequence, a significant hold-up potential is reduced, along with an important range of transaction costs.

NOTES

I am grateful to Harold Demsetz, Kevin James, Timothy Opler, and Oliver Williamson for useful comments.

1. The contractual agreement between Fisher Body and General Motors can be found in the minutes of the Board of Directors of Fisher Body Corporation for November 7, 1919. Analysis of this case is taken in part from Klein, Crawford, and Alchian (308–10).

2. This probabilistic equilibrium differs from the analysis in Klein, Crawford, and Alchian, where hold-ups were assumed not to be present in long-run equilibrium and existed solely because of transactor myopia or ignorance. Kenney and Klein present a discussion of the "self-enforcing range" and this equilibrium, together with the implications of the analysis for contract law.

3. *Sixteenth Annual Report*, General Motors Corporation, year ended December 31, 1924.

4. See deposition testimony of Alfred P. Sloan, Jr. in United States *v.* Dupont & Co., 366 U.S. 316 (1961), 186–90 (April 28, 1952) and 2908–14 (March 14, 1953).

5. In addition to the transaction costs associated with negotiating contractual arrangements and the transitional transaction costs associated with the renegotiating process when these arrangements do not work out in practice, there are the social costs associated with transactors not making specific investments and entering contractual arrangements to begin with. Transactors anticipate the rent-dissipating transaction costs associated with contractual negotiation and renegotiation because they recognize the limits to their reputation capital, the uncertainty of the world, and the necessary imperfections of contracts. Therefore, independent of any risk aversion, transactors will avoid entering contractual arrangements where there is a significant probability that the arrangement will not work out. The equilibrium contractual arrangements that transactors voluntarily adopt in the marketplace may appear, consistent with Coase's assertion, to handle opportunistic behavior—in the sense that we are unlikely to observe opportunism occurring very frequently. However, we do not see all the specific investments not made and the contractual arrangements not adopted when transactors anticipate a significant probability of being outside the self-enforcing range.

6. See, for example, the discussion in Klein, Crawford, and Alchian (313–19) and Williamson (240–45).

7. Coase discusses this as a particular contractual solution to the hold-up problem (chapter 3). See also Monteverde and Teece. Fisher's cost advantage was unlikely due to economies of scale in the production process. Evidence for this is the fact that, after demand growth and integration, Fisher supplied bodies solely to General Motors. This is one difference between the Fisher Body case and the A. O. Smith case discussed by Coase (chapter 3). There appears to be significantly greater economies of scale in producing automobile frames than producing automobile bodies, with Smith supplying frames then and now to multiple automobile manufacturers, thereby raising the cost of vertical integration as a solution to the hold-up problem (see Stigler). It is also important to note that the investment in automobile frame production is, apparently, less buyer-specific than the investment in automobile body production.

8. For example, one contract term that is used in employment arrangements in the entertainment industry, where the employer may make a substantial transactor-specific investment, is a right of first refusal clause. This clause reduces the credibility of hold-up threats since it requires the employee attempting to increase his wage by the amount of the quasi-rents from the employer's investment to threaten to quit working completely, rather than merely to threaten to quit the firm and work elsewhere.

9. See Coase (chapter 5) where he identifies this as the main weakness of his 1937 article.

10. The concept of specific knowledge which affects a firm's production technology and which is vested in and transferable with the firm has been discussed by numerous authors. Rosen notes that such a firm-specific information asset may be created over time by the discovery of trade connections and the assembly of an efficient "production team" and presents a model where specific knowledge is acquired through (or as a by-product of) a firm's production experience. A similar concept is developed in Prescott and Visscher and is related to the evolutionary theory of the firm presented by Nelson and Winter. The importance of information accumulation within the firm as a kind of progress function was originally discussed by Alchian (1959) and Arrow. This concept may explain why bankruptcy law provisions, which are designed to prevent the production team from disbanding, make economic sense. While physical assets generally may be salvageable, bankruptcy, accompanied by the discontinuance of a firm's operations, may destroy the organizational assets of the firm. The analysis also provides an economic justification for the "failing firm" defense in merger law.

11. In contrast, the Grossman and Hart model of vertical integration consists of single person firms where, by definition, ownership of organizational assets cannot be transferred or consolidated. Grossman and Hart concentrate solely on physical assets and the question of which particular physical assets firms own. However, the essential question of vertical integration is not asset ownership but the make-or-buy decisions of firms. General Motors may own all the physical capital in the Fisher plant yet buy the bodies from an independent Fisher Body Corporation. The Grossman and Hart answer to the question of the distribution of physical asset ownership, which relies on employee incentive effects, cannot explain the incidence of vertical integration. Although vertical integration of Fisher and General Motors may lead to increased monitoring of the Fisher brothers because they no longer bear the full value consequences of their behavior, most of the managers at Fisher Body, both before and after integration with General Motors, are employees and not owners of Fisher physical capital.

12. See, for example, Alchian and Demsetz, and Klein (1983).

REFERENCES

Alchian, Armen A. 1959. "Costs and Outputs." In M. Abramovitz, ed., *The Allocation of Economic Resources*. Stanford: Stanford University Press.

_____, and Harold Demsetz. 1972. "Production, Information Costs, and Economic Organization," 62 *American Economic Review* 777.

Arrow, Kenneth J. 1962. "The Economic Implications of Learning by Doing," 29 *Review of Economic Studies* 155.

Coase, Ronald H. 1937. "The Nature of the Firm," 4 *Economica* n.s. 386 [chapter 2 of this volume].

_____. 1988. "The Nature of the Firm: Origin, Meaning, Influence," 4 *Journal of Law, Economics, and Organization* 3–47.

Grossman, Sanford, and Oliver Hart. 1986. "The Costs and Benefits of Ownership: A Theory of Vertical and Lateral Organization," 94 *Journal of Political Economy* 691.

Joskow, Paul L. 1988. "Asset Specificity and the Structure of Vertical Relationships: Empirical Evidence," 4 *Journal of Law, Economics, and Organization* 95–118 [chapter 8 of this volume].

Kenney, Roy, and Benjamin Klein. 1985. "The Law and Economics of Contractual Flexibility," UCLA Department of Economics Working paper no. 388.

Klein, Benjamin. 1983. "Contracting Costs and Residual Claims: The Separation of Ownership and Control," 26 *Journal of Law and Economics* 367.

———, Robert Crawford, and Armen Alchian. 1978. "Vertical Integration, Appropriable Rents and the Competitive Contracting Process," 21 *Journal of Law and Economics* 297.

Monteverde, K. M., and David J. Teece. 1982. "Appropriable Rents and Quasi-Vertical Integration," 25 *Journal of Law and Economics* 321.

Nelson, Richard R., and Sidney G. Winter. 1982. *An Evolutionary Theory of Economic Change.* Cambridge: Harvard University Press.

Prescott, Edward C., and Michael Visscher. 1980. "Organizational Capital," 88 *Journal of Political Economy* 466.

Rosen, Sherwin. 1972. "Learning by Experience as Joint Production," 86 *Quarterly Journal of Economics* 366.

Stigler, George. 1951. "The Division of Labor Is Limited by the Extent of the Market," 59 *Journal of Political Economy* 185.

Williamson, Oliver E. 1979. "Transaction Cost Economics: The Governance of Contractual Relations," 22 *Journal of Law and Economics* 233.

1991 Nobel Lecture: The Institutional Structure of Production

R. H. COASE

In my long life I have known some great economists but I have never counted myself among their number nor walked in their company. I have made no innovations in high theory. My contribution to economics has been to urge the inclusion in our analysis of features of the economic system so obvious that, like the postman in G. K. Chesterton's Father Brown tale, "The Invisible Man," they have tended to be overlooked. Nonetheless, once included in the analysis, they will, as I believe, bring about a complete change in the structure of economic theory, at least in what is called price theory or microeconomics. What I have done is to show the importance for the working of the economic system of what may be termed the institutional structure of production. In this lecture I shall explain why, in my view, these features of the economic system were ignored and why their recognition will lead to a change in the way we analyse the working of the economic system and in the way we think about economic policy, changes which are already beginning to occur. I will also speak about the empirical work that needs to be done if this transformation in our approach is to increase our understanding. In speaking about this transformation, I do not wish to suggest that it is the result of my work alone. Oliver Williamson, Harold Demsetz, Steven Cheung, among others, have made outstanding contributions to the subject and without their work and that of many others, I doubt whether the significance of my writings would have been recognized. While it has been a great advantage of the creation of the Prize in Economic Sciences in Memory of Alfred Nobel that, by drawing attention to the significance of particular fields of economics, it encourages further research in them, the highlighting of the work of a few scholars, or, in my case, one scholar, tends to obscure the importance of the contributions of other able scholars whose researches have been crucial to the development of the field.

I will be speaking of that part of economics which has come to be called industrial organization but, to understand its present state, it is necessary to say something about the development of economics in general. During the two centuries since the publication of *The Wealth of Nations*, the main activity of economists, it seems to me, has been to fill the gaps in Adam Smith's system, to correct his errors and to make his analysis vastly more exact. A principal theme of *The Wealth of Nations* was that government regulation or centralised planning were not necessary to make an economic system function in an orderly way. The economy could be co-ordinated by a system of prices (the "invisible hand") and, furthermore, with beneficial results. A major task of economists since the publication of *The Wealth of Nations*, as Harold Demsetz has explained,[1] has been to formalize this proposition of Adam Smith. The given factors are technology and the tastes of consumers, and individuals, who follow their own interest, are governed in their choices by a system of prices. Economists have uncovered the conditions necessary if Adam Smith's results are to be achieved and where, in the real world, such conditions do not appear to be found, they have proposed changes which are designed to bring them about. It is what one finds in the textbooks. Harold Demsetz has said rightly that what this theory analyses is a system of extreme decentralization. It has been a great intellectual achievement and it throws light on many aspects of the economic system. But it has not been by any means all gain. The concentration on the determination of prices has led to a narrowing of focus which has had as a result the neglect of other aspects of the economic system. Sometimes, indeed, it seems as though economists conceive of their subject as being concerned only with the pricing system and anything outside this is considered as no part of their business. Thus, my old chief and wonderful human being, Lionel Robbins, wrote, in *The Nature and Significance of Economic Science*, about the "glaring deficiencies" of the old treatment of the theory of production with its discussion of peasant proprietorships and industrial forms: "It suggests that from the point of view of the economist 'organisation' is a matter of internal industrial (or agricultural) arrangement — if not internal to the firm, at any rate internal to 'the' industry. At the same time it tends to leave out completely the governing factor of all productive organisation — the relationship of prices and cost. . . ."[2] What this comes down to is that, in Robbins' view, an economist does not interest himself in the internal arrangements within organisations but only in what happens on the market, the purchase of factors of production and the sale of the goods that these factors produce. What happens in between the purchase of the factors of production and the sale of the goods that are produced by these factors is largely ignored. I do not know how far economists today share Robbins' attitude but it is undeniable that microeconomics is largely a study of the determination of prices and output, indeed this part of economics is often called price theory.

This neglect of other aspects of the system has been made easier by another feature of modern economic theory — the growing abstraction of the analysis, which does not seem to call for a detailed knowledge of the actual economic system or, at any rate, has managed to proceed without it. Holmstrom and Tirole writing on "The Theory of the Firm" in the recently published *Handbook of Industrial Organization*, conclude at the end of their article of 63 pages that "the evidence/theory ratio . . . is currently very low in this field."[3] Peltzman has written a scathing review of the *Handbook* in which he points out how much of the discussion in it is theory without any empirical basis.[4] What is studied is a system which lives in the minds of economists but not on earth. I have called the result "blackboard economics." The firm and the market appear by name but they lack any substance. The firm in mainstream economic theory has often been described as a "black box." And so it is. This is very extraordinary given that most resources in a modern economic system are employed within firms, with how these resources are used dependent on administrative decisions and not directly on the operation of a market. Consequently, the efficiency of the economic system depends to a very considerable extent on how these organisations conduct their affairs, particularly, of course, the modern corporation. Even more surprising, given their interest in the pricing system, is the neglect of the market or more specifically the institutional arrangements which govern the process of exchange. As these institutional arrangements determine to a large extent what is produced, what we have is a very incomplete theory. All this is beginning to change and in this process I am glad to have played my part. The value of including such institutional factors in the corpus of mainstream economics is made clear by recent events in Eastern Europe. These ex-communist countries are advised to move to a market economy, and their leaders wish to do so, but without the appropriate institutions no market economy of any significance is possible. If we knew more about our own economy, we would be in a better position to advise them.

What I endeavoured to do in the two articles cited by the Royal Swedish Academy of Sciences was to attempt to fill these gaps or more exactly to indicate the direction in which we should move if they are ultimately to be filled. Let me start with "The Nature of the Firm." I went as a student to the London School of Economics in 1929 to study for a Bachelor of Commerce degree, specialising in the Industry group, supposedly designed for people who wished to become works managers, a choice of occupation for which I was singularly ill-suited. However, in 1931 I had a great stroke of luck. Arnold Plant was appointed Professor of Commerce in 1930. He was a wonderful teacher. I began to attend his seminar in 1931, some five months before I took the final examinations. It was a revelation. He quoted Sir Arthur Salter: "The normal economic system works itself." And he explained how a competitive economic system co-ordinated by prices would lead to the production of goods and services which consumers valued most highly. Before being exposed to Plant's teaching, my notions on how the economy worked were extremely woolly. After Plant's seminar I had a coherent view of the economic system. He introduced me to Adam Smith's "invisible hand." As I had taken the first year of University work while still at High School, I managed to complete the requirements for a degree in two years. However, University regulations required three years of residence before a degree could be granted. I had therefore a year to spare. I then had another stroke of luck. I was awarded a Cassel travelling scholarship by the University of London. I decided to spend the year in the United States, this being treated as a year's residence at the London School of Economics, the regulations being somewhat loosely interpreted.

I decided to study vertical and lateral integration of industry in the United States. Plant had described in his lectures the different ways in which various industries were organised but we seemed to lack any theory which would explain these differences. I set out to find it. There was also another puzzle which, in my mind, needed to be solved and which seemed to be related to my main project. The view of the pricing system as a co-ordinating mechanism was clearly right but there were aspects of the argument which troubled me. Plant was opposed to all schemes, then very fashionable during the Great Depression, for the co-ordination of industrial production by some form of planning. Competition, according to Plant, acting through a system of prices, would do all the co-ordination necessary. And yet we had a factor of production, management, whose function was to co-ordinate. Why was it needed if the pricing system provided all the co-ordination necessary? The same problem presented itself to me at that time in another guise. The Russian Revolution had taken place only fourteen years earlier. We knew then very little about how planning would actually be carried out in a communist system. Lenin had said that the economic system in Russia would be run as one big factory. However, many economists in the West maintained that this was an impossibility. And yet there were factories in the West and some of them were extremely large. How did one reconcile the views expressed by economists on the role of the pricing system and the impossibility of successful central economic planning with the existence of management and of these apparently planned societies, firms, operating within our own economy?[5]

I found the answer by the summer of 1932. It was to realise that there were costs of using the pricing mechanism. What the prices are have to be discovered. There are negotiations to be undertaken, contracts have to be drawn up, inspections have to be made, arrangements have to be made to settle disputes, and so on. These costs have come to be known as transaction costs. Their existence implies that methods of co-ordination alternative to the market, which are themselves costly and in various ways imperfect, may nonetheless be preferable to relying on the pricing mechanism, the only method of co-ordination normally analysed by economists. It was the avoidance of the costs of carrying out transactions through the market that could explain the existence of the firm in which the allocation of factors came about as a result of administrative decisions (and I thought it did). In my 1937 article I argued that in a competitive system there would be an optimum of planning since a firm, that little planned society, could only continue to exist if it performed its co-ordination function at a lower cost than would be incurred if it were achieved by means of market transactions and also at a lower cost than this same function could be performed by another firm. To have an efficient economic system it is necessary not only to have markets but also areas of planning within organizations of the appropriate size. What this mix should be we find as a result of competition. This is what I said in my article of 1937. However, as we know from a letter I wrote in 1932 which has been preserved, all the essentials of this argument had been presented in a lecture I gave in Dundee at the beginning of October, 1932.[6] I was then twenty-one years of age and the sun never ceased to shine. I could never have imagined that these ideas would become some 60 years later a major justification for the award of a Nobel Prize. And it is a strange experience to be praised in my eighties for work I did in my twenties.

There is no doubt that the recognition by economists of the importance of the role of the firm in the functioning of the economy will prompt them to investigate its activities more closely. The work of Oliver Williamson and others has led to a greater understanding of the factors which govern what a firm does and how it does it. And we can also hope to learn much more in future from the studies of the activities of firms which have recently been initiated by the Center for Economic Studies of the Bureau of the Census of the United States. But it would be wrong to think that the most important consequence for economics of the publication of "The Nature of the Firm" has been to direct attention to the importance of the firm in our modern economy, a result which, in my view, would have come about in any case. What I think will be considered in future to have been the important contribution of this article is the explicit introduction of transaction costs into economic analysis. I argued in "The Nature of the Firm" that the existence of transaction costs leads to the emergence of the firm. But the effects are pervasive in the economy. Businessmen in deciding on their ways of doing business and on what to produce have to take into account transaction costs. If the costs of making an exchange are greater than the gains which that exchange would bring, that exchange would not take place and the greater production that would flow from specialisation would not be realised. In this way transaction costs affect not only contractual arrangements but also what goods and services are produced. Not to include transaction costs in the theory leaves many aspects of the working of the economic system unexplained, including the emergence of the firm, but much else besides. In fact, a large part of what we think of as economic activity is designed to accomplish what high transaction costs would otherwise prevent or to reduce transaction costs so that individuals can freely negotiate and we can take advantage of that diffused knowledge of which Hayek has told us.

I know of only one part of economics in which transaction costs have been used to explain a major feature of the economic system and that relates to the evolution and use of money. Adam Smith pointed out the hindrances to commerce that would arise in an economic system in which there was a division of labour but in which all exchange had to take the form of barter. No one would be able to buy anything unless he possessed something that the producer wanted. This difficulty, he explained, could be overcome by the use of money. A person wishing to buy something in a barter system has to find someone who has this product for sale but who also wants some of the goods possessed by the potential buyer. Similarly, a person wishing to sell something has to find someone who both wants what he has to offer and also possesses something that the potential seller wants. Exchange in a barter system requires what Jevons called "this double coincidence." Clearly the search for partners in exchange with suitable qualifications is likely to be very costly and will prevent many potentially beneficial exchanges from taking place. The benefit brought about by the use of money consists of a reduction in transaction costs. The use of money also reduces transaction costs by facilitating the drawing up of contracts as well as by reducing the quantity of goods that need to be held for purposes of exchange. However, the nature of the benefits secured by the use of money seems to have faded into the background so far as economists are concerned and it does not seem to have been noticed that there are other features of the economic system which exist because of the need to mitigate transaction costs.

I now turn to that other article cited by the Swedish Academy, "The Problem of Social Cost," published some 30 years ago. I will not say much here about its influence on legal scholarship, which has been immense, but will mainly consider its influence on economics, which has not been immense, although I believe that in time it will be. It is my view that the approach used in that article will ultimately transform the structure of microeconomics—and I will explain why. I should add that in writing this article I had no such general aim in mind. I thought that I was exposing the weaknesses of Pigou's analysis of the divergence between private and social products, an analysis generally accepted by economists, and that was all. It was only later, and in part as a result of conversations with Steven Cheung in the 1960's that I came to see the general significance for economic theory of what I had written in that article and also to see more clearly what questions needed to be further investigated.

Pigou's conclusion and that of most economists using standard economic theory was (and perhaps still is) that some kind of government action (usually the imposition of taxes) was required to restrain those whose actions had harmful effects on others (often termed negative externalities). What I showed in that article, as I thought, was that in a regime of zero transaction costs, an assumption of standard economic theory, negotiations between the parties would lead to those arrangements being made which would maximise wealth and this irrespective of the initial assignment of rights. This is the infamous Coase Theorem, named and formulated by Stigler, although it is based on work of mine. Stigler argues that the Coase Theorem follows from the standard assumptions of economic theory. Its logic cannot be questioned, only its domain.[7] I do not disagree with Stigler. However, I tend to regard the Coase Theorem as a stepping stone on the way to an analysis of an economy with positive transaction costs. The significance to me of the Coase Theorem is that it undermines the Pigovian system. Since standard economic theory assumes transaction costs to be zero, the Coase Theorem demonstrates that the Pigovian solutions are unnecessary in these circumstances. Of course, it does not imply, when transaction costs are positive, that government actions (such as government operation, regulation or taxation, including subsidies) could not produce a better result than relying on negotiations between individuals in the market. Whether this would be so could be discovered not by studying imaginary governments but what real governments actually do. My conclusion: let us study the world of positive transaction costs.

If we move from a regime of zero transaction costs to one of positive transaction costs, what becomes immediately clear is the crucial importance of the legal system in this new world. I explained in "The Problem of Social Cost" that what are traded on the market are not, as is often supposed by economists, physical entities but the rights to perform certain actions and the rights which individuals possess are established by the legal system. While we can imagine in the hypothetical world of zero transaction costs that the parties to an exchange would negotiate to change any provision of the law which prevents them from taking whatever steps are required to increase the value of production, in the real world of positive transaction costs, such a procedure would be extremely costly, and would make unprofitable, even where it was allowed, a great deal of such contracting around the law. Because of this, the rights which individuals possess, with their duties and privileges, will be, to a large extent, what the law determines. As a result, the legal system will have a profound effect on the working of the economic system and may in certain respects be said to control it. It is obviously desirable that these rights should be assigned to those who can use them most productively and with incentives that lead them to do so and that, to discover (and maintain) such a distribution of rights, the costs of their transference should be low, through clarity in the law and by making the legal requirements for such transfers less onerous. Since this can come about only if there is an appropriate system of property rights (and they are enforced), it is easy to understand why so many academic lawyers (at least in the United States) have found so attractive the task of uncovering the character of such a property rights system and why the subject of "law and economics" has flourished in American law schools. Indeed, work is going forward at such a pace that I do not consider it overoptimistic to believe that the main outlines of the subject will be drawn within five or ten years.

Until quite recently most economists seem to have been unaware of this relationship between the economic and legal systems except in the most general way. Stock and produce exchanges are often used by economists as examples of perfect or near-perfect competition. But these exchanges regulate in great detail the activities of traders (and this quite apart from any public regulation there may be). What can be traded, when it can be traded, the terms of settlement and so on are all laid down by the authorities of the exchange. There is, in effect, a private law. Without such rules and regulations, the speedy conclusion of trades would not be possible. Of course, when trading takes place outside exchanges (and this is almost all trading) and where the dealers are scattered in space and have very divergent interests, as in retailing and wholesaling, such a private law would be difficult to establish and their activities will be regulated by the laws of the State. It makes little sense for economists to discuss the process of exchange without specifying the institutional setting within which the trading takes place since this affects the incentives to produce and the costs of transacting. I think this is now beginning to be recognized and has been made crystal-clear by what is going on in Eastern Europe today. The time has surely gone in which economists could analyse in great detail two individuals exchanging nuts for berries on the edge of the forest and then feel that their analysis of the process of exchange was complete, illuminating though this analysis may be in certain respects. The process of contracting needs to be studied in a real world setting. We would then learn of the problems that are encountered and of how they are overcome and we would certainly become aware of the richness of the institutional alternatives between which we have to choose.

Oliver Williamson has ascribed the non-use or limited use of my thesis in "The Nature of the Firm" to the fact that it has not been made "operational," by which he means that the concept of transaction costs has not been incorporated into a general theory. I think this is correct. There have been two reasons for this. First, incorporating transaction costs into standard economic theory, which has been based on the assumption that they are zero, would be very difficult and economists who, like most scientists, as Thomas Kuhn has told us, are extremely conservative in their methods, have not been inclined to attempt it. Second, Williamson has also pointed out that although I was correct in making the choice between organization within the firm or through the market the center piece of my analysis, I did not indicate what the factors were that determined the outcome of this choice and thus made it difficult for others to build on what is often described as a "fundamental insight." This also is true. But the interrelationships which govern the mix of market and hierarchy, to use Williamson's terms, are extremely complex and in our present state of ignorance it will not be easy to discover what these factors are. What we need is more empirical work. In a paper written for a conference of the National Bureau of Economic Research I explained why I thought this was so. This is what I said: "An inspired theoretician might do as well without such empirical work, but my own feeling is that the inspiration is most likely to come through the stimulus provided by the patterns, puzzles and anomalies revealed by the systematic gathering of data, particularly when the prime need is to break our existing habits of thought."[8] This statement was made in 1970. I still think that in essentials it is true today. Although much interesting and important research was done in the seventies and eighties and we certainly know much more than we did in 1970, there is little doubt that a great deal more empirical work is needed. However, I have come to the conclusion that the main obstacle faced by researchers in industrial organization is the lack of available data on contracts and the activities of firms. I have therefore decided to do something about it.

Believing that there is a great deal of data on contracts and the activities of firms in the United States available in government departments and agencies in Washington, D. C., and that this information is largely unknown to economists, I organized a conference at the University of Chicago Law School in the summer of 1990 at which government officials presented papers in which they described what data was available and how to get access to it and also reported on some of the research being carried out within their departments. The audience consisted of academic economists. It was, as a colleague remarked, a case of supply meeting demand. The proceedings of this conference will be published in a special issue of the *Journal of Law and Economics*. Another development with which I am associated is the establishment of the Center for the Study of Contracts and the Structure of Enterprise at the Business School of the University of Pittsburgh. This Center will make large-scale collections of business contracts and will prepare databases which will be made available to all researchers, whatever their institution. Nor should we forget the work now getting started at the Center for Economic Studies of the Bureau of the Census. This greater availability of data and the encouragement given to all researchers working on the institutional structure of production by the award to me of the Nobel Prize should result in a reduction in that elegant but sterile theorizing so commonly found in the economics literature on industrial organization and should lead to studies which increase our understanding of how the real economic system works.

My remarks have sometimes been interpreted as implying that I am hostile to the mathematization of economic theory. This is untrue. Indeed, once we begin to uncover the real factors affecting the performance of the economic system, the complicated interrelations between them will clearly necessitate a mathematical treatment, as in the natural sciences, and economists like myself, who write in prose, will take their bow. May this period soon come.

I am very much aware that many economists whom I respect and admire will not agree with the opinions I have expressed and some may even be offended by them. But a scholar must be content with the knowledge that what is false in what he says will soon be exposed and, as for what is true, he can count on ultimately seeing it accepted, if only he lives long enough.

NOTES

1. Harold Demsetz, *Ownership, Control and the Firm* Volume 1, page 145.

2. Lionel Robbins, *The Nature and Significance of Economic Science* (1932), page 70.

3. Richard Schmalensee and Robert D. Willig (editors), *Handbook of Industrial Organization*, page 126.

4. Sam Peltzman, "The Handbook of Industrial Organization: A Review Article," *Journal of Political Economy*, February, 1991, pages 201–217.

5. A fuller account of these events will be found in Oliver E. Williamson and Sidney G. Winter (editors), *The Nature of the Firm, Origins, Evolution and Development*, pages 34–47.

6. *Ibid*, pages 34–35.

7. George J. Stigler, "Two Notes on the Coase Theorem," *Yale Law Journal*, December, 1989, pages 631–633.

8. R.H. Coase, *The Firm, the Market and the Law*, page 71.

Index

Cheung, Steven N. S., 61–62, 62–63, 198
Chicago, University of, 34, 44, 50. *See also* Regenstein Library
Clark, J. B., 19
Clark, Robert, 200–201, 210n.6
"Classificatory Note of the Determinateness of Equilibrium, A" (Kaldor), 31n.18
Coase, Ronald Harry, v, vi, 3, 12, 118, 122, 159, 179, 186, 189, 193n.1, 196–97, 209, 223. *See also* "Nature of the Firm, The"; "Problem of Social Cost, The"
   A. O. Smith case and, 224n.7
   Arnold Plant's influence on, 6, 37, 188
   on asset specificity, 109–10n.5, 134n.7, 154–55n.4
   autobiography of, 5–6
   colleagues of, 37–38
   on contract theory, 56–57, 67–69
   correspondence with Ronald Fowler, 34–35, 36, 38, 39–47, 48, 49, 50, 52, 70, 71
   employer-employee relationship and, 7, 29, 56, 57, 64–65, 152, 154n.3, 166–67, 219
   on firm's role, 220–22
   Ford and General Motors visited by, 43–44, 71
   on integration and specialization, 40–47
   Knight and, 48–49
   lectures by, 5, 51, 52, 67
   market mechanism costs estimated by, 221
   method of investigating a firm used by, 43–44, 183
   orthodoxy critiqued by, 182–83
   papers collected at Regenstein Library (University of Chicago), 36, 56–57, 59n.1, 60n.11
   pig cycle work of, 75
   price mode v. quantity mode and, 138–39, 140
   on realism in economics, 52, 183–84
   on "The Nature of the Firm," 3–4, 52–57
   training and career of, 36–40
   transaction cost economics and, 4, 11, 90–91, 175
   U.S. manufacturing firms studied by, 6–7, 38, 39–47, 183–84

and Viner, 44–45
as writer, 8, 49–50
Coffee, John, 112n.18
Colloquium on Industrial Organization. *See under* National Bureau of Economic Research
Combination, 25, 32n.33
Commons, John R., 91, 93
Comparative governance. *See under* Economic organization
Comparative systems, 14
Conglomerate, 107, 171
Continuity of association, 174
Contracts, 13, 56, 120
   and asset specificity, 94
   complete, 140–41
   costs of, 207, 214, 223
   definitions of, 198
   employment v. commercial transaction, 204–7
   within firms, 21, 55–56, 197–98
   hold-up problems and, 213, 214–17
   incomplete, 141–42
   informal, 131
   long-term, 67–73, 130–33, 134n.15
   opportunism and, 109n.3
   reputation and, 215
   residual rights of control in, 141–42
   theory of, 9
Control. *See* Residual rights of control
Corporate Control and Business Behavior (Williamson), 63
Corporate culture, 153
Cost accounting, 43
Cost-curve, 28–29
Courts, 102–3
Crawford, Robert G., 54–55, 71, 111n.8, 121, 139–42, 147, 151, 168
Crose, Ronald Harry, and Knight, 27

Dawes, Harry, 31n.15
Decentralization, 160–61, 164
Dedicated assets, 126, 132
Demsetz, Harold, 10, 139, 167–68, 208
Department of Energy. *See* U.S. Department of Energy
Depreciation of Capital (Fowler), 40
Deregulation. *See under* Regulation Division of Labor, firms and, 25–29
"Division of Labor Is Limited by the Extent of the Market, The" (Stigler), 40, 72